To Sam, Denise, and Sam —
With sincere best
wishes from your cousin.
God bless!

Earl Hutto
(aKa Captain Supreme)

7/27/97

CAPTAIN SUPREME GOES TO WASHINGTON

CAPTAIN SUPREME GOES TO WASHINGTON

A MEMOIR

BY

EARL HUTTO

 ENHUTT PUBLISHERS
Pensacola, Florida 32514

Requests for permission to make copies of any
part of the work should be mailed to:
ENHUTT PUBLISHERS
P. O. Box 15244
Pensacola, Florida 32514

Library of Congress Cataloging-in-Publication Data

Hutto, Earl, 1926-
    Captain Supreme Goes to Washington : a memoir / by Earl Hutto.
        p.   cm.
    1. Hutto, Earl, 1926-   2. Legislators--United States-
-Biography. 3. United States.   Congress. House--Biography.
4. Sportscasters--Florida--Biography.   I. Title.
E840,8,H93A3   1997
328. 73 ' 092--dc21
{B}   97-11208
                                                                CIP
                ISBN 0-9657381-9-1

Inside cover photographs courtesy Architect of the U. S. Capitol

Printed in the United States of America

CONTENTS

*To my wife, Nancy; our daughters,
Lori and Amy; and to our many
devoted friends*

BUCKING THE ODDS

As I awoke early one Spring morning in 1975 at our home, 3015 State Avenue in Panama City, Florida, I turned to my wife, Nancy, nudged her into waking and made a startling comment that I will probably never forget.

"You know," I said as she slowly opened her eyes, "Bob Sikes is bound to retire from Congress one of these days and I think I could win that congressional seat to represent the First District of Florida." Nancy's eyes were wide open by then, but she had a quizzical look on her face, understandably so because I had never mentioned such a thought before. "But I do not want to go to Washington, do you?"

"No way!," she responded without a moment's hesitation.

"But I think we should be thinking about some good person to run when Congressman Sikes retires and encourage him or her to start anticipating such a venture," I suggested. Nancy agreed.

Over the course of the next several weeks I made a point of talking to two or three people whom I thought were honorable people who could serve our district well. But, for one reason or another, although intrigued, they indicated they would be unable to run.

In reality, I knew in my heart of hearts that when Sikes decided to hang it up candidates would be coming out of the woodwork to run for the highest office in all of Northwest Florida. And I am sure that a whole bunch of them had already started thinking about this possibility inasmuch as Sikes was the subject of critical news media reports about conflict of interest charges made by Common Cause. The Watergate Class of 1974 was making waves in Congress aimed at more senior members. These upstart freshmen had made headlines by persuading the Democratic Caucus to oust three long-serving committee chairmen, and Congressman Sikes, who at that time had been in Congress for 35 years, seemed to be the next target of Common Cause and, as Mr. Sikes put it, "the liberal news media," especially the New York Times and even some of the newspapers in Florida.

Since none of those whom I considered to be topnotch people would run when the vacancy would occur in Florida's First Congressional District, I kept thinking that maybe I ought to do it.

Reflecting back on that morning I had sprung my astonishing assessment of congressional politics on Nancy I remember that we both had expressed our belief that I would have a good shot at winning. Our analysis made a lot of sense to both of us.

Why did we think I could win such a high office? Well, our reasoning went something like this: I was in my second two-year term in the Florida House of Representatives and I had won a high percentage of the vote in each of my two elections. My district included my home county of Bay and portions of Washington and Walton counties. I was well known not only because of my work in the Legislature, but also as a result of my daily exposure on television for several years in my work as sports director and state news editor on WJHG-TV, Channel 7, in Panama City.

The aforementioned counties, plus five others--Gulf, Holmes, Okaloosa, Santa Rosa, and Escambia--comprised the First Congressional District. Channel 7's coverage area included not only the three counties with which I was involved in my legislative district, but also Gulf County to the east as well as Holmes County to the north and to some extent Okaloosa County to the West. We believed we could garner the same high percentage vote in each of the three counties I presently represented, plus Gulf and Holmes Counties. We figured that we could do well in Okaloosa county, but probably would not carry it. Escambia, with Pensacola as the largest city in the district, and Santa Rosa County, both at the western end of the district would be where we would have to work the hardest since my TV coverage did not reach that far. But, I had begun my TV career in Pensacola years before and still had a nucleus of friends there. We opined that despite the fact that the population density, with about 80 per cent of the people, was 75 to l00 miles away on the other end of the district, we could still do well.

There was no question that uprooting our young family and moving from Panama City to Washington, D. C. had little appeal in the Hutto household, so after my contact with potential candidates, we pretty much dropped the subject. But I could not help but think about it. What an opportunity to serve one's country at the highest level! Would it be possible for a little cotton picking son of an Alabama tenant farmer to be elected to Congress? The more I thought about it the more I began wondering if I would be making a mistake not to run when the seat would come open. At this point I did more than think about it. I prayed about it. Silently , of course.

The practice in our household each evening was to listen to both of our little girls, Lori and Amy, say their goodnight prayers. Then, as now, when we retire for the night, Nancy and I alternate with one leading our prayers one night and the other the next. One night when it was my turn to pray I surprised Nancy by praying for guidance on whether or not I should plan to run for Congress. Needless to say, after the prayers, a lengthy discussion ensued, and to make a long story short, my dear wife reinforced her initial sentiment that she had no interest in forsaking the warm southerly climes of Florida for our nation's capitol.

As the days went by, I continued to harbor in my mind the notion that I could possibly someday be a U. S. Congressman. But it was definitely on the backburner as far as my conversations with my wife were concerned, although I somehow sensed that she might also have that in the back of her mind. My intuition was right. One morning, reminiscent of that first morning when the subject was broached, as we arose from a good night's rest, Nancy said, "Okay, Sweetie, I'm with you on running for Congress."

I cannot tell you how relieved I was that my spouse was now with me on this. I knew that she had no misgivings about it. We both believed, without a shadow of doubt, that this is what we should do.

Okay, so now that this momentous decision had been made, what do we do?   Obviously, we started making some plans. Immediately we started talking about it more frequently among ourselves -- and having a little fun in the process. One thing for sure, we would never become socialites in the big city. We are not party people. Since we do not drink, smoke, or cuss, we might be a little out of place in Washington. Tongue in cheek, I suggested to Nancy that perhaps our campaign motto should be "ELECT A SQUARE TO CONGRESS." We laughed.

Keep in mind that this was 1975, the Florida Legislature was in session and consequently I was as busy as a bee. There had really been no indication from Congressman Sikes that he might not run for reelection next year. But because of the treatment that Mr. Sikes was getting from Common Cause and the news media, it was just possible that he might decide to step down. Anyway, if Earl Hutto was to be the one to succeed him, we needed to start working now. Of course, we were not going to make any public announcement. But it was necessary to start talking to folks for two reasons--to line up support and possibly to discourage others from running. It seemed plausible to get the jump on other contenders. It would be low key, but nonetheless a lot of people would know my hat was in the ring.

"You know, Bob Sikes is getting on up there in age and with all the criticism he has been getting he possibly may not run next year. I have a strong desire to serve in Congress and believe I could do a good job. I think I'm going to run and would appreciate your support." This was the general thrust of my comments to people with whom I came in contact. The reactions ranged from the sublime to the ridiculous. Most were encouraging. Some were "Yeah, I will support you, but frankly I don't think you have a chance, Earl, with all the votes on the other end of the district."

This was not an exploratory expedition as I sought out friends and acquaintances all across Northwest Florida. This was simply doing my homework and laying the foundation for a congressional campaign, be it in 1976 or some future year. This was not a maybe. It was for real.

Nancy and I started visiting beyond my state legislative district and my phone bill went up exponentially as I scanned directories of cities and towns and made calls to many people I knew and others I knew about. The first get-together we had in Pensacola was at the home of my good friend, Homer Singletary, a technician with whom I worked at Channel 3 back in the days when we were both single. Homer and Laura invited a number of friends, mostly from their church, to a coffee to meet Nancy and me. I told those assembled about myself and that I planned to run for Congress when the seat opened up and I wanted their help in drumming up support for me.

We held a number of coffee and tea parties similar to this in the Pensacola area and a few in other localities. We were grateful to get a warm reception and a lot of encouragement. These early contacts were sandwiched around my legislative duties and handling the small one man advertising agency I owned to supplement my very modest state salary. Oftentimes, if we did not have a gathering in someone's home on Saturday, we would try to attend some public event so that I could meet more people and have more visibility. On some Sundays we were invited by friends to attend church with them. I shook a lot of hands. I also wrote down a lot of addresses and phone numbers. The type of campaigning we were doing at this time was not intense, but was done more casually. There was no doubt that we were sowing some good seeds and were uplifted by the acceptance of our plans by our old friends and a lot of new ones.

I have often said that politics did a lot to help my personality. Frankly, I can see how some people would view me as rather dull, or at least introverted and on the quiet side. But, I'm here to tell you that if you want to be successful in the political arena, you cannot hide in a closet. Ever since I got into politics I seem to carry a smile on my face and am quick to extend a cheery greeting to just about everyone with whom I come in contact. For example, I recall one time when the family was traveling in another state we stopped at a restaurant for dinner. As we entered we were speaking to everyone very pleasantly and inquiring of their health. When we got to the table Nancy said "We don't have to be so friendly to these people, they can't vote for us." We got a good chuckle out of that. But we do love people. If we did not, it would be terrible serving in public office.

After the legislative session was adjourned, Nancy and I decided we would take a trip in June, 1975, to Washington, D. C. We had written to Congressman Sikes and he agreed that he would be there on the date we chose and would be glad to see us. Our drive to our nation's capitol did nothing to specifically boost nor did it do anything to discourage our plans. The purpose was twofold -- the first was to share with the "He-Coon," as Sikes was fond of being called, our plans for running when he retired and try to determine when that eventuality might take place, and the second was to size up the place and dream about what it would be like to serve there.

Congressman Sikes was very gracious in receiving us. He invited us to eat with him in the House Dining Room, introduced us to congressmen in the elevator as we walked with him from his office over to the Capitol for a vote, and even invited me to attend a meeting of the Defense Appropriations Subcommittee, of which he was a member. He advised us that he did not yet know if he would be running for re-election next year, but we sensed he looked with favor on my running if he did call it quits. I later remarked, facetiously, to Nancy that, in introducing me as State Representative Earl Hutto to his colleagues, however, he did not add "my likely successor."

I had only passed through Washington very briefly once before and had driven by the Capitol, but I had never been inside. It certainly was a thrill for us to see the seat of government of the world's greatest nation. Though I knew the names of a number of congressmen, I only knew Mr. Sikes and Congressman Don Fuqua, of the adjacent Florida district. Though visitors are not allowed on the House floor, I asked the doorkeeper if he would ask Mr. Fuqua to come outside the chamber and see us. I had a good conversation with Congressman Fuqua and tried to feel him out about Sikes's plans, but he assured me he did not have the faintest idea as to whether Sikes would retire soon.

Fast forward to 1976. This was the great bicentennial year for our nation. But for Florida's First District Congressman Bob Sikes, it was, as he described it, "a grim nightmare." The attacks on him by the news media, including especially the New York Times, CBS's Sixty Minutes, and the original perpetrator, Common Cause, continued unabated. Common Cause filed complaints with the House Committee on Standards of Official Conduct (Ethics Committee) and that committee on July 29th brought to the floor a resolution recommending that Sikes be reprimanded. The vote to reprimand was overwhelming with only three members voting against it. Mr. Sikes, who did not speak for himself, but submitted a written statement for the record during the debate, denied the allegations of conflict of interest in connection with land on Holiday Isle in Destin, stock ownership in Fairchild Industries and in First Navy Bank on the Naval Air Station in Pensacola. He maintained that the committee had not found him guilty of breaking any law.

Being reprimanded is the least of three punishments that could be voted by the House. The severest, of course, is expulsion, and the next toughest is censure, where the member stands in the well before the House and is officially rebuked. So, Mr. Sikes got off with nothing more than his wrist slapped, so to speak, but it was quite devastating to him. He said he was deeply hurt, but asserted that he was not bitter and vowed to continue his service in Congress. This meant there was no way that Bob Sikes would not run for re-election. He had to seek a vote of confidence by the people of his district.

The opponent for Congressman Sikes in 1976 was John Benton, a Democrat and the son of a Panama City physician. Young Benton, a graduate of Duke University, resigned his job with the commerce department in Washington to make the run. He had apparently done volunteer work with Common Cause and Mr. Sikes declared that Benton's running was prompted by his old nemesis. In the end, the Congressman was vindicated with a solid vote at the polls and was in for two more years.

I have often stated, with strong conviction mind you, that the best way to run a campaign for public office is without an opponent. In the bicentennial year of 1976, I was blessed with that luxury as no one qualified to run against me for the Florida House of Representatives in District 8. This tied in well with our humble efforts to lay the groundwork for a possible congressional race two years hence. It would give us an opportunity to make the rounds of a lot of events, political and non-political, and to see a lot of people without the pressure of a campaign of our own.

Though Bob Sikes had received the blessings of his people at the polls in 1976, following his reprimand by the House, things did not get better for him as he returned to Washington for the 95th Congress. Following the precedent they set two years earlier in removing several committee chairmen, the Watergate class in the House, abetted by continuing pressure from Common Cause, now persuaded the Democratic Caucus to remove Mr. Sikes as Chairman of the Military Construction Appropriations Subcommittee. This was another crushing blow to the Florida panhandle Congressman.

As the next election cycle dawned in 1978 there was absolutely no indication that Congressman Sikes was going to retire, despite his problems. But, from the time of his last election, there had been speculation that he would not run again. The Florida Legislature, in those days, met during April and May, and that year there was a subtle feeling that my colleague, Representative Jerry Melvin, of Fort Walton Beach, a former staffer with Mr. Sikes, was going to run for the seat of his old boss if it came open. This was manifested a few times when he and I debated some of the bills on the House floor. Jerry seemed to oppose, or at least to question, some of my bills or positions I took. By that time there had been some rumors about individuals who might run for Congress should Sikes step down. Jerry Melvin was among those mentioned. Although Nancy and I had been discreet in our strategy and there was not a whole lot of talk about me running, probably because most people did not seriously think I had a chance, it was obvious to me that Melvin knew it. Toward the end of the session in late May our colleagues in the House would be aware of Hutto's and Melvin's interest in Congress.

There is an expression "It was no Sunday School Picnic."

Well, in this case, it was. That is exactly where our family was on Saturday, May 27, 1978, Memorial Day weekend. We were having a relaxing time swimming at Shell Island, a barrier island off the coast of Panama City, when some late arrivals to the picnic said they had heard on their car radio that Bob Sikes had just announced that he was retiring from Congress. Wow! What a bombshell!

Nancy and I looked at each other. This was the announcement we had been waiting to hear for a long time. Our hearts beat faster. We had to get to work. Our friends pretty well knew that I would be running and we confirmed that to them when they heard the news. We left the picnic early to get back home to get more details. Our phone was already ringing....a Miami radio station...the Pensacola News-Journal. Was I going to run? "Yes, I will run."

The He-Coon was calling it quits at age 72 after serving in Congress for 38 years, at that time a record tenure for a Florida congressman. Bob Sikes was something of a legend. He had been given great credit for building the strong military establishments in Northwest Florida. The military was, and is, the biggest thing going for the Panhandle economy. The people were deeply concerned that the Sikes departure would mean the loss of hundreds, perhaps thousands, of jobs. Most were shocked that he would leave. He had been encouraged by business leaders and others to serve "two more years."   Close friends indicated they had talked to him only a day before and he had given no indication he was going to retire.

But Bob Sikes had considered retirement two or three terms before. Each time he had been encouraged to continue for another term. After his reprimand by the House in '76 he had to vindicate himself at the polls. Since he had been successful in doing that, there were many, including myself, who felt that would be his last time. Then, being stripped of his subcommittee chairmanship at the beginning of the 95th Congress in early '77 only added to his woes.

Though we anticipated this turn of events, it was still somewhat of a shocker. Here it was the end of May and qualifying for federal office was in July. We were beginning to wonder. Is Sikes going to run yet another time? If, indeed, he had chosen to run again it might have thrown a monkey wrench into our plans. We were ready. So, it was a relief to us that his decision was made, though there was a tinge of sadness for Mr. Sikes.

Congressman Sikes did not call a news conference, nor

assemble his supporters or wait for a scheduled speech to break the news. He simply asked his staff to release his statement to the news media and then left Washington to visit friends in Louisville, Kentucky, according to press reports. Part of his statement said, "I will not be a candidate for re-election. This decision has been one of the most difficult I have ever had to make. It was only after much soul-searching and with great reluctance that I have concluded the time has come for me to lay aside the responsibilities of public office."

I confirmed to the media that I would definitely be a candidate. So did Warren Briggs, the Republican Mayor of Pensacola, who would resign to make the race. There was speculation that a whole flock of candidates possibly would announce. The day after the big news broke the media reported that those considering tossing their hats into the ring were State Senator W. D. Childers, Pensacola; Representatives Jerry Melvin, Fort Walton Beach and Grover Robinson, Pensacola; Escambia County Commissioner Jack Kenney and County Administrator Joe Mooney, all Democrats. State Senator Dempsey Barron of Panama City said he had rather be on top of 40 state senators than on the bottom of 435 congressmen and would remain where he was, and he encouraged Childers to do likewise. Also, State Representative Ed Fortune, D-Pace, and State Senator Tom Tobiassen, R-Pensacola, stated they would not run.

The Hutto candidacy had its work cut out for it. Though we had done a lot of what might be called public relations type activity the last two or three years, there were a lot of specific things that had to be done. These included composing and printing brochures, planning media advertising, looking for headquarters locations, and the least palatable matter of trying to raise funds. I could not immediately get down to the nitty-gritty of working on these things because the legislature would be in session for another week.

In the ensuing days Representative Melvin, as well as State Attorney Curtis Golden of Pensacola, and Ike Williams of Niceville made decisions to run. Surprisingly, when qualifying took place in mid-July, these, along with Briggs and I, were the only candidates to qualify to seek the congressional seat in the first district of Florida. So, it would be Golden, Melvin, Hutto, and Williams in the Democratic primary, with the winner to take on Briggs in the general.

Though I emphatically stated the day of the Sikes announcement that I would run, I did not make my official announcement until a couple of weeks later, after the legislature had adjourned. I needed to get as much media play as I could, so I scheduled announcements in the three major cities--Pensacola, Fort Walton Beach, and Panama City--in a one day sweep across the district. I followed up in the next few days with appearances in the smaller towns and with news releases to the weekly newspapers.

Remember, with two "young'ns," ages 8 and 10, Nancy could not always join me in traipsing around the district, which was about 130 miles long and roughly 50 to 60 miles in width. So, I either went by myself, or had some friend to accompany me on many of the trips. But, on non-school days it was always good to have Nancy, Lori, and Amy with me. On the day of my official announcement, I put on my best looking three-piece suit and headed out early by myself on the 100-mile trek from our home in Panama City to Pensacola. I made my first announcement there at 10 a.m., then in the center of the district in Fort Walton Beach at one, and in Panama City at 3:30 p.m.

It would have been nice to have had a large gathering to which I could make my announcement, but the main thing was to have the media there to get the message out to the people. After all, who would come out for such a thing during a workday in the middle of the week and when the campaign was just starting? But I did invite a few friends to be there to support me. In Pensacola, Homer Singletary, Gerald Newman, John Hodges, and Dave Sellers were among those who turned out to show some semblance of support.

"I am today officially announcing my candidacy for the U. S. Congress from District One. In so doing I believe I am in tune with the people of Northwest Florida." This was about what I said at the beginning of my talk which lasted between five and ten minutes. I stressed that I was close to the people during my three terms in the Florida Legislature, that I listened to their problems with an understanding heart and worked to solve their problems. I pointed out that in each of my first two terms in the legislature, I received about 80 percent of the vote and was without opposition for my third term.

"In Washington I will not be out to climb the social ladder, but will be there to do a job. My life style is different from that of many in high public office," I stated. "I am not lavish and I enjoy living the simple family life that is typical of most Northwest Floridians, so I will be able to relate to you and understand your needs."

I went on to say that I believed I could do as well as anyone in maintaining the military facilities in Northwest Florida, a strong defense is essential for our national security and I would fight to keep it strong. Additionally, I would work with local communities to acquire much needed industries and jobs. "In the legislature I have been a stalwart supporter of education and, as the Panhandle's only member of the House Education Committee, I worked to provide equality in education for all Florida's children," I stressed.

"As a member of the Governmental Operations Committee I fought for greater efficiency in government, including the steering to passage of legislation to implement recommendations of the Governor's Management and Efficiency Study Commission which resulted in savings of millions of dollars," I continued. I further pointed out that my efforts to get the state on biennial budgeting passed and would be in effect next year.

That was the thrust of my announcement except for personal information such as being a native of southeast Alabama, a resident of Florida for over 20 years, a veteran of the U. S. Navy, a graduate of Troy State University with a B.S. Degree in Business-English-Education, graduate work in broadcasting at Northwestern University, a former high school teacher and broadcaster. Also listed in the announcement, a copy of which I gave to each media outlet, was the fact that I was married to the former Nancy Myers and we had two daughters, Lori and Amy, was a deacon in the Baptist Church, a member of Gideons, immediate past president of the Fellowship of Christian Politicians, and a lay speaker in churches.

The campaign was underway! What a venture! Earl Hutto running for the Congress of the United States! Who in the backwoods of south Alabama would ever believe that? I thought of my late mother and dad. How proud they would have been! But also how nervous my mother might have been, knowing that I might lose. She might have said, "Son, are you sure you want to get mixed up in politics?" But they would have been my biggest supporters, although they would not have been able to vote in Florida.

In looking back on it, I was taking quite a risk. If I had lost, I would essentially have had no job. I would no longer have a seat in the legislature. From a financial standpoint I would have had to depend on the Earl Hutto Agency, the little one-man business which I operated out of our home, because I would no longer have had the $12,000 a year pay from the state. I was thankful that I had a few advertising accounts with my agency that supplemented my legislative salary, but it didn't add up to a lot.

But, you know something, we did not really give these matters a thought. When we made that decision to run two or three years before, we knew without a shadow of doubt that that was the thing we should do and we had faith that the good Lord would take care of us. That faith also gave us confidence to believe that we were going to win. We felt good about what we were doing. We also knew that we had to put feet to those prayers and work hard.

Believe me, we had to work hard, mighty hard, because we had no money. No money and running for Congress? Yep. We had not yet even set up a campaign account. Personally, I still would have my state pay until a replacement was elected and sworn in to take my seat in the legislature. Nancy had a few bucks she had saved up from her teacher's pay to use to get our driveway paved. The driveway would have to wait until later. We spent that money for bumper stickers. After that, every time Nancy saw a Hutto for Congress bumper sticker she would say, "There goes a piece of my driveway."

Wallace Kendrick, a local businessman, who had helped me raise money for my previous two campaigns for the state house, was willing to help me do the same for Congress. But it was tough sledding in that first primary. Harold Phillips, another businessman who had contributed to my previous races, but who had never met Wallace, joined him in making calls on my behalf. They became good friends. Initially we were able to get a few contributions, mostly from my home county and a smattering from around the district.

Over in the Pensacola area, Al McLeod and Gerald Newman became the unofficial co-chairmen for finances and did a good job of soliciting funds. But, as I said, in the first primary this was a very tough job. Even at the volunteer meetings Al or Gerald, or both, would get up and say how badly we needed financial support and, though most of our volunteers could not afford much, they chipped in what they could. This was enough to buy gas and meals and pay the rent and utilities on our headquarters locations. Of course, contributions and expenditures had to go through our campaign account and reports made to the Federal Elections Commission.

I had my state legislative district office in the back of an old dwelling on Jenks Avenue in Panama City and since the rest of the building was vacant, we were able to rent it from John Harrell, a

Republican friend, for a small price and this became not only our Bay County Headquarters, but also Earl Hutto for Congress Campaign Headquarters for the district. We were able to rent small, but visible, one room headquarters in the two other major cities, Fort Walton Beach and Pensacola. They were staffed by volunteers.

I had always managed my own campaigns and essentially that is what I did in the congressional race. I did have some good help. I could not afford a full-time campaign manager. I was blessed, however, by having three young men from Panama City who were dying to work in a big time campaign, like one for Congress. Steve Strickland, Robert Higdon, and Tommy Todd were bright young fellows who would serve me well. None had finished college, although Tommy was a little older and married. These "Whiz Kids" all had ideas, some good and some pretty bad...but youthful enthusiasm they did have. Steve, who had been away for a year or so studying at Beloit College in Wisconsin, was concerned about my physical image. The first thing he wanted me to do was to get some high heeled shoes so that I would look taller. I merely shrugged off this suggestion with a hearty laugh. But each of these guys was helpful in his own way. I could only pay them minimum wage and sometimes they had to wait on that. They did a lot of errand running, especially between Panama City and Pensacola and were good sounding boards for what they were hearing about other candidates. They helped in placing my ads, putting up signs, making telephone calls, and a multitude of other things that had to be done. I think each thought of himself as running the show and at times they were at odds with each other, but generally they worked well together.

Northwest Florida is one of the most conservative areas of the nation. In fact, in later years a survey by National Journal reported that it was the most conservative. The Panhandle at that time was better than 80 per cent Democratic registration and for many years we did not know what a Republican looked like. Someone joked that Republicans in Northwest Florida could meet in a phone booth. But the conservative Democrats did not mind crossing party lines in voting for president and occasionally in statewide races.

I disavowed the Democratic national party platform as being too liberal. Most people in the south felt the same way. But I did receive good support from some of our county Democratic committees. In this 1978 race this was probably more evident in

Okaloosa County than elsewhere and I was pleased to have several committee members to operate my campaign office to be available to people who might stop by for brochures and information about me.

In Pensacola the headquarters was in a good location right downtown in a vacant store on Garden Street. We were able to put up large signs in the windows and the facility was large enough for us to have campaign gatherings. Because this was the biggest population center, I felt I needed someone full-time in Pensacola and Escambia County. I hired a young man by the name of Tim Hyatt who was willing to work for minimum wage since he had no job. Fortunately, his vivacious wife, Brenda, who was an excellent volunteer helper, did have a job. Tim had absolutely no experience with campaigns, but he was all I could afford and he did his best.

Nowadays practically every campaign for Congress has a consulting firm to do polling, produce campaign commercials, and, in essence, run the campaign. Even in 1978 apparently a lot of campaigns were beginning to utilize such consultants. I could not afford one and would not have one even if I could afford it. I cannot and will not be packaged. I believe in campaigning the old-fashioned way by shaking a lot of hands, getting to know the people, and carrying my message at the grassroots level.

Fortunately for me I had media experience. I knew how to write and my radio and television background equipped me to get my message out and to do it at minimal cost. I saved thousands of dollars, which I did not have, by writing and producing my own radio and TV spots and newspaper ads. My theme was "He Stands for What is Right". I used a picture taken by Louie Walker, photographer for WJHG-TV with whom I had worked, that was a full length photo of me standing speaking into a microphone. This is what I used on the front of my brochure and on the few billboards we bought late in the campaign. Inside the brochure we put a lot of action pictures, several of me speaking before the Florida House, some with family, some with military people and veterans, one of me with a hardhat inside a factory, and one with Nancy and the girls and me riding on top of a load of watermelons in Mr. Farrell Nelson's truck in the Watermelon Festival Parade in Chipley. The narrative stated my positions on a number of issues such as the economy, inflation and deficit spending, gun control, environment, energy, senior citizens, and so on.

In Pensacola I felt I needed to jog folks' memories that I used to be one of them, that I lived there and worked at WEAR-TV in its early days back in the middle and late fifties. Back then I signed off my daily sportscasts with a motto, "Remember fans, in the game of life, as in any game of ball, play it clean, play it fair, or not at all." I came up with this early in my broadcasting career as a takeoff on a quote from the renowned sportswriter, Grantland Rice, who wrote, "When the one great scorer comes to write against your name, it is not whether you won or lost, but how you played the game." During this campaign a number of people remembered my motto. So, I knew I was no stranger to them.

I thought it might be a little difficult to fit that motto into a TV spot, so I chose to jog those memories in a more visible way. Supreme Ice Cream had been one of my big sponsors. They not only sponsored my sportscasts, but they also sponsored a kids show in primetime titled "Rocky Jones, Space Ranger". I became CAPTAIN SUPREME and in my space-like uniform I did the Supreme Ice Cream commercials inside the show. It was a popular program and the series lasted about six months, but I continued to be Captain Supreme when Rocky Jones was replaced by Jet Jackson. I made quite a few personal appearances at schools and youth gatherings and appeared in several parades such as the Fiesta of Five Flags in Pensacola and The National Peanut Festival in Dothan, Alabama, the home of Supreme Ice Cream. So, in this campaign for Congress, I used a picture in one of my TV ads of Captain Supreme riding on a float in the Fiesta of Five Flags Parade in downtown Pensacola. It was well received and we got several nice comments about it.

Though I had a good following in the rural counties, I did not want to take them for granted, so I campaigned in each one, generally going into stores and leaving brochures, handing them out on the streets, and making my way through the courthouses shaking every hand in sight. But I had found out long ago that in most small counties and cities there seem to be two factions....and if one faction is for something, or somebody, the other faction is going to be automatically against. So, I did not want to align myself in those counties with any particular group and felt that it was better not to have any kind of formal organization. I wanted to be friends and to receive all of their votes, regardless of their politics.

In Pensacola, Panama City, and Fort Walton Beach we held volunteer meetings once each week. As I recall, it was Panama City

Monday nights, Fort Walton Beach Tuesday nights, and Pensacola on Thursday nights. The meetings were generally held at our headquarters and I tried to fire up our volunteers to work harder, to get our message out, and to let me know what they were hearing out there. Oftentimes they would tell me of places I needed to go, people I needed to see, and things I should be doing. I will always be grateful to these fine people who gave us such great support and who were willing to put in a lot of time working on my behalf.

At the outset of the campaign State Attorney Curtis Golden was established as the favorite. The media pointed out that his family was well off financially and he indicated that he would spend as much of his own funds as necessary. His name was also well known since the First Judicial Circuit he served, and still serves, is made up of Escambia, Santa Rosa, Okaloosa, and Walton Counties, which accounted for a very high percentage of the population of District One. At the time he had been in office for about ten years.

What a blessing it was for Mr. Golden to be tabbed the frontrunner. It meant that Jerry Melvin would aim his artillery at Golden and not me. This was good not only from a political standpoint, but a personal one as well. I mentioned earlier about the little jabs from Jerry in our last days in the legislative session and I anticipated that I would be on the receiving end of his attacks in the campaign. Jerry was a hardworking and effective legislator, but he possessed a pretty sharp tongue and thus it was great that not only did we get along like the friends we were during the campaign, but our limited staffs and volunteers seemed to hit it off as well. All his firepower was aimed at Golden, and Jerry did not hesitate to express his disdain for lawyers.

So, in the first primary Melvin and Golden fought it out while Ike Williams and I were pretty well ignored by those two as far as their rhetoric went. Williams was a very colorful individual who had been a soldier of fortune in the Rhodesian Army, claimed to be the only candidate with international experience, and rode a horse around the district. I thought he conducted himself well in speeches and debates. Apparently the public did not see him as a serious candidate.

It was not my nature to run a negative campaign and it was good that I did not have to answer any charges from other candidates. Our campaign was going well, in our opinion. People were saying good things and giving us encouragement, but still some of our best friends, although fully supporting us and wishing us well, did not believe that we would win.

Thankfully I felt extremely well, physically and mentally, throughout this campaign. I went from early to late. I tried to get back home at night as much as possible to be with my wife and daughters. By the time I got in bed I was so tired that I was asleep by the time my head hit the pillow. Oftentimes I would leave home well before daybreak and head to the other end of the district. At times I spent the night with friends so as to be in that area the next morning.

One of my friends and volunteers was Bill Bruhmuller, a husky former Navy Seal, who quite often agreed to drive me around the district. This was very helpful in that Bill not only drove me, he gave the appearance of being a good body guard, and also made friendships and helped me campaign. Since the campaign could not afford a motel bill, I was glad that we did have friends who offered to put us up from time to time. Also, more than once, I took pillow and blankets from my car and slept on the hard floor of our headquarters in Pensacola so as to get a quick start in the morning.

The very early part of the campaign Nancy and I attended a regional banking reception held at Bay Point on the banks of Grand Lagoon in our home county. It was a very nice occasion with several hundred people enjoying the hospitality on the terrace of this beautiful resort. For a political candidate, and I was not the only one present, this was a good group with which to mingle. Nancy and I met a young redheaded fellow and his date and learned that he worked for Barnett Bank in Fort Walton Beach. We were quite impressed with him, perhaps because it was apparent that he was not drinking anything stronger than coke. "Fort Walton, huh?" "Yessir, that's right," responded the serious appearing redhead who wore a name tag that identified him as Randy Knepper.

Boy, oh boy, I thought, this may be another prayer answered. Did I ever need help in Fort Walton Beach. I knew very few people there and maybe my new acquaintance could lend a hand. "Randy, I am running for Congress," I said. "I do not know if you know anything about me, but I would like to talk to you about supporting me. Could I set up a time to meet with you over in Fort Walton?" Randy seemed excited and agreed to have me come by to talk about the campaign. Within a few days, I paid a visit to Randy at his office in the bank where he worked as a loan officer. We had a great deal in common, not the least of which was our Baptist faith and agreement on the moral issues of our nation. Randy made suggestions on a number of people that could be helpful in my behalf and introduced me to several folks who became supporters. In essence, although I am not sure his superiors would have looked favorably on his having an official title, he became my defacto campaign manager in south Okaloosa county. Randy and his parents gave me a lot of help.

One of the best ways to draw a crowd in Northwest Florida is to throw a fish fry. Mullet, which is delicious when fried fresh on the day it is caught, is sometimes referred to as the "soul food of politicians." We attended several fish fries and rallies during the course of the campaign. A number of them were public events where all the candidates, usually by alphabetical order, were allowed to speak about three minutes. At the free fish fries, we usually had a good turnout, but at the rallies where free food was not offered the attendance was on the sparse side. The rally crowds mostly consisted of candidates, their relatives, and close supporters. Sometimes a hotly contested race would bring out more people.

At the Bay County Democratic Rallies there was an old gentleman by the name of Pete Monaco who was the official timekeeper for the speeches. People got to noticing that I seemed to have more time than the other candidates. Pete really liked me and he did not want to cut me off before I finished what I wanted to say. When he was reproached about this, he said, "Well, at the age of 92, I sometimes have a little trouble reading my stopwatch."

Jim Seaton, a newspaper writer, devoted his column to a political rally he attended. On the congressional race he had this to say about the primary candidates: "Earl Hutto talked with the smoothness of experience. If I hear Jerry Melvin say `I worked for Bob Sikes for three years' one more time, I may be sick. Ike Williams lays it on the line and dislikes Ted Kennedy and Andrew Young as much as I do. I think more closet conservatives agree with him than will admit it. Curtis Golden sent tee shirts and hats, but didn't make roll call."

Most of the rural counties held Democratic rallies on Friday and Saturday nights for several weeks leading up to the election. Usually candidates for federal and state offices were given the courtesy of speaking first to be followed by the candidates for local offices. But occasionally the chairman put federal and state offices last, supposedly to hold the crowd. But, more often than not, some of the county races, such as that for sheriff, were more hotly contested and might command more interest. Anyway, there was no way that I could personally attend each of these rallies, but I tried to get to as many as I could. If I could not be there, I would try to have someone there to speak on my behalf.

Except for just a very small amount of media advertising, the Hutto campaign had relied mostly on getting up the limited number of yard signs we had, passing out brochures, and hustling every possible moment to line up support. I knew we needed more on-the-air and newspaper exposure and time was running out for the first primary on September 12th. We had to get on the air, especially in the Pensacola area, but had no funds. We just did not have the money to do it. So, I prevailed on Wallace Kendrick and Harold Phillips to lend me $5,000 each and, though we could not match Golden, we were able to get necessary exposure the last ten days before the election.

The League of Women Voters sponsored a candidates forum in Panama City, Fort Walton Beach, and Pensacola each election where all the candidates were given time to speak and to respond to questions. In Pensacola and Panama City, these programs were broadcast on television. WCOA Radio in Pensacola also invited the candidates to appear on their "Pensacola Speaks" program. I tried to be up on the issues and seemingly my appearances on these programs went quite well. At least I did not feel that they hurt me.

On election day Nancy and I arose early and got to the polls before the lines began forming. We were greeted warmly by those on hand who wished us well. Bay County had never had anyone elected to Congress and we were all hoping that this would be a first. In everyone's mind, this would be a longshot. How could someone from the eastern part of the district win when most of the voters lived on the other side? Despite this mindset, the Huttos still had a good confident feeling about what was about to take place.

Election day in the past had been an off day as I figured the die had been cast and there was nothing else I could do. This time the stakes were higher. The district was bigger and I thought I should make use of all the time I could. So I campaigned some on election day before getting back home to freshen up for the outcome.

Many candidates hold their election parties in fancy hotels, but we had always held them in our home. In reality, although we had a core of good workers, we were not that well organized in Pensacola and Fort Walton Beach. So we decided home was the best place to be. In my elections to the state legislature our Sunday School class had generally spearheaded the get-together by helping with the food and so on. The practice was also to have Daddy, while he was alive, my brother Rex, and sister Merle, and their families down from Ozark, Alabama to join us and spend the night. On this occasion, my first race for Congress, a lot of friends and supporters filled our house and the excitement was building as we awaited the first returns.

The noise level was naturally quite high with that many people and one could barely hear the TV. But, as the stations made their break-in reports, the crowd grew silent. Some were huddled by several radios trying to get returns from Pensacola or anywhere in the district. The polls closed at 7:00 p.m. It wasn't long before the first returns were announced. A cheer went up. Hutto was a big winner in the precincts that had reported. Good news! But the night was young and these returns were from our home county.

We couldn't wait to hear how it was going elsewhere, so we had advised friends in Pensacola and around the district that we would be calling to get the results. In Pensacola early returns showed us leading in some precincts, but overall Golden was leading in Escambia and Santa Rosa Counties, as expected. Within the next couple of hours we all would be filled with joy. Hutto was surprising the pundits by leading the entire district, and by a sizeable margin. Our pastor, Dr. N. B. Langford, led a victory prayer of thanksgiving.

It was a grand night. When the final tally was in it showed the following results: Hutto 39,982; Golden 29,692; Melvin 21,186; and Williams 3,687. A smashing victory! Hutto led second place finisher Golden by over 10,000 votes. I had won five of the eight counties in the district--Bay, Gulf, Washington, Holmes, and Walton--by huge margins. Golden had won two counties in his home area-- Escambia and Santa Rosa-- and Melvin carried his home county of Okaloosa. But I had done well in the other counties, placing a good second in populous Escambia and a close third in Santa Rosa and Okaloosa. Remember, in our "pillow talk" three years before, Nancy and I strategized that we could win big in those five counties and could do pretty well in the western counties. Bingo! That is exactly how it turned out. CAPTAIN SUPREME comes up a big winner!

Reached in Washington by the news media the day after the election, Congressman Bob Sikes called the primary "an interesting election," adding that "It is never safe to predict how a political race will come out. Of course, I was surprised, but I saw the way Hutto was coming up fast. It was pretty obvious he was moving up fast."

Curtis Golden was shocked! According to media reports he had spent more than twice as much as I had and he had expected to lead the ticket. The State Attorney, who at this point had rarely had opposition and incidentally has had none for his position since, did carry his native Santa Rosa county by a good margin, but in more densely populated Escambia his margin over me was only 13-9 and Melvin had run right behind me. We would have a highly contested runoff, but we were in the driver's seat unless I blew it, and there was no way I was going to do that.

This was the first runoff I had experienced in my short political career and it would be a challenge. Despite the contentious battle between Golden and Melvin in the first primary, Golden now courted Melvin for his support. So did I. But I had told the media I could win without Jerry's endorsement. I was a little embarrassed, though, the way it came out in the paper. It appeared that I did not care whether or not Melvin was for me. I certainly did not mean it that way and expressed that to Melvin, who understood. But he decided not to endorse anyone.

The collegiality of the Melvin and Hutto staffs in the first primary did, however, inure to my benefit in the runoff because I got his top staffer to coordinate my runoff. I did not know Carol Biven, but those three "whiz kids" who worked with me had observed her work in Jerry's campaign and urged me to hire her. It was a good move. Carol endeared herself to our campaign volunteers, many of whom my friend, Homer Singletary, had lined up from the Warrington Presbyterian Church, and fired them up....got them more excited. We gained a lot of other volunteers.

Coming out of the first primary with such a good vote made me humble and grateful to the people for such a show of support. I expressed this through the media and to those with whom I came in contact. Everybody loves a winner! Now, we began getting pledges of support from around the district. My close friends, who had been sort of ambivalent about my running, now were highly enthusiastic. For example, Tax Collector Donnell Brookins, with whom I worked at the TV station before he ran for office, started typing out letters on my old Royal portable typewriter right there at my house, on election night, to people asking them for financial support. We started getting checks in the mail. Though it was certainly not enough to run a profuse campaign it did mean that we could breathe a little easier about not having to skimp so much.

Golden, keenly aware of the overwhelming vote I had received in the five eastern-most counties, used a strategy in the runoff of playing off Escambia, Santa Rosa, and Okaloosa Counties--the more densely populated areas on his side of the district--against Gulf, Bay, Washington, Holmes, and Walton counties where I had done so well. There were 200,062 democrats registered in the district and 136,728 were in the three western counties targeted by Golden with only 63,334 in the five smaller eastern counties.

Curtis charged that I would favor the eastern part of the district in my home area by working harder for Tyndall Air Force Base in Panama City than I would for Eglin Air Force Base, Whiting Field, and the Pensacola Navy complex. His strategy did not work. I responded that I would be a congressman for all District One and would work equally hard for every county.

The mere fact that District One would have a different congressman after nearly four decades made this a very important election for Florida's Panhandle area. Mark O'Brien wrote an article in the Pensacola News-Journal with the headline "Candidates Sparring in Fight for Congress" in which he related a few of Golden's charges and my response to them. Golden reiterated that I had received a "block vote" from the eastern part of the district and would be a sectional representative. I responded that "Yes, I am proud of the fact that such a high percentage of the people in those counties voted for me. They are the ones who know me best. I will not divide the district, but will unite it."

As in the first primary, I felt the best way for me to campaign was to see as many voters and work as hard as I could. I was up and at it early each day. I attended early morning breakfasts. Some mornings I was outside the gate of factories and other facilities greeting the workers and handing them a brochure as they arrived. Still on other mornings I waved to motorists as they headed to work. People said I was everywhere. I'm glad they noticed! Waving at street corners was not new to me, but in the past I had done it by myself or perhaps with Nancy. Now, Carol, who had really utilized this technique with Melvin in the first primary, organized groups to get out and wave with my campaign signs.

Even though I had to spend a lot of time away from home during this campaign year,I tried to keep things in perspective. I dearly love my family and did not like being away from them. All of us were caught up in this thing and anytime the girls were not in school I tried to have us all together as much as possible. I remember one time when Lori and Amy took several of their friends from Northside Elementary along when Nancy and others traveled the 100-mile stretch from Panama City to a rally at Seville Square in Pensacola. These little friends were real interested and excited that Lori and Amy's Dad was running for Congress, though they might not have understood a whole lot about politics. Our campaign was bereft of a lot of the frills because we just could not afford them. We did have a few tee shirts emblazoned with "Earl Hutto for Congress" on the front and back for family and close supporters . Our kids and their friends were excited to be wearing them.

Being the active youngsters they were, during the rally they found something more captivating to do.They started playing on one of the rides in the park when they became engaged with a bunch of little Golden supporters. When these youngsters wearing Golden shirts found out that the father of Lori and Amy was Earl Hutto they started taunting our group by saying that Golden is going to "beat your Dad". "No he won't," "Yes, he will" went on for a spell. Though it might have started good naturedly, they almost came to blows before the rally was over. On the way home, these young'uns were all wired and wound up about this confrontation in Pensacola.

Everyone was upbeat as the second primary election day arrived October 5, 1978. We felt we had run a good campaign, but one never knows until those ballots are tabulated. The Golden-Hutto campaign had been a clean one, at least in comparison to today's negative fiascos. To Curtis Golden's credit, I do not recall seeing any negative or mudslinging ads by him on television. In our face-to-face meetings we had discussed legitimate issues and conducted campaigns worthy of the high office we were seeking.

Elections in Florida are held on Tuesdays, but this runoff was on Thursday due to Jewish holidays. This day was similar to the first primary day for me as far as my activities were concerned. But where to be election night? Our Pensacola volunteers wanted me to be with them and, of course, the homefolks wanted me in Panama City. I tried to accommodate both. Late in the day Bill Sowell of Sowell Aviation flew Wallace Kendrick and me to Pensacola.

The volunteers brought in worlds of food for a covered dish supper at Hutto Headquarters in Pensacola and they decorated the place beautifully. It was a festive occasion. Everyone was in a good mood and there was a real closeness and love one for another as we waited for the show to begin. The first precincts in Pensacola reported that Hutto was ahead. It was what we wanted to hear. I called home to Panama City. It was thumbs up there, too. The shorter runoff ballot made for quicker tabulations and before long I was being projected as the winner. The news media interviewed me amid cheers from our supporters. What a glorious feeling!

Before leaving Pensacola we went by the Escambia County Democratic Headquarters and as I entered, Chairman Bill Marshall said "Let's give a big cheer for our Democratic Candidate for Congress." The next day in the Pensacola News-Journal there was a feature story with a headline: "CAPT. SUPREME," with a sub-headline "Demo Workers Cheer Hutto!" In the article by Ira Brock the first paragraph read "Ole Captain Supreme did better than Superman or any other make-believe heroes of early television."

By the time we flew back to Panama City, it was getting a little late, but still a good crowd was waiting on the tarmac of the airport. As I disembarked, there was a big cheer! My hands went up spontaneously in a victory pose as I smiled broadly. I was grateful that the homefolks were there to greet me. It was emotional as I embraced Nancy and the girls and there were a few tears of joy. I accepted the congratulations of the crowd with a lot of hugs and handshakes, plus a brief victory speech.

On runoff day, in addition to our race, the Governor-Lieutenant Governor contest, as well as a couple of other state and local races brought a good turnout of voters. Over 94,000, the almost identical number that voted in the first primary, expressed themselves at the polls. The final tally showed Hutto with 58,352 and Golden 35,721. I had carried seven of the eight counties and Curtis had carried his native county of Santa Rosa, but not by a great margin. A good victory--and I gave thanks. It was two down and one to go.

The stage was set. Lights...camera...action! This was the big show, the one that counted...the general election for U. S. Representative to Congress from Florida's First District pitting Earl

Hutto against Warren Briggs. This was for the marbles. The winner will be a Congressman!

The Hutto camp was ready for the run. We had momentum. We had confidence, but were not cocky. We had our work cut out for us. Republicans wanted to win this seat that had been in Democratic hands always. That's right! There was never a Republican in Congress from Northwest Florida.

Warren Briggs, who stepped down from his appointive non-partisan position as Mayor of Pensacola, was a worthy opponent and no newcomer to politics. He served a two year term as a Democrat in the Florida House, 1966-68. He was well respected and would not be hampered by lack of money. The Republican National Committee had this district targeted and would provide personnel and funding.

A side-by-side profile of Briggs and me was written by Mary Barrineau for the Pensacola News-Journal. The big headline was "West Florida's Next Congressman..." On one side the sub headline was "Warren Briggs..The Right Man to Fill Big Shoes," and on the other side "Earl Hutto: Play It Clean, Play It Fair, or Not at All" (a reference to my old sportscasts sign off). The article provided an in depth look at both of us. This is what it showed about Warren's background: born and raised in Minnesota, graduated from West Point, served in U. S. Army Air Corps, taught at Military Academy, brought to north Escambia county town of Century by his father-in-law to run his sawmill in 1957. Included in the story were several complimentary comments from Warren's friends.

I thought Mary did a super job in her writing, but I was a little embarrassed at some of the comments she quoted from some of my friends. Gerald Newman, whose father's place we lived on when my dad was a sharecropper back in Alabama, said, "You never heard him make a fuss about what he was doing, but you'd look around and the job always got done. He was a kid who never did anything but work. After school he'd work in the field with his dad."

Homer Singletary had this to say, "It may sound corny, but I'd have to describe Earl as Mr. Nice Guy. I've never known him to take a drink, smoke a cigarette, say a cuss word or even lose his temper. He wouldn't get upset with people who did any of those things, but he just wouldn't do them." These were true friends speaking, but they were probably setting me higher on a pedestal than I deserved to be.

Warren Briggs might have been just as hard a worker as I was.

Although a Republican had a tough time getting the spotlight while the Democratic primary was going on, Warren worked throughout the district and even showed up at some Democratic Rallies. Some Democrats complained about it and thought this was rather "bold or brash" on his part.. But, after all, these rallies were open to the public and there was nothing illegal about a Republican attending.

One of the biggest flaps in the campaign revolved around a TV spot I taped with Congressman Sikes. I was playing on the theme "From one Conservative Democrat to another, Pass it on." I wrote a 30-second spot that embodied that theme and at a Democratic Rally at Ferdinand Plaza in Pensacola I showed it to Bob Sikes and asked his approval. "It looks good to me," he said. I had a film crew there and I asked Bob if we could be filmed walking down the sidewalk together. He readily agreed. The effort turned out well and I soon had it on the tube. When some of Mr. Sikes's Pensacola cronies saw it, they hit the ceiling. One of them, Vince Whibbs, who would in later years as Mayor of Pensacola become a good friend and supporter of mine, called Sikes at his home in Crestview to complain about it. The next morning, Briggs went to Crestview and did a tape with Sikes in which the He-Coon was quoted as saying "Warren, I invited you here because I felt we should discuss a situation neither of us anticipated. That is the ad depicting me with your opponent. He's a good friend and you are a good friend, but I have tried to make it clear that I am not telling people who to vote for."

Bob Sikes was caught in a difficult situation. It was hard to play both sides. The News-Journal, indeed, had quoted Sikes, at Gubernatorial Candidate Bob Graham's Headquarters, as saying he was endorsing Hutto and the entire Democratic slate. I had not really asked him for his endorsement as such. I told the media "The advertisement was done with the approval of Mr. Sikes and the point it makes is that the district has been served by a conservative Democrat in Congress for 38 years and the tradition should be continued. It did not say Sikes is endorsing me. For that matter, the copy could have been voiced over a file picture."

Later that day my wife, Nancy, represented me at a groundbreaking ceremony at Tyndall Air Force Base. She was seated next to Congressman Sikes on the platform. While someone else was at the podium Sikes leaned over to Nancy and brought up the TV ad. He suggested to her that I take it off the air. Alma Butler, his administrative assistant in Washington, also called me. When Nancy called to advise me of this episode I acted immediately to comply by calling the stations and removing the spot. In so doing I stated "I would not have used the ad without Mr. Sikes's approval and I am pulling it off the air to ease the tension."

In a campaign trip to the northern end of Escambia county I stopped in at crossroads stores or any place I could find people. At a couple of stops in the Century area I was told "Yes, we"ll vote for you. We can't support the other fella because he's part of that silk stocking crowd." This ignited a thought for another commercial.

We were having good crowds at our Thursday night volunteer meetings. So I taped a "made for TV speech" of 30-seconds duration which in essence said "My friends, I am not a member of the silk stocking crowd and when you elect me to Congress I will serve all the people." Our volunteers responded spontaneously with cheers and applause. The ad looked good on television.

Warren constantly rapped the liberal Democrats in Congress and Speaker Tip O'Neill , exclaiming that he would not work with O'Neill and the Democrats but with people who think as the people in this district. That gave me a wonderful opening of which I took advantage. To that assertion I answered, "I can't imagine someone lashing out at the Speaker and then expecting to go up there and get anything done. My work in the legislature shows I can work with people and I will work with Tip O'Neill, though we have philosophical differences, for the betterment of our country and this district." It resonated well as I emphasized the importance of keeping someone in the majority in this seat.

I believe that Warren Briggs was uncomfortable at times because he had people from Washington telling him how to run his campaign and what to say. He had staff people from the Republican National Committee working out of his office and I am sure that, philosophically, he agreed with them. But Warren, I think, would have preferred being more of his own man. Anyway, we were able to emphasize we had nobody from Washington running our campaign.

There were a couple of other occasions during the course of the contest where the situation arose that gave me a "lob ball to hit out of the park." While Congressman Phil Crane (R-Illinois) was down in the district campaigning for Warren, he made the statement that Briggs would come to Washington as a freshman representative and "succumb to either the arm twisting of House Speaker Tip O'Neill, which is no way to represent this district, or else come to Washington as an independent voice and be relegated to limbo." Crane shouldn't have said it because at every meeting thereafter where Warren and I spoke I would pull out the clipping and say "See, right here in the paper one of the leading Republicans says that Warren would be relegated to limbo if he doesn't work with the speaker." Warren cringed every time I reached inside my coat pocket.

The other occasion that provided fodder for a response was when then Congressman Trent Lott (R-Mississippi) of Pascagoula, made airport stops in support of Briggs. Lott, when asked about Briggs's chances of getting on the defense committees, downplayed those possibilities for a freshman congressman. I did not hesitate to point out Lott's comments along the trail from time to time.

Actually, I did have one congressman to come into the district to see me during the campaign. Andy Ireland, a freshman Democrat from Winter Haven, had called and arranged to meet me at the Okaloosa Air Terminal in Fort Walton Beach. As I recall, I believe he brought me a campaign check, but I don't remember if it was from his campaign account or if it was the one and only check that I received from the Democratic Congressional Campaign Committee. But the main reason Andy, who had just a short stay between flights, wanted to see me was to lobby me to support him for the Appropriations Committee from the Florida delegation. I had met Andy once before when he had visited the Florida Legislature and, since he was a good conservative who shared the philosophy of Northwest Floridians, I told him I would try to help, but had to get elected first. I took comfort in the fact he thought I would have no trouble doing that.

I did not mean to be presumptuous, but during the general election campaign I made a one day trip to Washington to meet with people about my own possibilities of getting on the Armed Services Committee. Among those I met with was Congressman Charlie Bennett, a senior member of the Florida delegation and a Subcommittee Chairman on the House Armed Services Committee. Mr. Bennett pledged his support in trying to get me a slot on the committee, but warned that it might not be easy for a freshman since it would give Florida two members on the committee. He was being cautious because I already knew there were two or three states that had two members on the HASC.

Sunday, as much as possible, was a day of rest and attending church for the Hutto family. I remember sitting in church several times, reflecting on what a wonderful respite it was from the rigors of the campaign trail, and counting the days before the election would be over. I loved campaigning, but anything can wear one out. It was nice though, as I made the trek to and fro between Panama City and Pensacola, that I was traveling the Miracle Strip and along the way I had a spectacular view of the world's most beautiful beaches, especially the emerald waters around Destin. What a district to represent...if I ever make it to election day!

November 7, 1978, finally arrived and was I glad to see it. This had been a great experience over the last six months, but I was ready for it to end.We had worked hard and done our very best. I was keyed up. Nancy, Lori and Amy were keyed up. Our supporters were keyed up. This would be one of the most significant days of our lives. It was a good day for an election, partly cloudy and pleasant.

Florida on this day would elect a new Governor and a new Lieutenant Governor. Other state cabinet officials would be elected. There was a state senatorial race in the western end of the district and a smattering of state legislative contests. At this time there were not enough Republicans in Northwest Florida for them to successfully try local races, but there were a few competing. Also on the ballot were some important constitutional amendments.

There was no question that this was an important election. To some observers it was the most important election ever for our area. It was not a presidential election year. There was no U. S. Senate race. But the focus was on the contest that would see the election of a new Congressman for Northwest Florida for the first time in nearly four decades. I was in the center of this focus. I had a right to be awfully nervous, but I was not. Someone described me with an old southern saying "He is as cool as a cucumber."

On Monday before the election I stood on Palafox Street and Brent Lane in Pensacola from 6:30 to 9:30 a.m. waving to everyone in the mass of cars that transited that busy intersection. How uplifting to see occupants of the vehicles roll down their windows and holler comments such as "Good luck, Earl, we're with you." Blowing car horns in acknowledgment of my campaign was quite gratifying.

I spent the night in Pensacola and early on election morning I was in Gulf Breeze waving to the onslaught of motorists headed onto the bay bridge bound for their jobs in Pensacola. As on the previous day, I had a few of my volunteers waving signs and reminding people to vote. Again, the reception was very positive. Afterwards I headed eastward for a scheduled stop in Fort Walton at mid-morning and then was back home in Panama City about noon.

Nancy and I breathed a sigh of relief. How good it was to know that the long arduous campaign, though a wonderful time in our life, was over. We had been the underdog, in the minds of most, from day one. We were on the eastern end of a district heavily weighted with voters on the other end. We had no money. Yet we had come through two elections on top. We had run the course and spent about $70,000 through three elections-- a first primary, second primary runoff, and the general election. That was fantastic considering that nowadays it is not unusual for a candidate to spend a million dollars or more, just on a primary. We had paid back the $5,000 each we had borrowed from Wallace and Harold and had about $2,000 balance. Through it all, we had been blessed.

At Nancy's insistence I took a hot bath and headed for bed and had no trouble going right to sleep. I was reinvigorated when awakened from my nap a couple of hours later and eager for what the next few hours would bring.

In order for me to spend some time with supporters in our three major cities that night, it was necessary to have some special arrangements. We had to move quickly in order to cram this busy itinerary into the relatively brief period from the time the polls closed until most people's bedtime. So, in late afternoon Nancy and I, accompanied by Wallace and Edith Kendrick, headed to Pensacola, driven in a Florida Highway Patrol car at normal speed.

On arrival in Pensacola, it was well past closing time for the downtown stores, but it was not apparent because of the cars parked on Garden Street. A big crowd was on hand. As we entered our headquarters there was a lot of hugging, greeting, and well wishing. A great air of expectancy filled the place. These people had a lot of confidence in me. Indeed, it went well beyond that. Many of them were newly found friends who had worked so hard on my behalf. Now, as we came down to the wire, they showed a lot of love and affection for Nancy and me. We felt the same way about them and were so grateful for this close relationship.

For the third time in about two months a bountiful covered

dish supper was spread in the midst of the festively decorated Hutto Headquarters. Fortuitous as it might have been, the cake inscribed with "Congratulations Congressman Hutto" was not only beautiful, but delicious. We had a great time eating, socializing, and just enjoying each other's company....all this with sober people. No alcohol was served.

A little after 7 o'clock, the returns began coming in. Shh..shh..quiet folks, let's listen to the radio: "Our first report on that important race for U.S. Congress...in Precinct 53, for Earl Hutto 459, and for Warren Briggs 277....in Precinct 49 the tally is in and it shows Hutto walloped Briggs 282 to 52." The crowd went wild! It was looking good, but I reminded them it was not over yet. Still I was mighty happy. Within the next hour or so Don Priest, the venerable News Director of WCOA, reported "Folks, district-wide Earl Hutto has taken a big lead in the race for the U. S. Congress and we are projecting that Mr. Hutto has been elected and will succeed Bob Sikes in Washington". .The place was ecstatic!

We began receiving congratulations. "We'll be up to Washington to see you," some of them were saying. "Better get you some longhandles, it's gonna get cold up there, Earl." This was a great celebration. But we knew we had to be moving on so that we could share some of our time in the two other locations. Members of the media were there, so I did interviews with them. Still others were on the phone. Everybody wanted to chat with us....it was hard to get away, but finally we were able to move on.

Lieutenant Gilbert put his foot to the pedal and it did not take very long for us to get to Fort Walton Beach. After doing an interview at the radio station, talking to reporters, and visiting with our volunteers, we were on our way home....at least I thought so.

The Highway Patrol car that carried the Kendricks and us zoomed down U. S. Highway 98 at a high rate of speed. But as we got through Panama City Beach, instead of heading on across Hathaway Bridge into Panama City, trooper Gilbert turned right and, with blue lights flashing and siren blaring, headed south. I knew that something was up. My wife had conspired with some of our good friends who, knowing that there were so many people in the vicinity who had been working, hoping, and praying for me to be elected to Congress, decided our victory party should be some place larger than our home. We were headed to Captain Anderson's on Grand

Lagoon, the biggest restaurant in the area.

It was nothing new for Captain Anderson's to be crowded with hundreds of diners during the tourist season, but this was November and as we pulled up to the restaurant, it was evident a tremendous crowd was on hand. It was hard to believe that this many people were gathered because of me.

What a thrill it was as we entered the restaurant to receive such an uproarious reception. I was ushered right on up to the head table before even getting a chance to visit personally with anyone. Donnell Brookins was the emcee and I am sure he had done a good job of keeping the crowd entertained with his wit and humor. They had been patiently waiting all this time for us. For some it was well past their bedtime, especially our children. But everyone was having a good time. Nancy and I were having the best time of all.

As I looked out over the audience I saw many good friends, some of whom I had known for a long time, but also a lot of people whom I did not recognize. Relatives were there. My kinfolks from Ozark and Dothan, Alabama, had brought along some family friends. Nancy's parents and her brother from Oviedo, Florida, and a number of her relatives from Albany, Georgia, Panama City, and DeFuniak Springs were present. As we came in, Nancy had joined her family members who were seated in front of the podium with Lori and Amy. I was not close enough to talk to them from up there, but we did exchange greetings from a distance.

It was so good, also, to see my coordinator from Pensacola, Carol Biven, there with good friends Homer and Laura Singletary. They were able to get there before us because they had not stopped in Fort Walton Beach. Among those attending from Fort Walton were Randy Knepper and his parents, Harold and Myrtle. I recognized these special people when I came to the microphone.

The first plaque I received after being elected to Congress was presented by our neighbors in Panama City, Steve and Mary Sue Southerland. The inscription read: "Presented to the Honorable Earl Hutto..Congressman of the United States of America..District One, State of Florida. 'If my people, which are called by my name, shall humble themselves and pray, and seek my face, and turn from their wicked ways, then will I hear from Heaven, and will forgive their sins, and will heal their land.'...II Chronicles 7:14....In helping to lead our great nation, may these words of God be foremost in your mind and influence you in all decisions." This was so meaningful and the plaque would go on my office wall.

I don't remember exactly how Donnell introduced me, but I do know, in keeping with his style, it was done in a light-hearted mood. I do remember while I was at the mike he kept answering the phone and telling me that this one or that one, mostly from the news media, was calling me for comment. One of the calls was from Congressman Bill Lehman (D-Florida) from Miami. I kept telling Donnell to get their numbers. He did and I called them back later. Congressman Lehman congratulated me and said he was looking forward to working with me. He did not mention it, but I knew there was another reason for his call...he was seeking support for the Appropriations Committee, but I had already committed to Andy Ireland. Hey, I couldn't believe I was already involved in Washington politics and my votes were not all counted!

Though there was good-natured frivolity, this occasion also was very touching and I came close to choking up a time or two. I told the crowd about how surprised I was that we did not head home when nearing Panama City and how thrilled that they had honored us with their presence.

I briefly related the humble beginnings of our quest for congress some three years ago and how all the prayers, hard work, and good support had given me an opportunity very few people receive. About this point I called Nancy to the podium to share the moment. As usual she pulled another surprise, taking off the Hutto for Congress pin I was wearing and throwing it to the audience. Then, to the delight of the crowd,she pinned one on that said "Congressman Earl Hutto."

I closed by expressing our gratitude for their friendship and saying "With your continued prayers and support, I pledge to you that I am going to do my very best to make you a good congressman, one who will work hard for you and the best nation in the world, the United States of America."

It was time for cake cutting. The cake, provided by our supporters, was in the shape of the U. S. Capitol and was as pretty as any wedding cake imaginable. It bore the inscription "Congressman Earl Hutto." Nancy and I had the honor of cutting the first pieces...and then we could finally mix and mingle. It was an unforgettable joyous occasion to end the eventful day!

At last we were home with our loved ones, tired, but relaxed and happy.

Warren Briggs called the day after the election and was very gracious in his congratulations.

By the way, the final tally district-wide was Hutto 85,608, Briggs 49,715.

CAPTAIN SUPREME GOES TO WASHINGTON!!!

2

HUMBLE BEGINNING

The Halls of Congress are a long way from Midland City, Alabama where I first saw the light of day. Actually, it is stretching it a bit to say that I was born in Midland City because it was really several miles back of the water tank of the town, on what was Route #2, and still is, I think. Maybe the only thing that was remarkable about my birth was the fact I was delivered by a doctor. The reason I know that is because ol' Doc Espy's name is on my birth certificate.

Actually, I do not recall ever having seen the place of my birth. Was it a log cabin a la Abe Lincoln? I really do not know. If I had known that to have been the case, I would, as some politicians have done, probably taken delight in using it in my campaigns later on. That would be a mark of distinction to put on one's brochure or to state in a speech, "I was born in a log cabin, the son of poor parents, in rural south Alabama." For me, it might not have been a log cabin, but it was no mansion, and the rest of that phrase is accurate.

My first recollections in life are of another place that is on a certain street corner in the town of Midland City. The house we lived in at that time took on some added significance one day in 1993. That is when Congressman Terry Everett (R-Alabama) brought a picture to me on the floor of the U. S. House of Representatives where we were both members and said "Have you ever seen this house?" Surprised, I responded, "Yes, it's in Midland City, Alabama, and I used to live in it." He replied, "I did, too."

It turns out that the Everett family lived there in that same house some years after the Hutto family. Now, as the picture revealed, it has been made into a small church. Congressman Everett and I both surmised that this may be the first situation ever that two Members of Congress, non-related, had lived in the same house.

This house was no palace. It was what we called in Alabama a "shotgun house," just a simple straight back house without fancy architectural features. But, it had running water and an indoor toilet.

My memories of life in this house are not good ones. When I was about four or five years old, my grandfather and grandmother, on my mother's side, Mr. and Mrs. Will Mathis, were killed in a terrible accident. They were riding to church in a buggy pulled by a mule when they were hit from the rear by a drinking automobile driver. Even then, drinking drivers were killing innocent people.

Ma and Pa's tragic death almost killed Mama. She was so deeply grieved that, I believe, this kept her depressed, in some ways, for a long long time. I remember many years later Mama would get upset every time she heard an ambulance.

My mother, Ellie Mathis, was born in Barbour County, just to the north of our home county of Dale. Mama had four brothers and one sister. I do not know how she and Daddy, Lemmie Hutto, got together, but I do remember them telling us about eloping across the state line to Fort Gaines, Georgia, to get married. Their reason for eloping was that Pa, my granddaddy, did not care much for Lem, as he was called, or at least did not want him marrying his daughter.

Mama, a deeply caring person, loved all her family, but she was especially close to Joyce Godwin, her only sister. Joyce, who was the baby of the Mathis family, had been married a couple of years to Hubert Godwin. Hubert had no job, things were tough, so Mama and Daddy let them have a room in our house there in Midland City. My parents did a lot for this couple and during Joyce's difficult pregnancy Mama looked after her sister ever so closely.

During childbirth, Joyce died. This, coming not too long after Ma and Pa's passing, was almost more than Mama could bear. But, still there was more trouble to come. Shortly after the birth of the little baby girl, named Delores, and the supervening passing of Joyce, Pearl Godwin, a sister-in-law of Hubert, grabbed up the infant, and against my mother's will, took the child on the pretense that she would take care of her until after the funeral. After the funeral, this lady would not give up the baby. By rights, my mother should have been the one to take Delores and raise her. Hubert wanted Mama to have her, but Pearl Godwin was a domineering woman and Hubert was a rather meek man who would not speak up.

If my mother had not had a lot of faith, I do not believe she could have endured all the tragedy that prevailed in her life during this time. She was so hurt by all these happenings and to have someone, who had not had great success in raising another adoptive child, to take Delores away, made it hard for her to keep going. But Mama was not a quitter and God gave her the strength to carry on.

There are two other not-so-fond memories I have of the period in which we lived in that house. One was when a firecracker exploded in my hand. My sister, Merle, who was three years younger, and I did not get a whole lot of presents at Christmas time, simply because my folks couldn't afford it. But I liked Christmas fireworks like Roman candles, sparklers, and firecrackers. Mama wasn't crazy about her little boy shooting firecrackers, but reluctantly agreed. One night it was a bit chilly and I kept badgering Daddy to go out with me to shoot a firecracker. These were the kind where you light the fuse and throw it before it "pops." This time, I struck the match, lit the fuse, and prepared to sling it away, but unfortunately it must have been a short fuse. The explosion really hurt my hand, but did not do any permanent damage. It did make me wary of fireworks after that.

The other memory would have long-term ramifications on my life, but not pleasant at the outset. This revolved around my starting school for the very first time. Not having any older siblings in school, I had a vision of school being something very bad. I had heard talk about students getting whippings at school. Despite my Mama's explanation that only those boys and girls who were bad in school would get those whippings, I still was terrified.

The school was within walking distance. In fact, there was only Johnny Daniel's Drugstore and Marshall's Meat Market and not much more in Midland City, so everything there was within walking distance. As my parents walked me to school, they took me kicking and screaming. I did not want to go to that horrible place where I would be whipped. I was not at all happy when they left me there, and in my anxiety I messed up my britches. But I finally settled down. In retrospect, I wonder if all the trauma experienced in our home in the recent past had a bearing on my lack of security and confidence.

I got through that first year in school without any whippings, but I apparently was not a brilliant student. Oh, I got promoted alright. But it wasn't to the second grade. Back then, at least in Midland City, they had a high-first grade. So, instead of the second grade, I went to high-first the next year. Those formative years are very important and even in my early school years the educators must have realized that it is essential not to move students up just because of age. My teacher obviously knew that it was better for me to be held back a year. Anyway, I did not have to stay in first grade, I was in high-first. Big deal. Maybe it was some consolation to my parents that I was promoted to high-first....and now, I do believe, as I look back analytically, it was a blessing because I developed confidence and became a better performer among my peers.

My early childhood was spent during the great depression. Times were hard for everybody. But, it was a very difficult time for families like ours who were already poor. We moved from Midland City to a place out in the country, on Mr. Bryant Walding's place, so Daddy could try to get work with farmers in the area. He only had a sixth grade education and Mama had gone through eighth grade. Not many among their peers had finished high school. But even with a college degree it would have been tough back in the early thirties.

Merle and I didn't know anything about the depression. We didn't know there was anything better. Economics was not our game. But there were a lot of other games. I remember when, without our parents' consent, we went out to a pasture and tried to ride a young bull. We were having fun and after I had helped Merle ride him a short distance, I mounted up for my turn. The bull suddenly lunged forward and started bucking his hind legs up and down and dumped me on the ground. It didn't hurt much, but we were not eager to mess with that buckaroo anymore.

Merle had entered school by now and we both took the bus early each morning to go back to the same school in Midland City. After that first year I had come to love school and did well. I was rather small for my age. Some of my friends nicknamed me "Pee Wee" or "Runt." I didn't mind Pee Wee too much, but I didn't care for the Runt tag. I might have been little, but I could run faster than just about anybody and I became very determined and competitive.

During my school-age years, I can think of several teachers who really played a key role in my future. Most all of them were good, but in particular there are two that stood out. My second grade teacher was Miss Allie Bagwell, a spinster. Remember, I was fresh out of high-first, so I think she felt an obligation to bring me along and further my confidence. My desk was near the back of the room one time when Miss Bagwell caught me banging on my desk like a piano. She said, "Earl, if you want to play the piano just come on up in front and play for the whole class." She made me do it. Everybody laughed and I got tickled, too. Really, instead of punishment, I think the teacher realized that this attention would be good for me. It was. That bit of show biz was likely another little boost to my confidence.

My fourth grade teacher, Miss Napier, was one of my favorites. She entertained the class with readings. One of the readings that fascinated me was about a character called Rastus who had stolen a watermelon and had to explain his way out of it. I listened so intently that I memorized the reading. When I got home I practiced it myself. My parents heard me saying it around the house, and, I think were kind of proud of how I recited it. When we were in the company of others they would often ask me to tell about Rastus stealing the watermelon. Miss Napier did not know I had been doing this and when she found out she asked me to do it for the class. I was bashful about it, but when I got up there I tried to use all the animation and inflection she had used. My classmates liked it and this endeared me to Miss Napier and the class. It really did a lot for my ego!

While we had some of the amenities of life when we lived in Midland City, we had none of those where we lived in the country. There was no running water, no indoor plumbing, and no electricity. Our toilet facility was outside and we drew water from a deep well. To see at night, we had dimly lit kerosene lamps. When we got home from school, we had chores to perform. Merle and I toted in firewood and stove wood. We had to draw water and bring it in for drinking and for bathing. The water was in buckets and we kept a dipper in the buckets for dipping out to drink or putting into the washpan. Clothes washers, dryers, and dishwashers were unheard of. Mama washed clothes in a washtub outside. She then used a washpaddle to beat stubborn dirt out of the clothes before putting them into a big black washpot under which was placed a fire to boil and sanitize them.

After the daily chores were taken care of, I could then go out to play. It doesn't sound exciting, but simple things like rolling an old tire or bending a wire into a staff and using it to propel a small iron wheel around the neighborhood was a good way to occupy my time.

Since our family, like most, didn't have any money, it was necessary to try to grow enough food to exist. For us, it meant planting vegetables in a garden, the small plot of land provided by the landlord. From the garden we had peas, beans, cabbage, turnips, okra, tomatoes, corn, and other produce that Mama would cook. Daddy would help at hog killings so the owner would pay him off in meat for the family table. We ate a lot of cornbread from meal that had been ground at a grist mill down at the river and when possible my folks might get enough money to buy flour for biscuits.

My mother used plain flour instead of self-rising flour and put in her own seasoning. She could make biscuits that would almost melt in your mouth. They were especially good with a generous coat of butter. Sometimes we mashed the butter into locally made sugar cane syrup and then sopped it with our biscuits.   Talk about good eatin'...that was a breakfast for kings! We managed to get along fine, but there was little knowledge about nutrition. So what if this kind of good 'eatin had a little cholesterol or maybe some fat?

Daddy was quite healthy, except for a double hernia that precluded him from doing much heavy work, but Mama was not the healthiest person around. She caught a dreaded disease called palagra. It seemed that quite a number of women were getting this disease. Mama did not have any energy and one of the symptoms was a breaking out and scaling of the legs. We had no car. There were not many around, but a neighbor in the area was kind enough to take some of the ladies to the doctor in Midland City at certain times. We were worried about Mama being sick.

We moved a lot. We had never owned a home. We had to get by the best we could and, when my folks could find a house with the slightest possibility of Daddy getting some work in the area to provide for the family, we would move on. We moved to an area south of Echo, still in Dale County, to Mr. Tom Newman's place in 1937 for Daddy to be one of Mr. Tom's farmhands when he could use him. Mama's palagra, which apparently was nothing more than malnutrition, got better and later disappeared.

This was the year that Rex was born. Merle and I were proud of our baby brother, who was eleven years younger than I and eight years behind Merle. We lived in this little house for only about a year, but I remember that while living there I made the first money I ever earned in my life. Mr. Tom told me if I would dig up some Bermuda grass next to his barn he would pay me for it. I jumped at the opportunity, took a hoe and got busy. He paid me with some change, about seventy five cents, and I was proud as a peacock.

But it was not a peacock that got me into trouble around there. Mr. Murphy, who lived a couple of hundred yards from us, had a big turkey gobbler. We used the Murphy's well from which to draw our water and often times I made the trek up there to fetch water for the house. One day as I was carrying a bucket of water a big turkey gobbler was about to jump all over me. I ran as fast as I could to get away from him. From then on I carried a stick with which to fight him. Once I hit him so hard I thought I had killed him. I was scared of what the Murphys would do, but the old gobbler recovered and after that he didn't seem to bother me as much.

Our next move was not far away, right to the center of Echo. Now, Echo is no thriving metropolis. It was a crossroads with three country stores on three of the four corners of the intersection. We moved into an old empty store building on the fourth corner. There was a Lodge in Echo and I remember that Daddy's brother, Uncle Noah, was a Mason and member of that Lodge. The Echo Methodist Church was there. The community was very proud of Echo School which went from first through the ninth grades, with most of the students bussed in from rural areas.

I enjoyed living in that old store building, not because it was such a great house to live in, but because there was a lot more activity in the area. We could watch the traffic that passed right in front on State Highway 27 and we liked to watch people going and coming from the three stores. One day there was a car with a loudspeaker on top of it that stopped and the tallest man I ever saw got out of it. This fellow went inside the store to get a cold drink and when he came back out I was standing there admiring his car with the big speaker on top. The tall man said "Young man, would you like to say something on the loudspeaker?" "I don't know what to say," I replied.

The tall man that charmed everybody in Echo was James E. "Big Jim" Folsom who was running for congress. I was only 12 years old and I didn't know a thing about politics, but when Big Jim told me to get in his car behind the steering wheel, press the microphone button and say "Vote for Big Jim Folsom for Congress" I got excited. I blurted it out real good and became a Big Jim Folsom fan.

After the election was over, I inquired about Big Jim. Daddy laughed and said that Big Jim got walloped. He had been running against Congressman Henry B. Steagall, who was something of an institution. Mr. Steagall, the co-author of the Glass-Steagall Act, probably the most significant banking legislation ever enacted, had been in congress for a long time. But that didn't keep me from liking Big Jim, who in later years gained fame as the "Kissing Governor" of Alabama. I must give credit to this man because when he gave me the opportunity to tell everyone in Echo to "Vote for Big Jim Folsom" it was my very first political speech, and it pricked my interest enough that from that day on I have pretty well kept up with politics...and eventually became a politician...er, statesman, that is, myself!

Echo is not a whole lot different today than it was back in the late thirties when we lived there. So, one can imagine how surprised I was a few years ago when I was riding in the subway trolley car from the Rayburn House Office Building to the Capitol to vote with a bunch of other congressman that I heard Congressman Jerry Solomon (R-New York) mention something about "Echo." I was seated close by and I said "Jerry, did I hear you say something about Echo? Did you mean Echo, Alabama?" He assured me that was exactly the Echo he was talking about. "What do you know about Echo?," I wanted to know. Small world. Jerry said that Echo is where his adoptive parents came from and that they had left Echo many years ago to become fruit pickers in Frostproof, Florida where he had grown up. Since that time we have good-naturedly referred to each other as "Cuzz." Since Congressman Terry Everett represents Echo, and was born and raised in Dale county, the three of us had a picture taken together in front of the Capitol and we refer to ourselves as the "Dale County Boys." We were the subject of an article in The Southern Star in the county seat of Ozark.

Echo holds other good memories. Mr. T. A. Hartzog, the Principal at Echo School, lived there in Echo. He had a son, Lamar Hartzog, about my age and we, along with other youngsters, had a good time playing. It was in Echo School that I first saw an indoor basketball court. The first time I took a shot I put it through the hoop. At that time I was still a small boy and I had to shoot pretty high to get the ball to the goal. But, if I had a clear shot I could put it through the basket and it was a lot of fun when we could get up a game.

Marbles and tops were two other games that I enjoyed playing. There were two games in marbles that were fun -- ring marbles and hole marbles. In ring marbles, a ring would be drawn in the dirt into which each player would put a marble. Then each would throw a "taw," the marble one used to shoot at other marbles, toward the shooting line that was drawn. Closeness to the line would determine the order for shooting at the marbles in the ring.. Each player could throw from a standing position at the marbles in the ring and try to knock them out. After all players had thrown from the line, they then, in the same order and from the same spot where their line shot landed, take turns at shooting at the marbles by thumping the taw from a kneeling or crouched position. This game could either be for "fun," where you got your own marbles back or for "keeps," where each player kept marbles they knocked out of the ring. My mother did not like for me to play "keeps" because she feared I would lose all my marbles or that some other kid would lose all his. I seldom lost all my marbles then, but some people may think that I have now.

I think I liked playing hole marbles better than ring marbles. In this game, played by two or more players, there are four holes that are dug in the dirt, three of them in a row and the fourth at an angle. It is wise to use a big heavy taw in this game. Each player shoots from the ground by thumping for the hole. If Player A makes the hole there is an option to lie in wait and if Player B misses the hole, Player A can take his taw and knock the opponent's marble as far away from the hole as possible so that it is difficult to make the hole on the next shot. Then Player A can go on and make the other holes, the object being to make all the holes going out and then coming back while at the same time fending off the other player or players. The player that wins gets "knucks," as we called it. That means that the losing player or players put their fist over the edge of the hole and the winner takes his taw and shoots the loser's knuckles as hard as possible. Sometimes this can really hurt, because some players used steel balls or big stone marbles and I can remember there were times when my knuckles were as red as could be.

Spinning a top, which is another game we played during school recess, is another skill that I achieved to some degree. This is a game that can be played alone or with a bunch of people. When you are just spinning a top all that is necessary is to wind the string around the top and then throw it down and it starts spinning. Good hard ground or some other hard surface is best to spin it on. When you throw it, and it is spinning, you may just wish to scoop your hand under it and pick it up while it is spinning. Another way to play is to draw a rather large circle on the ground. Each player spins inside the ring and, as the top's spin dies, if the top doesn't roll out of the ring, it is fair game for other players to shoot at with their tops. It takes pretty good precision to make the top hit where you want it, but I have seen some who could make it hit on a dime. Some tops that fail to spin out of the ring, and are not made of good wood, are subject to be split open by other spinners.

These are hardly high tech games. Can you imagine some of today's youngsters playing such archaic contests? Although they may have the latest electronic or computer games, I doubt that any kids nowadays had any more fun than we did. A lot of games we made up, and that is creativity which is important in one's development. At home we sometimes played horseshoes or we went round and round on a Flying Jenny that Daddy had made for us. He did this by bolting a pole loosely onto a stump or center post. One of us straddled the pole on each end and held onto the handlebars, which were just strips of wood nailed across the pole. Then both of us took our feet and pushed around simultaneously until we got it going real fast and let it coast. What a thrill!

Because of lack of equipment, it was often necessary to improvise on some of these recreational pursuits. Often, when we played baseball, it was with a sponge ball. We would put down most anything to serve for bases, and for a bat we used some sort of handle or board that we could get our hands around and swing. At C'. stmas time, we often made a kerosene ball to play with at night. This was simply done by taking a ball, made of string, soaking it in kerosene for a few days and then taking it out at night, striking a match to light it, and throwing it up into the air or to each other as a lighted ball. It would not burn us unless we held it too long at a time. Such was the life in rural Alabama in the days of my upbringing. Never a dull moment!

After a year or so in "downtown" Echo, a non-incorporated settlement of maybe a hundred or so people, but which drew from a pretty large surrounding area, we moved away, but not too far. In the ensuing years we lived in several different places, but all were still in the vicinity of Echo and Merle and I still took the bus to Echo School.

Rex was only about a year and a half old when he became ill. My parents had to get someone to take Rex to a doctor in Ozark, about 15 or 20 miles away. It was determined that our little brother had pneumonia and he needed to be near a doctor and have constant care. This was long before Ozark ever got a hospital. Since the nearest doctor was in Ozark, our family was in a difficult situation, but it was worked out when a dear lady in Ozark, Mrs. Lena Young, let Mama bring Rex to her home so she could stay with him and be near to the doctor. We had no telephone, but Daddy would walk some distance to a store each day to call Mama to find out how Rex was doing.

Rex's condition worsened. We were very worried about him. He was in critical condition and the doctor feared that he would not make it. But in a week or more he began to get better. The good Lord had spared our baby brother's life and we all were so thankful. He continued to improve and in a few days Daddy got someone to drive him to Ozark to get him and Mama. When they arrived back home we were so happy to see Rex and he was mighty glad to see us. He hardly looked like himself as he was very thin and pale. But before long, he was back to normal and our anxieties eased.

Franklin D. Roosevelt, who had been in office for a couple of years, had started some programs that were helping people get jobs and the economy was improving in the nation. Daddy was farming on halves, or sharecropping as it was known, with Mr. Johnny Bell. But it was not a good crop year and besides we were only able to borrow a little subsistence money until the crops would be harvested in the Fall. For the Huttos, the recession was still on. As a result, there was not much food in our household. We sometimes were able to get a few canned vegetables during the winter and early spring months before the fresh vegetables came along, but I remember distinctly that for the longest time we were on a steady diet of mostly tomato gravy and biscuits. Not a very nutritious regimen. But we survived!

Generally speaking, we children were in pretty good health. We had the usual childhood diseases such as whooping cough, measles, and mumps. Sometimes there were contagious diseases going around school. One time we caught the itch. Bad news! Both Merle and I caught it. This was a disgrace. You would never let anyone know you had the itch. But, how does one keep from scratching? It is impossible not to scratch as bad as that stuff itched. So anybody that had it usually tipped it off by scratching. A remedy for this was a medicine called "Sit-a-side" which we put all over our bodies before going to bed. When that was applied to the itch it burned like everything. I'm not sure it helped all that much. I think the itch just ran its course over a matter of days.

My tonsils were bad and this caused me to have sore throats, a common problem for a lot of children. So, the Ozark Kiwanis Club sponsored a free tonsillectomy clinic so that impoverished kids could have their tonsils removed. I remember Mr. M. W. Redd, a Kiwanian, drove out to our house to get Daddy and me and took us to Ozark. The surgery was done in the court room of the Dale County courthouse. The procedure did not hurt, because I was asleep. But being put to sleep with that ether is an ordeal that I will never forget.

I made one career decision, really about the only one, early in life. That decision: to never be a farmer. Working so hard in the fields, taking care of the mules, hogs, cows, and chickens and not making much money was not for me. There was no way I wanted to be a farmer when I grew up.

I never got to plow much, although that was something that I wanted to do. There were no tractors to do the plowing back then. It was done with a mule hitched to a plowstock to pull the plow that was guided by the farmer. Sometimes when Daddy was plowing, he would let me try it for a row or two. But I was really too small and I had a hard time keeping the mule moving properly and guiding the plow in the furrow. If the rows were not completely straight, the one doing the plowing would have to slightly pull the reins of the mule in the direction needed to turn. Depending on the gentleness and obedience of the mule it would sometimes suffice to say "gee" to get him to go right or "ha" to bring him left. Of course, the signal to stop the mule was "woe" and to start him it was necessary to make a clucking sound with the tongue and say "get up mule!" Sometimes one could hear a farmer in the distance hollering to a contrary mule.

Picking cotton, though, prepared me well for congress. Years later, while serving in those hallowed halls, I sometimes made the point, facetiously, to some of my colleagues, that everyone there should have picked some cotton. I might add that eating grits would have also added another good dimension to those making such momentous decisions. For the record, I have picked a lot of cotton and I have eaten a lot of grits. I still love grits, but cotton picking is another matter. Thank God for technology and the invention of the mechanical cotton picker. Picking cotton by hand is a backbreaking job that I do not wish on anybody.

When I picked cotton, it was because I had to do it, either because we had to get the cotton crop picked before the school term started or because I wanted to make a little money with which to buy books or maybe some school clothes. The way we did it was to strap a sack over our shoulder and let it drag on the ground behind us. When, and if, we filled the bag before quitting time, we would take it to have it weighed and emptied on a common pile in a barn or shed which protected it in case of rain.

The going rate for picking cotton when I was a youngster was fifty cents per hundred pounds. About the most I could pick was 100 or 150 pounds a day, so at the end of the week I didn't have a whole lot of money, but prices were low back then and I was just glad to be able to buy something.

The best time to pick cotton was in the early morning when the dew was on the cotton. This made it weigh more and one could make more money. We would pick the cotton by walking or crawling on our knees between the rows. The adults would use a longer sack and most would wear knee pads. The better pickers would take two rows, picking the row to their left and the one to the right.

Picking cotton under a boiling hot sun in the middle of summer is no picnic. Sometimes it was agonizing and I couldn't wait to get to the end of the row so I could rest briefly under a shade tree or get a drink of water. But one of the things we kids did enjoy was playing on the picked cotton, or even better, riding atop a wagon load of cotton on the way to the cotton gin in town. When we got paid, it was fun to get a cold drink, Baby Ruth candy bar, or bubblegum.

Most of the students in Echo School, including myself, were in the 4-H Club. It was, and still is a very fine organization. Each student was supposed to have an annual project like raising a pig, a calf, or growing a potato patch or something related to agriculture. One of the highlights of the year was the big county-wide 4-H Rally. Several busses loaded up and took us to the big event in Ozark. We would carry a packed lunch and Mama would try to make something special for me to take to the rally. To illustrate how poor we were, I remember one year I was embarrassed because I had biscuits my mother made and most of the other kids had sandwiches made with store bought lightbread. I have never forgotten that and I have great compassion for the underprivileged.

It was exciting for us country kids to be able to go to town. For us, town was Ozark, the county seat for Dale County and we made it there infrequently. It was enjoyable to walk around town with my parents, go into a few stores, and see if they could find a few bargains on some new clothes for us kids. We did not have the greatest clothes to wear to school and sometimes our clothing had a few patches where Mama had mended them. To her credit, regardless of the condition of the clothing, it was always clean. My folks had no patience with uncleanness in our house or on our person.

One day we were in Ozark when a gentleman asked me if I wanted to sell boiled peanuts and make some money. Yeah, I liked the idea and when I asked Daddy, he said it was okay. So, the man put several bags in a box for me and I went around town, and like the other boys I had seen doing it, I yelled "Fresh boiled peanuts, a nickel a bag." I did quite well, selling about 50 bags. I got a penny for each bag I sold. With the money, I went to a hamburger stand and bought me a hamburger. It was the first one I ever ate, and mmm...was it delicious. I still had about forty cents left and I don't remember how I spent it. Anyway, selling peanuts was my first venture into business.

Sometimes when we were in Ozark, Daddy and I would take a walk down the residential areas of Broad or Eufaula Street. We would look at the nice houses, and though my folks had taught me not to be envious or wish for things I could not get, I could not help thinking how nice it would be to live in one of those beautiful homes.

At Echo I had two teachers I really loved. They gave me motivation that I have always appreciated. Mrs. Glass formed a jazz band in her class made up of little jazz horns, tambourines, and perhaps another instrument or two. She put me on one of the tambourines and did I ever enjoy beating that instrument. Mrs. Glass also had regular spelling bees in her class. Spelling is one thing I seemed to have a knack for, so most times I was the last one standing after all of my classmates had missed a word and had to sit down.

Mrs. Crim was a sister to Mrs. Glass and she inspired me by getting me to write poetry and plays. In fact, it was under Mrs. Crim's tutelage that I decided I wanted to be a poet when I grew up. Remember, my other career decision was a negative one in which I decided I would never be a farmer. But I liked poetry and it was fun to come up with words that rhymed. One of my poems was titled "School Days" and it was published with other poems in The Ozark Sun. I kept that clipping for many years. I still enjoy poetry, but ambitions for being a poet was a passing childhood fancy.

In Mrs. Crim's sixth grade class we used to do a lot of playwriting and acting. This was something that really was appealing to me. Some of the plays were out of books and Mrs. Crim would choose the cast and do the directing. We would even have costumes and some of the plays were presented in the school assembly where our parents were invited to come and see them. It made me put my thinking cap on and come up with ideas for plays. I wrote several that received the approval of Mrs. Crim and this made me happy. I look back on it as another time where a personal interest by the teacher in a pupil means so much. It was a definite plus in my development.

3

THE GROWING YEARS

$\mathbb{F}$or several years we had lived around Echo or in the area a short distance to the south near Bethel Methodist Church where Daddy was born and raised. Echo was the landmark for a pretty big hunk of rural Dale County. It was fascinating to me that Echo seemed to always be the point of reference when someone was seeking directions. The likely response the locals would give would be to point a certain way and say "It's back thataway from Echo," not north, south, west, or east of Echo, just "thataway from Echo."

Anyway, when I was in the eighth grade, we upped and moved again. This time it was further away, completely out of Dale County. Daddy had given up farming and had no job. We had relatives, Mama's Uncle Charlie and Aunt Vick Mathis and family, living in Union Springs, Alabama. Several of them worked at the cotton mill and Daddy was hoping to get a job in the mill. So, we moved north about 75 miles.

We first moved in with Uncle Seebie and Aunt Golious Helms, Mama's double first cousin, until we could find a house. When we found a place it was a fascinating old house at the train depot in Union Springs which had been used as a combination house and snack bar, a place where train passengers used to get a hamburger or a cup of coffee along their journey. We found it interesting to see the trains come and go, especially the passenger trains loading and unloading.

The move was a big change for Merle and me as we were going to live in a city for the first time since our early days in Midland City. But Union Springs, which depended almost solely on the cotton mill, was larger than Midland City.

We had never owned a radio. In fact, we had gone to a neighbor's house back in Dale County to listen to the Joe Louis-Max Schmelling heavyweight championship fight. But while we lived with relatives in Union Springs, we listened to their radio a lot. I remember Daddy and Uncle Seebie staying up at night listening to news from London on shortwave radio about what Hitler was doing in Europe.

It is always difficult for children to change schools and it was that way for Merle and me. The school seemed to be okay, but different. There didn't seem to be as much closeness between teachers and students. I do, however, remember two attractive young teachers I liked--Mr. Rawls and Miss Mary. It was obvious to us students that they cared a lot about each other. In later years I heard that Mr. Rawls had gone off to the service, but I always wondered if these two nice people ever married each other.

Union Springs was not much kinder to the Huttos economically than Dale County. Daddy would go in at the start of the three shifts each day to see if he could get on. He was able to work a few days as a substitute, but he never got a full-time job at the mill. In later years, I would be thankful for this. Environmentally, it was not a very healthy job. Many of the employees, who worked around all that lint and apparently in pretty bad conditions, were quite pale and had medical problems. Several of our relatives who worked in cotton mills died at less than normal longevity.

Being in Union Springs, though, did expose me to football for the first time. I got to attend some of the high school games and this was exciting. Instead of playing marbles, I started playing tag football, mostly with my cousins.

About the time we were getting adjusted to life in Union Springs, here we go again. If there was no possibility of employment here, then why not head back home? That's just what we did. We pulled up stakes and headed back to Dale County. We did not go back to a rural area, but to a place in Ozark called Boggy Bottom, just off Eufaula Street.

We didn't return to Dale County because Daddy was offered a job. That was not the case. He just thought his chances in Ozark were as good as Union Springs. At least we were back in our home county. Daddy, with only limited education and no skills, was able to get menial jobs from time to time to keep the family going.

The little house we moved into in Ozark was a good house, but very small. It had no more than a thousand square feet. It did have running water, electricity, and indoor plumbing, which we had gotten used to in Union Springs. To help with our finances, we rented the smallest of the two bedrooms to Daddy's brother, Fred, for a while.

Fred was a bachelor, probably in his thirties, and looked a lot like Humphrey Bogart, ruggedly handsome. He liked to drink and run around with women. This was not to the liking of my mother. I think they liked and respected each other, but Mama let Fred know that she was not going to tolerate any drinking around our house. This arrangement lasted for a while, but one night Fred and one of the Richardson brothers came in late and apparently the latter was going to spend the night with Fred; both of them were drunk. During the night they were loud and rowdy enough for the whole neighborhood to hear them. It was the last night Fred stayed in that house. Mama told him he would have to leave.

Several years later, however, Fred boarded with us again and there was no problem. I looked up to Uncle Fred in some ways as a hero because he was a good lefthanded baseball pitcher who pitched with a semi-pro team. Some folks believed that if Fred had stayed away from alcohol and women, he would have made it to the major leagues. He did settle down and got married at about 40 years of age.

We did not know it at the time, but we had moved back to Dale County to stay. That does not mean, however, that we continued to live in the same house. We did not. We moved a lot during the years that Merle, Rex, and I were growing up. When we moved to Ozark I began the ninth grade at Dale County High. Merle was in Emma Flowers Elementary and Rex was only four and not in school.

Our house in Boggy Bottom was less than a mile from the stadium in Ozark. This was where practically all the organized sports activities, which I enjoyed, took place. At this point I was still too young and still too small to play on a high school team, but I was always ready to play a game of tag football or sandlot baseball. At school there was an outdoor basketball court and a classmate, Frank Gillian, and I were always out there shooting basketball.

Oftentimes, I would take my little four-year old brother by the hand and go see the Ozark Eagles football team at practice. Even at that young age, Rex enjoyed sports. Coach Phil Crigler would be giving the team a hard workout. Some of his top players were the Price brothers, Martin and Glen, both star running backs. I wanted so badly to see the Friday night home games, but my folks just could not afford to pay my way. There was one occasion when I wanted to see a big game so much that a friend and I slipped in. We went into the stadium early and stayed in a bathroom until the fans started coming in. I would never do a thing like that again.

Somehow my folks scraped up enough money to get me a used bicycle. I not only had a great time riding it, but it helped me to earn a little money. I got a job as delivery boy at City Market, which was mostly a meat market, although they did carry a small assortment of groceries. The store provided free delivery and when someone called for a pound of beef or pork or whatever, the meatcutter would wrap it up and I would deliver it directly to the customer. Sometimes it might be cold or rainy, but I did my job and made a little money.

After that, I sold the Grit, a weekly paper published in Pennsylvania, that runs a lot of different feature stories instead of timely news items. I would go out selling the Grit around the neighborhood and, in fact, all around the area since I had a bicycle. These were good little jobs that instilled in me a work ethic that put me in good stead later on.

I was not a straight "A" student, but I was a good student who made decent grades. Our parents struggled to give us the best life possible and to see that we got a good education, which they were never able to achieve. Most of all they wanted us to be good, to do our very best in all we attempted to do, to serve God and people.

We continued to move a lot, but not necessarily to get a better house. It might have been that my folks tried to find places that charged less rent. We lived in three or four other places in Ozark. One residence was in an area called "Tin Top," where all the houses had tin roofs. It was a hot place in summer and cold in winter, but one delightful thing about living in a tin-topped house was the sound of rain pattering on the roof. That made for mighty good sleeping.

It was about my sophomore year in high school that the family moved to Ewell, a community about five miles east of Ozark on the Abbeville Highway. In the ensuing years, the Huttos would live in three different houses. The first was an old unpainted house that had the kitchen separated from the rest of the house, with a little open-air walkway between. This was okay except in the cold of winter. We kept fairly comfortable, except for the few steps in-between, by having a fire in the fireplace, our only source of heat, and in the kitchen the wood stove kept the temperature at a reasonable level.

Mama knew how to cook better than anyone I ever knew. That's not just my opinion. A lot of people liked to come and see us and get some of "Miss Ellie's" cooking. When we would go to a covered dish event, such as the Kelly-Mathis family reunion, everybody wanted to find where her dishes were. The trouble, sometimes, was just being able to afford to buy the necessary groceries. Mama could make everything so tasty. Her cakes and pies would melt in your mouth. Back then we did not know anything about cholesterol and some of these other maladies. As far as we knew all these foods were good and healthy and we thrived on them.

I remember December 7, 1941 President Roosevelt addressed the congress to ask for a Declaration of War against the Japanese. This was the start of World War II.

Camp Rucker, later to become permanent as Fort Rucker, was being built between Ozark and Enterprise. This new Army base would bring jobs and a big economic boost to the whole Southeast Alabama area, known as the Wiregrass. Before long we were seeing a lot of soldiers around, and Ozark welcomed them with open arms.

Camp Rucker did not immediately help my father get a job. He still was bothered by the hernia problem he had had for years, and it was worse. Then, too, Daddy was not a very aggressive person. He did not have the determination of my mother. My sister, brother, and I were brought up in a wonderful, loving home. But, there were a few times that Mama was on Daddy's case about looking for a job. This was one of the few things I recall my parents arguing about.

While in high school I got a job in which I earned more money than I had ever made. A man from Chicago, Frank Harrison, came into town with a franchise from the Atlanta Journal to sell papers at Camp Rucker. I was one of the boys he hired to peddle those papers. Mr. Harrison, who wanted us to call him Frank, was a nice, but hard-driving man. After school each day the dozen or so guys he hired would board Frank's covered truck for the trip to the base. Each of us was assigned an area to work and we would be dropped off with our bundle of papers. Frank did not have to motivate me. I hustled in and out of the barracks yelling, "Get your Atlanta Journal..covers Dixie like the dew." I sold a lot of papers, more than anyone, even the boy who had the hospital area.

Frank was a good business man. If he found out that a particular company or battalion was a National Guard outfit called up together from the same locale, he would make arrangements to get their local paper, at least the Sunday edition. We already were selling the Sunday edition of the Chicago Herald American about two days late and I remember also that we sold the Denver Post.

The truck would get us back to Ozark after dark each day and I would ride my bike, with flashlight wrapped around the handlebars, the five miles to Ewell. I made about twenty five or thirty dollars a week, which was good for a school boy at that time. I gave most of the money to my parents because I knew they needed it. They were hesitant to take it, saying "Son, we don't want to take your money."

I was happy to help my family. I never regretted giving my parents one penny. I helped them financially as long as they lived. They did not have much in the way of material things to give us children, but the love and example they provided for us was worth more than riches and gold. I could never repay them for the sacrifices they had made for us.

The war brought sacrifices. There was a scaling back of a lot of activities and there were shortages due to the conflict. At school we lost our coach. Coach Phil Crigler went into the service and this caused a revamping and sometimes cancellation of sports schedules.

There were volunteers who answered the need to fill in for those who went into the service. One of those was Reverend Walkup, the pastor of the Presbyterian Church in Ozark, who became the coach. Coach Walkup put in as much time as he could with the school on a part-time basis.

My small physical stature did not keep me from participating in athletics. I made the starting lineup as a forward on the basketball team. Boy, was I proud to be an Ozark Eagle! This was in my junior year. Other starters that varied some included senior Graves Riley as well as Nathan Byrd, Raymond Creel, Maurice Johnson, and Jimmy Clouse of my class. The problem was more than having a part-time coach. We had no schedule. We did not even have a gym. We practiced and played in the National Guard Armory.

The school finally lined up a couple of games with teams from Camp Rucker. All I knew to do was dribble and shoot. I really needed some coaching and I was grateful that Reverend Walkup was able to give us as much of his time as he did. In those couple of games we played, I think I was the high point man with about 10 or 12 points. Graves Riley would tip the ball to Nathan or one of my teammates who would pass the ball to me and I dribbled toward the goal. I was faster than the soldier guarding me, but I could tell he was right behind me, so I faked a layup to avoid his blocking the shot, and as he went on by me I tossed the ball into the net for two points. I seldom got to use my "patented" turning hook shot, though.

I always regretted not being able to earn a letter which I could sport on a sweater or jacket. Also, it was unfortunate that we did not field a school baseball team. I played well in that sport in unorganized competition and later would play some in semi-pro baseball. If we had only had a full-time coach and a schedule I would have been able to get those coveted letters playing with the Ozark Eagles.

When I sold papers at Rucker, I occasionally was invited by the Mess Sergeant to eat in the mess hall before the troops started converging on the place. The food was quite good, especially the desserts. I got a pretty good taste of army life, except the hard training out in the field and woods. I watched them stand in formation and march. I learned to march and do about face, right face, left face, forward march and all of those routines. I also learned to salute.

Another thing I learned about the military was the discipline and what all of the insignias meant, especially the ratings of the enlisted personnel and the rankings of the commissioned officers. I was in awe at seeing higher ranked officers, like a full bird colonel. When I saw a jeep or automobile with a flag that had stars I really got excited because I knew it was a general's car. I was impressed and much in awe when I saw a general with stars on his shoulders.

After selling papers for a period of time, I was able to get a government job with the Army Post Exchange Service. This was while I was still in high school and I was able to get credit for my work in conjunction with classroom study. The program was called Diversified Occupations, or D. O. and the instructor was Mr. E. D. Bittner. Mr. Bittner had a dynamic outgoing personality and was good at lining up jobs for students and maintaining liaison between job and classroom. It was easy to get a good grade in his class and he had an excellent rapport with all of us. He didn't mind our calling him Dan or E. D. He was one of those teachers who was special.

My job was at PX number three. It had a pool hall and bowling alley. It did not sell beer. It had a soda fountain and a soft drink-cigarette counter. My job was to run the soft drink-cigarette counter. I had to be quick and efficient to handle that job because, when the soldiers flooded in there after the movie turned out, it was chaos. Everybody wanted to be waited on first. All were amazed at how quickly I could open four drinks at a time and make change without looking down at the cash register.

Two pretty girls, considerably older than I, handled the soda fountain. Sometimes, if both could not be there, I dished up the ice cream, made the milkshakes, and served the soda fountain customers.

I loved my job and was pulling down fifty three cents an hour. What a bonanza for a teenager!

On May 12 of my junior year I became 18 years old and had to register for the draft. In anticipation that I possibly might have to go into the service before completing the requirements for high school graduation in the next school term, I went to summer school and gained some credit. My parents wanted me to be deferred from service until I could graduate. Miss Onnie Ard was head of the draft board and it was within the purview of the board to defer students such as myself. Miss Onnie was a distant cousin of Daddy's and he spoke to her about that. She was not receptive, apparently, because I was classified as I-A.

Mama had always been dead set against my playing tackle football, but realizing that I wanted to play the game very much and it appeared likely I would have to be leaving for the service, she consented for me to go out for football as my senior year was beginning. I weighed 118 pounds, dripping wet, and was no match for some of those big football players. But I hung in there with them until I got my notice that I was being called up. I remember Coach Walkup telling me to block a big strong guy by the name of Pete Beasley . When I went toward him, I just rolled down in front of him, hoping to trip him. Maybe Mama was right. This was no place for a little fellow like me.

When I received word that I would not be deferred to finish school, and had to report for duty on September 22, my parents were really upset. They were deeply hurt and disappointed that Miss Onnie would not defer me long enough to get the credits I needed for graduation. But, somehow, I was not upset. I took it with calmness and resolve. I wanted to graduate from high school, but I have always been patriotic and I wanted to serve my country.

I had never been more than 100 miles away from home. In a way, I was eager to be going somewhere that I had never been. But, it was hard leaving home and my family that I loved and who meant so much to me. It was a tearful farewell. Even as Mama prepared breakfast that morning she was crying, although she tried not to show it, and although Daddy never openly cried I could tell he was kind of sniffing. Merle and Rex were both sad about my going. I cried too.

A bus load of men, and young boys who were destined to be men, departed Ozark and traveled to Montgomery where we received our physicals and were assigned to one of the services. I had nothing against the Army, but I had spent a lot of time on base at Camp Rucker and learned a lot about soldiering. Now, I felt it would be exciting to go into another branch of service. Not all were able to get placed in the service they wanted, but I got my choice. It was Navy Blue!

Lem and Ellie Hutto with children Merle and Earl

4

NAVY BLUE

Although I had learned something about the military the last several years while selling papers and working at PX#3 at Camp Rucker, I did not know what it was like being away from home and family until I experienced that feeling after being sworn into the Navy.

Those of us who were assigned to the Navy before departure from Montgomery were all sent to the U. S. Naval Training Center at Great Lakes, Illinois. This is where we would receive our basic training, better known as "boot" training. Among the first things we did was go to the barbershop, but not for hair styling. Why did we need a barber for the kind of haircut we got? They sheared it all off.

We were not asked if we wanted to go shopping to get some new clothes. We were ushered through a line for our government-issued clothing. The amount of clothing didn't matter because we would not be going anywhere during the next two or three months and would not be needing an abundance of things to wear. During the issuance of clothing, there must have been a mixup in sizes because the white sailor's hat I got was too big for me. I was embarrassed, but I was stuck with it for the duration of boot training.

A lot of boot training consisted of physical training and discipline. We didn't actually wear boots per se. They were canvas-type leggings and a recruit had better not be caught outside the barracks without "boots" on. We were all Apprentice Seamen, the very lowest rating in the U. S. Navy...and we were treated as such. Strict requirements included washing our own clothes, making our beds correctly, and making sure that our shoes were shined to a sheen. It seemed that we were constantly being inspected.

I was thankful that we had two or three other trainees from our part of Alabama in our company, which was Company #1861. Saxon Dykes, who had been a teacher and principal, and Foy Love, a redheaded guy from Midland City, were Dale Countians in our unit. We were able to share information from back home and commiserate with one another about the tough life we were undergoing.

I understood that the rigors we were being put through were

necessary and that this regimen was the kind of discipline necessary for a military man. It did not, however, keep me from being homesick at times. We looked forward with great anticipation to every mail call. I listened intently for my name to be called. Mama wrote frequently to let me know how Daddy, Merle, and Rex were doing and kept me abreast of what was going on in Ozark. I wrote home often. There wasn't much else to do during the few hours of the day or night that we had some time in the barracks.

The Commanding Officer of Company #1861 was Petty Officer First Class Jim Shoulders. He was from Ohio and had been an athlete at Ohio State. He was certainly athletic looking, a well-built muscular guy....a tough cookie, but one who could occasionally be human, and show a smidgen of kindness. Mr. Shoulders, like a Marine drill sergeant, had the responsibility of whipping us into disciplined, physically fit sailors. He would not fail in that mission.

Mr. Shoulders took a liking to my friend, Saxon Dykes, mainly, I think, because he was more his age. Anyway, our commanding officer made Saxon one of his assistants. One time at an inspection, Mr. Shoulders, as we were required to call him, found something wrong with the way my bunk had been made that day. I thought I was going to get demerits for that, but Saxon informed me later that he had interceded for me and I would not be penalized.

Mr. Shoulders did not wear boots. We had to salute everyone not wearing boots. This surprised me greatly because at Camp Rucker only the commissioned officers were saluted. But this was the Navy. We did not see any commissioned officers and it was mandated that we must salute not only our company commander, but anyone else who was not wearing boots. If we met a Seaman First Class on the way to get a coke, we would salute. I was scared to death of anyone not wearing the so-called boots, like I had on.

It was tough at Great Lakes, but it was not unbearable. Some things I enjoyed...like marching. My buddies couldn't understand that. For me, it was putting into practice the things I had learned observing the Army at Camp Rucker. I had learned how to do these commands, but had never put them into practice. Now I was proving that I could do it for real. Ah, I should have been a platoon leader.

It is possible, if I had been more outgoing and aggressive, that I could have been a march leader, like the guy from Columbus, Georgia who was appointed by Mr. Shoulders to lead the marching.

I was just too shy, at that point in life, to let anyone know that this was old hat to me.

One added touch I did not see the Army doing was the singing and chanting we did as we marched. Not only did I enjoy our singing, but I enjoyed hearing other units singing as they marched at Camp Green Bay. "The biscuits in the Navy they say are very fine...One rolled off the table and killed a friend of mine...I don't want no more of Navy life, but gee, Mom, I wanna go home...left, right..left..right...You had a good home and you left....left...right...left...right." What fun!

A definite highlight of my time at Great Lakes was when our company was marched to the stadium on a Saturday afternoon to see a college football game. It was the Great Lakes Navy team going up against The University of Illinois. How exciting this was! Although an avid follower of sports, I had never seen a college game. The relatively few high school games I had seen were mostly low scoring contests, but this game was outstanding. It featured the sensational running of the great Buddy Young, who was destined for NFL stardom. This was a see-saw game all the way. The final score was a tie, 26-26. That 52 points now doesn't sound all that fantastic, but then I thought it was great. What a thrilling football game!

I had been to Montgomery, Alabama once during a high school trip and that was the biggest city I had ever seen until I was inducted into the Navy. When we finally got liberty from boot camp, it is understandable that I was awe-stricken when I saw the big city of Chicago. This was something to write home about. I also went to Waukegan, Illinois and visited the USO. It was good to sit and read a magazine, write letters and cards, and have a good feeling about being away from the regimentation of boot camp.

After ten and half weeks our boot training was over. It was emotional for everyone, including Mr. Shoulders, as we graduated from this phase of training. We were automatically promoted from Apprentice Seaman to Seaman Second Class, equivalent to Private First Class in the Marine Corps or Army. Now, we were going home-....and I couldn't wait to get there.

As I rode the train the thousand miles back to Ozark I was very excited, but also a little nervous about going home. Would everything be the same? Though it had been less than three months since I had been home, it seemed like an eternity.

It was so good to see Mama, Daddy, Merle, and Rex! They were happy to see me, too...and so was our dog, Brownie. We were a close-knit family and the love we shared with each other, though not always outwardly expressed, helped sustain me in this period of my life when I was making the transition to adulthood.

How joyous it was to be home in Ewell with my dear family, especially during the wonderful period of Christmas. The time slipped by so quickly, and now I had to leave again. It was the practice in our home to kneel around the table and have prayer before breakfast every morning. The words Mama prayed, on that morning of my departure to return to the Navy after this brief period at home, are still vivid. She prayed, "Dear Lord, let your guardian angel be with Earl to protect him wherever he goes and whatever he does." It was hard for all of us to hold back the tears. We tried to be strong and restrain those emotions, but intermittently the sniffles could be heard.

When the actual moment of saying goodbye came, we could not hold back the tears. My future was uncertain. The war was still going on. In Europe the allied forces seemed to be winning, but the outcome in the Pacific was undetermined. There was no telling where I would be headed when I got back to Great Lakes. Yet, as I parted from these loved ones, although difficult, I realized there was a positive feeling. We had faith that God would take care of me. I was not afraid. I wanted to serve my country and I was ready to do what was necessary for the United States of America.

Upon returning to Great Lakes, our Company 1861, along with other companies, was placed in the OGU (Outgoing Units), the place where assignments were made to sailors completing boot camp. It was a real large arena-type building with hundreds of bunks and a lot of guys waiting anxiously to find out where they were headed.

I believe that most people can recall significant happenings in their lives that have affected or influenced their future. One of these turning points in the road was about to happen to me. When I had returned from leave and reported to OGU I was feeling a little under the weather. My right side was hurting a bit and I decided to go check it out at Sick Bay. The doctor there thought I might have appendicitis. So, for the first time in my life, I was admitted to a hospital.

I stayed in Great Lakes Naval Hospital for several days, but they could not find anything wrong with me. Maybe what ailed me was eating too much of Mama's Christmas cooking. Mmm...as I thought back, how good that eating was--turkey and dressing, several kinds of cakes and pies that she cooked on those special occasions.

Anyway, when I got out of the hospital and went back to OGU, I found out that my company had shipped out. I would never see those friends I had trained with again. A few were assigned to special schools such as aircraft maintenance, storekeeping, and so on. But the largest number was assigned to the aircraft carrier, USS Franklin. This was one of those turning points I alluded to earlier.

I was assigned to the naval base in Newport, Rhode Island to await completion of a new ship, the USS Bremerton, being built at Naval Shipyard in Philadelphia. This was a turning point, a fortunate one for me. Was the good Lord looking out for me? I could have been aboard the Franklin and perished with a number of my friends who went down when the vessel was hit in the Pacific.

It was early 1945 and we were experiencing a severe winter in Newport, at least in the eyes of a lad from the deep south who had never seen snow before experiencing the excitement of the white stuff at Great Lakes when I reported to OGU. In Newport, it was worse. It would snow and then rain and the ground was always slushy.

I enjoyed Newport, however. For one thing, we had a lot more freedom without all the tight restrictions of boot camp. I was also slowly gaining more confidence and finding out that all my superiors were not monsters. I no longer had to salute enlisted people without boots. Although I did not mind saluting, I had a problem with exalting people just because they did not wear boots. Now, there were commissioned officers around, with gold braid. Though being respectful, I was not frightened out of my wits in their presence. I remember Lieutenant JG Culver as being nice and helpful as we received training in such subjects as ship and aircraft identification, and fire control. At Newport I was promoted to Seaman First Class.

There was one time when we were on the inspection field that I will never forget. The inspecting officer was a full commander, the highest ranking naval officer I had seen up to that time. You know, one of these fellows with scrambled eggs on his hat. I remember the man's name well. It was Commander Marshall. We were standing rigidly at attention and as the reviewing party neared I could hear Commander Marshall making critical remarks to our CO about this sailor or that sailor not having a clean hat or shined shoes. When he approached me he paused momentarily, looked me straight in the eyes in a manner that struck terror in my heart. He took his hand and pushed my sailor hat down and said, "Square your hat, mate" and moved on. Imagine how embarrassed I was. The nerve of this little guy no bigger than I, in fact smaller, humiliating me like that.

This little episode was just a part of the discipline I needed and a good lesson in being prepared. From then on my hat was squared, one inch above my eyebrows, the properly mandated regulation.

It was at the navy base in Newport that we heard the news of the death of President Franklin D. Roosevelt. The U. S. and the free world had lost a great leader The nation mourned its longest serving president, who was in his unprecedented fourth term. Much later I learned that my boot camp buddy, Saxon Dykes, was one of those who marched for the Navy in Roosevelt's funeral cortege in Washington, an honor for him, but sad nonetheless.

After being in Newport roughly two months we were transferred to Philadelphia, although our ship was still not ready. Part of us were assigned to the Wellsbach Building in nearby Camden, New Jersey to await further work on the ship. Within a few days we would, indeed, move on board this spanking brand new vessel.

Meanwhile, back in Alabama it was graduation time for my class. When I first went into the Navy I started taking correspondence courses from the Armed Forces Institute out of the University of Wisconsin so that I could complete the work necessary to get my high high school diploma at the time of graduation. At the ceremony, Principal J. O. Barnes passed out the diplomas as the seniors walked by. Then, he handed my diploma to my parents in the audience. They were embarrassed because my diploma was not in a nice folder like the others. They wrote a letter to The Southern Star the next week explaining that I was off in the service of my country and that they had not been contacted about purchasing a folder for my diploma.

The USS Bremerton (CA-l30) was a magnificent ship, a heavy cruiser so noted by the designation "CA," which stands for cruiser armament, as distinguished from CL, a light cruiser. Our ship was named for Bremerton, Washington. This was, at that time, the largest ship I ever saw. What a vessel! I was real proud to serve on board.

The official commissioning ceremony was held on the main deck with all the pomp and circumstance attendant to such events. High Navy officials, as well as civilian dignitaries and representatives of the cities of Bremerton and Philadelphia were on hand for the occasion. Relatives of some of the crew were there. It would have been great for my folks to be present, but there was no way that could happen. After the ceremony, tours were conducted and there were a lot of oohs and aahs as compliments to the Navy's newest ship.

I was placed in a gunnery division on the Bremerton which had living quarters on the third deck down. Our division had the responsibility of operating and maintaining the aft turret of the main battery on topside. The main battery consisted of three turrets of eight inch guns, two forward and one aft. Each turret had three guns which fired projectiles that weighed close to 300 pounds each. The ship also had several five inch gun turrets, as well as 40-millimeter and 20-millimeter gun placements. This baby was armed to the hilt!

My job aboard ship was a good one. I was blessed by not having to swab the deck, be subject to working in the kitchen, and other menial tasks. I was on the crew of Turret #3 which fired those big guns. I was named to be the Sight Setter. My duties were to sit in a little booth with the sight setting instrumentation. When I received the information on my sound-powered phone hookup I would set the sight angle and sight deflection that would guide the projectile to its target. That was heavy stuff. If I did not do my job the shot would miss its target. A Chief Gunners Mate was Captain of the turret and I also worked with several other Petty Officers. I was striking for Gunners Mate Third Class.

The USS Bremerton would be my home for the better part of a year. We had a period of time before taking her to sea to adjust to the ship and to acquaint ourselves with work stations and to carry out our responsibilities. In other words, this was a time of organization, getting to know the "Big B," each other, and establishing a team.

Philadelphia, the City of Brotherly Love, was a place that I really enjoyed. While making our ship ready for its maiden voyage, oftentimes we had liberty at night and on weekends. There had been only limited time to see Chicago and Newport. But, in Philadelphia I had a chance to go downtown, walk the streets and see the sights. Typically, a lot of the sailors wanted to frequent the bars and chase women. Without condemning anyone, let me say that this was not my style. I came from a dry county and a dry home. Alcohol was not a part of my life. I can have all the fun and enjoyment I want without it and the next day feel good, and remember everything.

There were a few other teetotalers in my division. One was

Richard Fox, of Norfolk, Virginia, and he and I often went out together, and sometimes were joined by other crew members. A night to remember was May 8, 1945, VE Day! What an exhilarating feeling to know the U. S. and allies had won the war in Europe. The country was euphoric. The streets of Philadelphia were filled with people... sirens sounding... car horns blaring... as America celebrated victory!

It was one down and one to go. The victory was won in Europe, but the Japanese had not been defeated in the Pacific. We were not ready to go home yet...and the preparations we were making to prepare the Bremerton as a fighting ship continued. It was an exciting time to be a part of ship's company as we got underway for the first time and headed out on our "shakedown" cruise, designed to work out all the bugs and make her combat ready.

At sea we did all the things we needed to do, including holding general alarm drills, manning battle stations....and getting used to being on the ocean with no land in sight. Many sailors can tell you that around Cape Hatteras, off the coast of North Carolina the water can be pretty rough. Sometimes turbulent seas would preclude our being topside unless absolutely necessary. Actually, if the pitching and rolling of the ship was not too excessive, I enjoyed it. I can remember some nights, however, in the Atlantic and later the Pacific Ocean, where it was almost impossible to sleep. At times I flipped over from one side to the other in my bunk every time the ship rolled. This was all part of being a sailor.

The Bremerton anchored offshore at Guantanamo Bay, Cuba. Talk about hot weather...it was steaming. Some nights we either did not have air conditioning or it was cut off. It was unbearable to try to sleep in our bunks, so some of us took blankets and pillows and slept topside on the open deck. Are we having fun yet? You bet! This is an experience I wouldn't miss. On some days our whale boats were lowered over the side of the ship to the water and we were taken ashore to the Navy facility, which the U. S. continues to utilize even with Castro's Cuba just over the fence. It was nice to go swimming and enjoy the club facilities on base at Guantanamo.

The Bremerton crew was on the receiving end of a wonderful serendipity when we got underway from Guantanamo presumably headed out for more sea trials. There were rumors we were headed to some unknown distant location. At sea we continued our general quarters alerts and practice firing. We did not know our destination, but it wasn't very long until we knew we were pretty far south. We knew it because all of us "Pollywogs" were initiated into the Ancient Order of the Deep as we crossed the equator. My recollection is that they stripped us down to our waist and made us crawl along the deck while the Shellbacks, those who had crossed the equator before, smeared us with paint and grease and prodded us like cattle. It was not severe punishment, and was fun. I still have my Shellback Certificate, so if I ever cross the equator again I won't be a Pollywog.

It turns out that our secret destination was one to our liking as we steamed into Rio de Janeiro, Brazil. I don't think that there was any deep dark secret or intelligence purpose for our not knowing to start with where we were going. I think the Skipper just wanted to provide the crew with a pleasant surprise. We docked in Rio with a view of Sugarloaf Mountain. This trip was my first time out of the USA and going on liberty into the city of Rio was a great opportunity.

After our shakedown cruise, we returned to the east coast, but this time we docked in Boston instead of Philadelphia. On August 6th and 9th the atomic bombs took their toll on Hiroshima and Nagasaki, and Japan was reeling. The Pacific war came to an end on August 14 with the formal surrender signed on September 2, 1945, in Tokyo Bay aboard the USS Missouri. So, the Bremerton was in Boston when VJ Day was celebrated in Mid-August. The scene in downtown Boston was much like it had been on VE Day in Philadelphia. The home front, which had been so supportive of American and Allied forces, was jubilant with celebrations going on around the nation. This was a meaningful time for Americans because the war had been won.

The end of the war had come, but the USS Bremerton would not remain moored to the pier in Boston. As a Seaman First Class I was not exactly tuned into the strategy or decisions coming out of Navy Headquarters in Washington. So, I must assume that the plans all along had been for the Bremerton to be deployed to the Pacific after its shakedown. Anyway, that's where we headed, via the Panama Canal, of course. Transiting the canal aboard this big ship was quite an interesting experience. So was the fact that when we exited the canal, we were in a different ocean, the Pacific, and this young sailor was seeing a lot of the world.

Out on the ocean blue sometimes there is little to do during off hours. This allows for pensive periods of deep thoughts and reflections. Many times I would go topside and enjoy the tranquility of the infinite miles of blue seas surrounding us as the ship plowed on at what seemed like a snail's pace. It was a good time to sit against a quiet area of the superstructure and write letters back home to family and friends...and also to think about my future.

What would I do when I got out of the Navy? One thought was that I would go to the University of Alabama and play basketball. In retrospect, this was pretty naive. Although I felt I was a good player, I was too short to play college basketball. But I was an Alabama fan, especially since I was hearing about a great young football player, Leapin' Harry Gilmer, a sensational passer.

As I pondered further about what I might do on the outside, I thought about the hydraulic lifts that brought those big projectiles up from the ship's bowels to the gun turret where they could be fired, and of hearing that the future of hydraulics was bright. I figured that this would be a big thing in the automotive world and that maybe I would work at a filling station and perhaps someday own one. Remember, my career decisions as a boy had been a definite no to farming and a passing fancy ambition to becoming a poet. Obviously, I was a long way from decision-making on a civilian future.

There was a stopover for the Bremerton at Pearl Harbor in Honolulu, Hawaii, the place where America's involvement in World War II began when the Japanese dropped their bombs and sunk our battleships. I do not recall how many days we were in Hawaii, but it was long enough for us to go on liberty and for us sailors to have our pictures made with a grass skirted "Hula" girl. I am not sure Mama was pleased with this when I sent photographs back home.

Our Asiatic Pacific journey next took us to Korea where we anchored off the coast near Inchon. Some of the guys took liberty and went ashore, but for some reason or another I did not get off the ship. Perhaps I was on duty during that time. However, another good thing about serving in turret #3 is that we had a periscope in it which allowed us to view a lot of the area surrounding the ship. We made good use of this perk while in port.

When we cruised into Shanghai, China, a few days later it provided my shipmates and me a chance to add another country to our list of places visited. We were in Shanghai for some time. The Chinese amazed me in many ways. For one thing, I could not believe how some of them could skull those sampans, small boats, continuously without ever stopping to rest. Likewise, when we went into the city and rode a ricksha, it was unbelievable that the man pulling us would run the whole distance in delivering us like a taxi to our destination. Several of us went to play basketball while in Shanghai. It was surprising to find a court since I do not believe that basketball was a widely played game in China at that time.

It was along about February of 1946 that the Bremerton moved on up the China coast and anchored off the city of Tsingtao. The duration of our stay in the Tsingtao area was fairly brief and then we were back to Shanghai. This visit to China was the first time that I came to realize the poverty and hard living of so many people around the world. I saw so many of these people sifting through garbage for food. There was evidence of deprivation all around. How great to be an American! This is a privilege we often take for granted.

Since the war was over, those of us in the active Naval Reserves were looking to the time when we would return to civilian life. A few men, all along, had left the ship and headed back to the states. In early to mid-March, I was among those who loaded seabags and said goodbye to the USS Bremerton for the last time. We boarded a troop-carrying ship, the USS Tazewell, loaded with other servicemen, and made our last trek across the ocean as sailors, landing in San Diego, California. Then we boarded a troop train and lumbered eastward through the western plains. Our destination was New Orleans. There I was processed, received my discharge and was a civilian. Date of separation - March 30. I received discharge compensation of eighty three dollars, plus twenty dollars travel expense, and headed to Ozark. Free at last!

A joyful reunion took place at our home in Ewell. As a skinny little kid, I had gone into the service of my country, done my duty, performed to the best of my ability. I must have been a pretty good sailor. For example, I harbor in my memory the time the Officer of the Deck, upon my return to the ship after a night of liberty, saying, "Mate, that's the only decent salute I have seen all night!"

Now, the good Lord had answered the prayers of my family. I was back in Dale County safe and sound...a civilian once again and ready to begin the rest of my life. I was proud to have been a sailor in the United States Navy and never regretted one minute of the time I gave to Uncle Sam.

Earl Hutto after completion of boot camp
at Great Lakes Naval Training Center.

The Hutto children--
Earl, Rex, and Merle

Earl served on the USS Bremerton while in the U. S. Navy

COLLEGE-WOULD YOU BELIEVE?

Earl Hutto going to college? Who in the world would ever believe that? Certainly, none of my kin folks. Only one person, a distant cousin, of all my relatives in the Hutto and Mathis families, had ever been to college. My entry into post-secondary education would definitely be breaking new ground.

Several of my high school classmates got out of the service about the time I did and it was good to reestablish old friendships. Our favorite meeting place in Ozark over the next few months was the Confederate Monument on the Dale County courthouse square. We would sit on the steps of the monument and trade war stories, talk about our class members and their whereabouts, and try to decide what we were going to do now that we were free to make that choice.

I had pretty well decided before I left the ship that I was going to take advantage of the GI Bill and go to college, notwithstanding my earlier consideration of working at a service station. Most of those in our group were likewise planning to go to college. Various colleges were talked about with a lot of discussion about Alabama, perhaps because of the glamor of 'Bama's great football team.

Somehow we got around to talking about Troy State Teachers College being a good school only 40 miles up the road. None of us really knew what we wanted to study and I doubt, at that time, that any in the bunch planned to go into teaching. Nonetheless, since we had not been at home much over the last few years it would be nice to go to Troy. That way, it would be easy to get home for the weekends. So, several of us seized on the idea that we ought to go to Troy State for a couple of years, take general courses, and then transfer to the University of Alabama and get a degree in engineering. Obviously, I had tempered my previous thoughts about becoming a basketball star at Alabama.

In the Fall of 1946, there we were, several people from Ozark, on hand to register for classes at the opening of the first quarter at Troy State Teachers College. The college did not have a men's dormitory at that time, but anticipating the onslaught of veterans beginning and returning to school, authorities erected temporary barracks on campus in the vicinity of Bibb Graves Hall, the administration building.

The men's barracks had been partitioned off into rooms that could accommodate three, or possibly four, students each. I got a room with Ted Parker and Brownie Andrews. Ted had been in my high school class and, like most of the others, had gone into the service at the end of our senior year, instead of the beginning as I had. Ted was in the Navy aboard the carrier USS Hornet and Brownie, who had been two classes ahead of us, was a former Marine.

Our accommodations were not the greatest. The barracks were no better than we had in the service. Sometimes in the morning, if there was a rush to use the limited bathroom facilities, some of us would go up to Bibb Graves Hall to shave. But, we could not complain. After all, there was no bugler that sounded reveille in the morning and we could sleep late if we did not have an early class that day....and we could go home on weekends!

There were very few students on campus who owned automobiles. On some Friday afternoons, if I could not get a ride with some student in a car headed south, I would get out on U. S. Highway 231 and thumb a ride to Ozark. Usually, I and other Troy students would catch a Greyhound bus back on Sunday nights. But I was beginning to really like college, so I started staying on campus more weekends.

Brownie, one of our roommates, up and got married, which was a surprise to Ted and me. Brownie and his bride, Vivian, moved into the apartments on campus that were being rented to married students. They rented a spare bedroom to Ted and me. This was an improvement over the barracks.

Some time during our freshman year, the first boys dormitory, Pace Hall, was completed and Ted and I were able to get a room on the top floor of the three store building. A third roommate was a redheaded fellow, Lawrence Sasser, of Dozier, Alabama. Pace was right across from Shackleford Hall, the girl's dorm, the only other dormitory on campus.

Troy State has a beautiful campus built on tree shaded property southeast of the city of Troy. In addition to the two dorms, the focal point was the administration building, Bibb Graves Hall. Other buildings were Wright Hall, the gymnasium and physical education department; and Kilby Hall, the Laboratory School, which was a regular six-grade elementary school where education majors did their practice teaching under full-time critic teachers.

There were a little less than 1,000 students enrolled, but the college was growing. About a year after I got there Troy State Teachers College was renamed Troy State College. Now it is Troy State University, with several thousand students on the main campus and at several other locations. TSU is one of the major institutions serving our U. S. Military, both domestically and overseas.

I doubt if any of the Ozark crowd registered for pre-engineering. I certainly did not. I felt that I did not have the technical aptitude to become an engineer, so I channeled my studies toward business and English. I later added education courses so that I could get a teacher's certificate, as a backup, if I could not get another job. Later, my qualifications to be a teacher came in handy.

Hey, I liked Troy State. I was making good grades. I wanted to stay there. I was not about to transfer to Alabama, Auburn, or anywhere else. Ted and Brownie, and several of the Ozark people, decided they wanted to stay at TSC also.

One of the most popular instructors at Troy was Professor Auxford Sartain. I took economics under him and learned a lot about the various economic systems of the world. One time in his class I got caught in a bit of his humor. I discovered he had excellent hearing. He had just finished explaining one of the economic theories, and then said, "Does that sound like mud?" I whispered to the young lady adjacent to me "Yes, just as clear." I didn't mean for the class to hear me, but Mr. Sartain heard it and said, "Just as clear, eh?" He and the class laughed. I was a wee bit embarrassed.

In another class, there was an incident I will never forget. George "Plowboy" Maddox was in that class. It was Mrs. Lenice Stephan's history class, held in an upstairs classroom with the windows open and a gentle breeze blowing in. Mrs. Stephan was a very straight-forward person and not one to admit any mistakes. At this particular time she asked a question and Plowboy raised his hand. "Yes, Mr. Maddox." He gave her the answer, but she said it was wrong. Plowboy said, "Mrs. Stephan, I just got it out of the book." She said, "Then, the book is wrong." Whereupon, Plowboy slammed the book closed and tossed it out the second floor window.

I have spoken earlier about special teachers. Let me tell you about another one who had a definite impact on my life, Janette Stout. She was the speech teacher. I had heard good comments about her classes and decided to sign up. With my background, I needed speech. I learned a lot. Proper articulation and inflection helped me get rid of my monotone. I learned to say "penny" instead of "pinny." I got rid of my South Alabama twang and became one of Miss Stout's stars.

The Troy area's first radio station had been on the air only a short time. WTBF was located close to the main campus and the station was beginning to do broadcasting from the college. Miss Stout had liked my voice when the speech class practiced speaking on the new tape recorder, so she assigned me to be the announcer for "The Singing Lady." This was a program that featured Mrs. Olivia Rainer, from the Music Department, in a half hour program that was beamed toward elementary students in Pike County's classrooms.

I was seated at a small table with an amplifier on it and I wore earphones as we got ready for that first program. I listened nervously to get my cue from the station. Finally, it came across, "Now, we take you to the campus of Troy State College." At that point, I turned on Mrs. Rainer's microphone and gave her the cue to begin. She began playing her theme song on the piano. After a few seconds, I faded her microphone, turned on my own mike and said, "Good morning boys and girls. Welcome to the Singing Lady program, with piano and songs by Mrs. Olivia Rainer direct from the campus of Troy State College. Now, here is the Singing Lady!" I sat and controlled the volume until time for the close. It went well. Little did I know I had just launched a broadcasting career.

I did other programs from the college, such as "Here's to Veterans," a 15-minute program from the VA that provided information for the many veterans of World War II. The first of these programs were scripted, but later it was received by the station on a large disc which we called a transcription.

Mr. Bill Needham, from Chicago, was Manager of WTBF. He and Sam Townsend, the Program Director, liked my voice and my presentations from the college and hired me to be a part-time announcer. I received some very valuable experience and also made a little money. Besides that, I became something of a celebrity with my fellow students. I was not all that taken with my voice, but if other people liked it, that was to my benefit and I appreciated their compliments. My folks were real proud of my being on radio when they heard about it. Unfortunately, they could not pick me up because the station did not quite reach Ozark.

One of my fans was Elizabeth Sorbet, a French lady from New Orleans, a professor in business at the college. Her course in accounting, which had an overflow enrollment at the beginning of the quarter, found students dropping out like flies after just a few days. Her course was hard. But Miss Sorbet took a liking to me and somehow I finished the course, though my memory is a little dim on the final grade I received.

One night Miss Sorbet invited the class over to her house for dinner. She commented about her radio needing repairs because it did not sound clear enough for the symphonic music she enjoyed. Good friend Gerald Newman and I decided we would try to fix the radio for our professor. We fixed it all right. When we finally gave up, the radio would not emit the slightest sound. I doubt it ever played again. Gerald and I still laugh about fixing Miss Sorbet's radio!

At Dale County High I had been the first sports editor of The Eagle's Cry, a student newspaper that Mr. Bittner, our DO teacher, had helped us get started. I enjoyed writing sports, so I got on the staff of the Tropolitan, the TSC newspaper, and before long became the sports editor. I thoroughly enjoyed writing about football, basketball, and baseball, or any sports, including the intramural leagues.

Asa Dudley, the manager (water boy and equipment manager) of the TSC Red Wave football team, told me he was interested in writing sports and asked if I would give him a try at it. I did, and Asa wrote very well, but that particular story required a lot of copy and Asa only gave me two paragraphs. After that he became a good writer and I was pleased, later on, in having a hand in helping Asa get started as an announcer at WTBF, where today he is the manager.

L. B. "Tex" Williams was another one of my talented friends. He not only had written sports, but many other articles for the Tropolitan. Tex and I were fortunate in getting jobs as co-directors of sports publicity at TSC. This was before the days of full-time sports information directors at Troy. In this job, we were doing something we enjoyed and getting paid for it. We often traveled with the athletic teams on road games. We kept team and individual statistics, wrote sports articles for radio, newspapers and the Associated Press.

I will never forget the night that Tex and I had on-campus dates with Gail Smitherman and Mary Ann Strawbridge. This was

Friday night before the Red Wave would go against Austin Peay College of Tennessee on Saturday. Tex and I had a problem. We were supposed to provide Max Moseley of the Montgomery Advertiser with the starting lineup for both teams for the Saturday morning paper. But the publicity people from Austin Peay had not sent the lineup. On this night Tex and I took the young ladies by our office where we tried to call again for the lineups. We had received copies of releases about individual players, so we tried our best to piece together a lineup. We were short a couple of players and we needed desperately to get this lineup in before the Advertiser's deadline. Suddenly, we got a brilliant idea! We put our dates' names down. At right tackle--Smitherman, and at left end--Strawbridge. You can imagine the fun we had seeing that in the paper the next morning. I am sure the opposing coach wondered who his new players were.

In recent years Troy State has had outstanding teams in a number of sports and has won national championships, first in NAIA, then, as the college has grown, in NCAA-Division II, and has come very close for the last couple of years in Division I-AA. When I was there, Red Wave football teams would do good to have break-even seasons.

The nickname for Troy State teams, as you have surmised, was Red Wave, interchangeable with Trojans. Now Trojans is the only nickname used. The football coach was Buddy McCollum, a tall former star at Auburn. Coach McCollum's nickname was "Bat Man" and his favorite saying, which he used often, was, "Now, here's the basis for it." He was a nice man...and very colorful. Tex and I also gave some of the players dandy nicknames, like "Doc" Bowden, "Goat" Carlton, "Go-Go" Hilyer, and "Snake-eye" Hicks.

It was exciting for me to do play-by-play on some of the local sports contests. It was kind of neat the way I got started. Ernie Bazemore, a fun-loving deep-voiced student from Columbus, Georgia had prevailed on WTBF to do some of the Troy High basketball games. There was no press box in their gym, but Ernie would locate in the stands about mid-court with his amplifier and microphone and tell the folks on the air what was happening. One night he saw me walk into the gym and motioned for me to come join him in the stands. All of a sudden, Ernie announced "..and now, to call the third quarter of tonight's contest between Troy and Union Springs is one of WTBF's announcers, Earl Hutto." He handed me the mike and I started calling play-by-play. What fun! Basketball was not hard to call, because there are fewer players who can very quickly be recognized by face as well as numbers.

Ernie Bazemore had provided me with a wonderful opportunity. This impromptu performance led to my doing some of the college sports. This experience which was unexpectedly handed me in the bleachers at the Troy-Union Springs basketball game was the beginning of sports broadcasting for me, later a major qualification for my employment.

Sports has been an interest of mine all my life. I played intramural basketball at Troy State and was a pitcher on the junior varsity baseball team. Actually, I think I made a mistake in going out for the wrong position. Had I gone out for second base I might have made the varsity because I was a good fielder and singles hitter.

While I was at TSU I played semi-pro baseball in the summer as a second baseman with Ariton, Alabama. Other teams in the league were Eufaula, Clayton, Clio, Louisville, Brundidge, Baker Hill, and Ozark. Bennie Sheppard, a student from Columbus, Georgia, played several games with us and thrilled the fans with his excellent hitting.

We played games on Thursdays and Sundays. It was special for me to play against my Uncle Fred Hutto, an idol of mine, who was a left-handed pitcher on the Ozark team. The amount we got paid was not much and it varied according to the attendance at each game. If a player had an outstanding performance the hat was passed and the collection was given to the star player as a bonus. I remember getting "the pot" once, when I had three straight singles in a game at Eufaula.

I never had anticipated that I would want to attend summer school, but I chose to do so for a number of reasons. First, and foremost, I was attending college on the GI Bill and I did not want to interrupt my compensation. Second, I did not want to leave my part-time job announcing with WTBF, and third, by going to summer school for three summers, I could graduate a year earlier.

In our junior year at Troy, my roommate and Ozark friend, Ted Parker, married a lovely young lady, Miriam McNair, from Troy. Ted's place as my roommate in the dorm was filled by another Dale Countian, Fred Johnson. One of my memories of Fred is that one Christmas he received an anonymous Christmas gift of a Bible. Fred was convinced it was I who gave it to him because I was the only one who knew him well enough to know that he needed it. But, he was wrong. I did not give him the Bible and we never found out who did.

I lost the only political race I remember losing when Howard Pelham defeated me by less than a half dozen votes for President of Pace Hall. Pace continued to be my place of abode for the rest of my college career. It was a pleasant place to live and we had a good dorm mother in Mrs. Mildred Montgomery, who had an apartment just inside the front door.

Just across the hall from my room in Pace lived a fellow by the name of Charlie Norris, from Mount Willing, Alabama. Charlie was interested in running for president of the student government. I urged him to run and I would be his campaign manager. Charlie knew absolutely nothing about campaigning. Though I had no real practical experience myself, I had a good idea of what needed to be done, so we threw Charlie's hat in the ring. I wrote his speeches, planned his activities and advertising, and anything else that came to mind. Guess what? Charlie Norris won. It gave me a good feeling because Charlie, though not a dynamic individual, was a good man and served us well.

From my humble beginning, it almost boggles the mind to realize that I grew so much while in college at Troy. Good teaching by committed professors, relationships with fellow students, and opportunities for personal development gave me a good foundation for future success. In essence I became, almost without realizing it, a student leader. But behind it all was a deep faith in God and the love of my family back home.

My grades were such that I was invited to join Kappa Delta Pi, honor society in education. Within a year I was elected president. The Palladium, the Troy State annual, reminds me that I also was elected secretary of the senior class. I have always been glad that I went beyond just taking and passing courses, but also involved myself in extracurricular activities.

After three years, I had sufficient credit hours for graduation and received my B.S. Degree in Business-English-Education from Troy State College. I graduated in the summer of 1949 with my family in attendance. A college education not only had been possible and believable for someone in my family, it had become a reality. My family and friends joined me in the pride of this achievement!

Earl and his father, Lem Hutto, at home in Ewell, Alabama

Earl on campus at Troy State College

The Hutto family home was completed at the time Earl graduated from college and was the only home his parents ever owned.

6

THE WORLD OF WORK

Okay, so I was a college graduate. What should I do? Well, I knew I must go out in the world and make a living. I was not afraid to do this, but was just a little undecided on which way to go. I had my teaching degree from Troy State College, one of the top teacher training institutions in America, but in addition to the prospect of being a teacher, the possibility of a broadcasting career intrigued me.

My dilemma, a pretty good one to be in, was settled when former roommate, Ted Parker, and wife, Miriam, accepted teaching jobs in Houston County, Alabama and suggested I get a job there. In a way, I did want to teach, so I went down to Dothan to see the Superintendent, Mr. Solomon Baxter, about it. When Mr. Baxter found out I was qualified to teach business subjects, he hired me on the spot to teach at Cottonwood High School. I would be working under Principal G. L. Baxter, a brother of the superintendent. Ted and Miriam were at Webb Junior High in the same county.

Before I left Troy, I bought myself an automobile--my first-- with some savings I had achieved. It was a used car, a 1940 Ford, but it ran pretty good, and I was proud of it. The only thing wrong with it that I could see was that someone had bashed in the left rear fender.

Prior to heading south to Cottonwood, I had a few days to spend with my folks at Ewell. What a happy time for the Hutto family. This was the time we moved into our new house, the first we ever owned. I was so proud of my parents for the determination they had shown in pursuing home ownership. Over a period of several years, they had bought building blocks and stacked them up until they had saved enough to build. This house was no mansion, but it was ours. It had two bedrooms, living room, dining room, and kitchen...and, of course, a bathroom with running water. It was rather nice, and Daddy and Mama continued to improve it through the years, including the addition of another bedroom. No more moving around for the Huttos! This place would be called "home" for the next 26 years and would be the only home for my parents for the remainder of their lives.

Cottonwood is 13 miles south of Dothan and close to the Florida line. It is about 30 miles south of the Ozark-Ewell area.

Cottonwood was a small town, but had a good-sized consolidated school, of which I was a new faculty member. When I reported for duty a week before the doors opened for the '49 Fall term of school, I found I would be working with several former Troy classmates.

Plowboy was there! Yep, Plowboy Maddox, the fellow who had tossed the book out of the second story window when the teacher said it was wrong and also was noted for running his old car into the campus lagoon, was to be the assistant football coach at Cottonwood. His wife, Faye, was also a new teacher. Betty Culbreth, Jonnie Sue Boswell, and Gene Ramage were others from TSU on the faculty. Another beginning teacher was Daphne Sue Wilkinson, an Auburn graduate, who would teach home economics. I was generally pleased with the rest of the faculty. We had a very collegial group and I looked forward to working with them.

There were not many places in town for a single man to stay. Mr. Barnes, a 40-year old bachelor on the Cottonwood faculty rented a room from Mr. and Mrs. Hart Snell and I rented there. It was a nice room Mr. Barnes and I shared, but I didn't like this arrangement and my second year I rented from John and Ernestine Lewis.

Except for the Maddoxes, the other new teachers at Cottonwood were all single. Jonnie Sue and Daphne Sue were the two beauties. They already had boy friends, but it didn't bother me. I was dating, though not steady, a young lady from another town. Anyway, we were all good friends and had a lot of fun together.

It was easy to tell that Cottonwood, like most towns of that size, had a lot of politics at play. The two sides were obvious, but I did not want to get mixed up with either side, so I tried to be friends with all. A real old gentleman, Mr. White, with an office downtown, seemed to be the leader of one group. I was impressed with Mr. White and believe he wanted to help the community. He oftentimes involved people from what one might call the "other side."

I was 23, but I must have looked even younger. Some of the high school girls were quite flirty, but I gave them no encouragement. There was no way I was going to date one of them. To me it was a "no no" for a teacher to date a student, despite no rule against it.

I was asked, however, on one occasion, to transport several of the cheerleaders to an out of town football game. When we got back into town I met some of the parents who were waiting for the cheerleaders. The next morning one of the students said her mother had asked her, "Do you mean that little shirttail boy is your teacher?"

I did, however, have a good rapport with my students. CHS did not offer courses such as business law, accounting, and so on. Most of my classes were typing and I taught one class of shorthand. The typing classes went well and it was rewarding to see how pleased the boys and girls were in mastering the touch system and being able to type without looking at the keys. I did not feel as comfortable teaching shorthand because I had only a minimum amount of shorthand in college. But it worked out okay and some of the young ladies were able to use shorthand in jobs after graduation.

Most weekends I would go out of town, either home, Troy, or some other place. I did spend some weekends in Cottonwood. My Principal and his wife, Mr. and Mrs. Baxter, as well as Mr. Barnes and others were members of the Methodist Church and I attended church with them. There wasn't much to do around Cottonwood other than events at church or school. For a single man, I was active in the community and was a member of the Cottonwood Lions Club.

I probably had not been in Cottonwood a week when Mr. Jess Swicegood, owner of radio station WDIG in Dothan, called and said he had heard that I had experience in radio and wondered if I would be interested in doing some part-time work at his station. I jumped at the idea. After school, I would drive up to Dothan for more work. I was a disk jockey and had a program in the afternoon called "Juke Box Varieties" on which I played popular requests both from write-ins and call-ins. Then, at 6:00 p.m. I had a 15-minute sportscast.

I was making twenty-two hundred dollars a year teaching. Now, that sounds like peanuts, but then it wasn't too bad as a starting salary. I made additional money with WDIG. It was enough for me to live on, help my folks, and save a little. It was also nice to be something of a radio celebrity in Cottonwood.

The Cottonwood Bears had some pretty good sports teams. I was asked to do the PA system at home football games. There was no press box, but I had the microphone in the stands, right in the middle of rabid Cottonwood fans. I sometimes dated Patsy, a young faculty member, and when she was sitting next to me I put the mike close to her face and the whole crowd heard her laughing. Now, I cannot imagine doing something like that as a sophisticated faculty member. Come to think of it, I guess I was not that sophisticated.

We started an independent basketball team in Cottonwood

made up of local guys outside of school and myself. Fellows like James Howard Lewis, Lamar Sellers, and David West were pretty good players. We played some of the city league teams out of Dothan. I remember one night I rushed from my job at WDIG back to Cottonwood and arrived shortly after the game had started. We were playing Nip & Ernie's (a Dothan drive-in restaurant). These Dothan folks had a good team. As soon as I got dressed and made it to the sidelines the coach put me in. I was as hot as a firecracker and couldn't miss with my hookshot from the corner. I made about a half dozen shots in a row and although we lost the game, the next day I was the talk of the school. I felt really good about this, especially since I didn't really get to play much when I was in school.

Mr. Swicegood wanted me to come to work full-time at WDIG as program director and sports director. He made a good offer, so after two years of teaching, I left Cottonwood for Dothan. I had enjoyed Cottonwood, but broadcasting had a stronger pull on me, and I yielded. I was satisfied, though, with my work with those young people in Cottonwood. Even now, I occasionally see one of my former students and will ask if they can type? Surprisingly, they can.

I had some education time left on my GI Bill of Rights and decided I wanted to attend the NBC-Northwestern TV-Radio Institute that summer before reporting to work at WDIG. My lodging in Evanston, Illinois, was in the Fisk Huts on the Northwestern campus. I had two classes on campus--programming taught by Dr. Hunter and news taught by the renowned Dr. Baskett Mosse--and an announcing class at NBC studios in the Merchandise Mart Building in Chicago taught by NBC's Louis Roen. This was a very meaningful summer and I not only learned more about radio, but a considerable amount about television by doing simulated sportscasts.

Being in Chicago was a revisit from my old Navy days, although I had seen very little of the city then. One of the more memorable things about this visit was seeing several performers at Chicago Theater such as Nat King Cole and Les Paul and Mary Ford whose hits I had been playing on radio. I also took in Cubs and White Sox games when Nellie Fox and Minnie Minoso were big stars.

When I got back to my full-time job at WDIG, I fell right into my duties of programming the station, recording commercials, and doing my sportscasts. Typing, which I taught at Cottonwood, is one of the best skills to have that I know of. I have used it so much in my life, both personally and in my jobs. Although we had some secretarial help at the radio station, I generally found it was quicker for me to type out the log for each day's broadcast, typing in the commercials in red. I also typed the scripts for local sports stories, which I combined with wire stories, for use on my nightly sportscasts.

Even while I was working part-time at WDIG, I did play-by-play on out-of-town football and basketball games of the Dothan High School Tigers. Now that I was full-time, we did even more sports, as this was an area where we could beat the competition from the other stations, WAGF and WOOF. As the expression goes, I was in "Hog Heaven." This was my forte. I loved sports and sports broadcasting.

I had replaced John Ingersoll as the program director of the station. Mr. Ingersoll left town and was never heard of in Dothan again. John had a nice rich voice and did a good job on the air as well as in programming. One of the shows he did, on which I succeeded him, was "Food for Facts." This was a live 15-minute program at 11:45 a.m. from the Charcoal Steakhouse and Cafeteria, a popular eating place in Dothan. The format was to table hop around the restaurant interviewing three guests per program and asking the jackpot question. The Charcoal Steakhouse provided two dollars for the jackpot each day and it was rolled over to the next day if the question was not answered correctly. I also signed the check of each guest I interviewed and they got their lunch free. The questions were on various subjects and if the jackpot question had been answered the day before, I had to dig to come up with a new question before I went downtown to do the show. One of the questions I remember using more than once in the three years I did the program would have a different answer today. The question was: Who holds the record for playing in the most consecutive major league games and how many? The answer was Lou Gehrig with 2,134 games, but in 1995 Cal Ripken of the Orioles received wide acclaim for breaking that record. Food for Facts was a program on which I had a lot of fun talking with the people, many of them from out of town, having lunch in Dothan.

Joe Holloway was one of the more popular radio personalities in Dothan. He did The Farm Hand Show from 5:00 to 8:00 a.m. and came back for Holloway's Hangout 10:00 a.m to noon. The earlier program was mostly country music and the Hangout segment was popular music. Joe had a gift of gab that people enjoyed listening to.

One of the favorite pastimes was trying to break up the person on the air and get him to laughing. Joe was good at that. He had big eyes and when he started rolling those eyes and making all kind of gestures it was hard for whomever was in the studio to maintain control. Wayne Moseley did our 12:40 p.m. local newscast. He would check with the police and other sources around town, and would generally adlib his well-listened-to newscast. I'll admit that Joe caused me to break down with guffaws more than once. Wayne would cup his left hand over his left ear to hear himself and was harder to break up, but if Joe got his attention, he was not immune.

The station received two or three sets of season tickets to the Dothan High football games each year. Joe, a graduate and big booster of Dothan High, would get one set of those season tickets. One year, as the season was approaching, Joe kept asking Mr. Swicegood if he had received the tickets yet. Finally, a few days before the first game, Joe got his tickets from the boss.

Despite the fact that the control room, where the on-duty announcer worked, got pretty warm from time to time, Mr. Swicegood was adamant about keeping the control room door closed to avoid extraneous noises getting on the air. One of the funniest things I witnessed at WDIG was Mr. Swicegood coming in one morning, the day after he had given Joe the tickets, and finding Joe announcing with the control room door open. This irked him so much that he went and slammed the door shut. This enraged Joe and when he had finished his announcement he jumped up, opened the door, and without saying a word, but with a very angry look, reached in his pocket and handed Mr. Swicegood the long-sought-after football tickets. It was not funny to Joe, but it was to all of us who had seen Joe sweating out those tickets.

One year Mr. Swicegood, who was active in the community, was Chairman of the National Peanut Festival in Dothan. The national celebrity that year was Sally Rand, the noted stripper. Mr. Swicegood worked out an agreement with the other two stations in town to carry some of the festival activities. Wouldn't you know, it fell my lot to interview Sally Rand on a three-station network and an audience that included everyone in the Wiregrass area who had their radio on. I only remember one thing about the interview and that was Sally Rand signing off by saying, "Until I see you again, I hope that you will be seeing more of me."

In doing the play-by-play of football and basketball I tried to put a lot of excitement into it to paint a word picture for the audience. This was before television had really come into our area, so we had a big audience. Both WDIG and WAGF did the Dothan High football games, but ours was the only station to do basketball. Mr. Swicegood finally worked out a deal for the football games where we would join forces with WAGF and have only one broadcast going to both stations. I did the play-by-play and Lamar Trammell of WAGF did the color. One time in Anniston we were broadcasting from a press box that had no glass enclosure when a rain and windstorm came and blew away our spotting board info. It was tough identifying the players and we had a miserable time getting through that game.

A new coach, coupled with our broadcasts, really put Dothan on the map with its basketball program. Coach Russell Taylor, who had great success as basketball coach at Enterprise, was hired by Dothan. He and athletic director Rip Hewes sought the best players they could find. If they heard of a good basketball player they would coax him into coming to Dothan.. Some fathers were given jobs in Dothan so that their sons could play for Dothan High. Two of Dothan's arch rivals were Eufaula High and Lanier of Montgomery.

Dothan won its way to the state tournament in Tuscaloosa just about every year after Coach Taylor came on board. I would go to Tuscaloosa to broadcast the games back to Dothan. I recall with a chuckle every time I think about an incident after one of the games Dothan had won. Afterwards, Coach Taylor invited me to go to dinner with the coaches. When we got in the car Coach Taylor said, "I could kill that Johnny Boyd. In the pre-game prayer he closed it by saying 'and dear Lord, please forgive Coach Taylor of his many, many sins'" I still laugh at that when I think about it. Johnny Boyd was the star center and is now a Baptist preacher.

A friend of mine, Chuck Gilmore, who was station manager at WULA in Eufaula, did the play-by-play for Eufaula. Once when the two rivals were playing each other, Chuck suggested that we have one broadcast back to both stations. I would do play-by-play when Dothan had the ball and he would do the same for Eufaula. It was rather unique, but it worked out all right for that one game.

Doing play-by-play of a lot of sports sparked a desire in me to move up the ladder to the networks. This would take not only a lot of talent, but also a lot of know-how in getting the attention of those folks in New York. I was humble enough and knew I was not the greatest sportscaster in the world. But, I always worked hard at being the best in whatever I attempted to do. I was convinced I could call a game as good as Bill Stern, Harry Wismer, or Lindsey Nelson, the famous sportscasters of that era. None of the network biggies could hear me way down in Dothan, but I felt that some time in the future I could be broadcasting nationally.

It was not New York calling. It was Pensacola, Florida. One day I got a call from old friend, Chuck Gilmore, who had left Eufaula and had gone to work as a salesman with the very first TV station for miles around. The station, WEAR-TV, had just gone on the air in Pensacola and Chuck suggested I should come down and interview for the sports director's job. This was intriguing. Ever since I had attended the NBC-Northwestern Institute three years earlier, I had just been waiting and preparing myself for television.

I went to Pensacola, talked to program director Jerry Williams, got the job and was thrilled at the prospects of working in Pensacola on Channel 3, which was already putting a signal into the Dothan area for the few people who had TV sets. When I gave Mr. Swicegood my two-week notice he tried to talk me out of it and made promises of higher pay and the opportunity to broadcast minor league baseball in the Alabama-Florida League.

There was no way that he could talk me into staying, but Mr. Swicegood said something that has stayed with me and kept me humble. His profound statement was that I had an acceptable voice, but not an exceptional voice. I was never infatuated with my voice, but his comment reminded me that humility would serve me well.

Earl Hutto was excited about television, but I would be leaving to live outside Alabama for the first time in my life except for the time I served in the Navy. Mama and Daddy and my teenage brother, Rex, did not want me to go. Merle had already married. Though they did not like the idea of my being that far from home they understood it was necessary to enhance my career and accepted it.

As I drove to Pensacola, I have to admit I cried a little on the way as I thought of leaving my family behind. At the time, Daddy and Mama were running a little store in Ewell, mostly pumping and selling gas. They were working very hard and not earning much money. But I consoled myself with the knowledge that this move was right. Pensacola was only about 160 miles away. I would continue to stay close to my folks and help them financially or in any way that I could.

7

FLORIDA SUNSHINE

The only people I knew in Pensacola, Florida, were two cousins, one from my father's side and one from my mother's side who did not know each other. I needed a place to stay, so I called both to get their recommendations. One had a friend who said a lady by the name of Mrs. Carrie Waite offered room and board. So, when I arrived in Pensacola, that is where I lived initially.

Mrs. Waite was a dear lady who used her home in caring for three or four elderly ladies downstairs. She had two rooms upstairs she rented and this is where I stayed. Mrs. Waite had an outstanding younger lady, an African American nurse named Chloe, who helped care for the ladies, one or two of whom were confined to wheelchairs.

Although I ate downstairs I did not see much of the aged ladies except when they were sitting on the front porch in good weather. A friend kidded me about living in an old folks home. But Mrs. Waite and Chloe treated me wonderfully well and surely will have stars in their crowns in Heaven for the loving treatment of those ladies entrusted to their care.

The new television station was still feeling its way, getting bugs worked out technically, and moving cautiously but steadily in adding and improving its programming. Only one person at the station had worked in TV and that was program director Jerry Williams. Channel 3 was only on for a few hours initially, from about 4:00 to 10:00 p.m. each day.

My big moment on the screen did not come immediately. When I arrived in Pensacola at age 27 ready to make my debut, WEAR-TV was not yet ready for me. Although I was hired as the first Sports Director, I was instead put to work at WEAR Radio at the old Smith's Shipyard spinning records and announcing on a six-hour daily shift. TV had not yet started a sportscast and I had to bide my time as a radio disk jockey until they were ready for me.

Bingo! I got my break quicker than expected, even before they were ready to start a live sportscast. Jack Ridner goofed up and the call went out for me to report for duty at TV. Jack was a staff announcer who had also been given a half hour on-camera live show about once a week. The guy was talented, but what a character! This particular night he and Charlie Huddleston, the engineer on duty, were clowning around during a movie. Charlie playfully turned on Jack's microphone just as he said something definitely not suitable for video land. One of those glued to his set and hearing it was Manager Mel Wheeler who called and fired Jack immediately. Tough luck, Jack, you've just launched Hutto's TV career!

My duties included much more than sportscasting. I did staff announcing and this entailed making announcements inside programs and between programs. Some of them were voice over film and some were voice over slides. Some were commercials and some were public service announcements. The announcer on duty also had the responsibility of loading the slide projector and film projectors for these spots. It did not take me long to learn how to do that and my proficiency made me known as the fastest loader in the business.

Sometimes it was necessary to be very swift in loading the projectors. The reason being that the slide projector had two carousels that held about ten slides each, alternating from one side to the other when the announcer punched a button in the booth. There were times when the copy called for more slides than there were slots during a break. There would be an intervening 20-second film and while it was running I would hurriedly rush out to the projector and replace slides and get back into the booth by the time the short film was over. There were times when I would have to load the other film projector while a 20-second film was airing on the other projector.

The life of the booth announcer could be hectic. But during long programs, there would be nothing to do but sit in the booth and watch what was going on the air, or read or take a brief stroll through the station. Thus, this is what I did for several weeks before I ever faced the cameras.

Finally, the big day arrived. My daily sports program was scheduled and I nervously waited for the red tally light on the front of the camera to come on and the cameraman to signal me that I was on the air. It was a five-minute sportscast and I was given a lot of leeway in how I conducted it. During baseball season I used a painted wooden scoreboard on which I hung names of major league teams. Before the show went on, I would write in the scores with chalk. I wrote letters to all the teams and received photos of players. I would staple pictures of stars like Mickey Mantle, Willie Mays, Whitey Ford, Al Kaline on a board and a second camera would pick them up while I talked about their performance that day.

We had about 60 employees at Channel 3. This compared to a half dozen or so at the radio station where I had worked. Actually, some of those people did not know much about what they were supposed to do. One who confessed to this was assistant program director Ray Carow, who joined the station following Navy service. But Ray obviously learned something because in later years he became head of Gray Communications which ran three TV stations.

One of Ray's duties was to direct the live segment of news, sports, and weather from 6:00 to 6:30 p.m. Other directors were assistant manager Milt DeReyna, production manager Ken Welch, and Jerry Williams. Jerry was the man everybody looked to since he had television experience.

Not long after I came over to TV, the radio station was moved over to operate in the same building as television. For a while, I did a sportscast on radio, but generally most of my work was on TV. There was a period of time, though, when Mel decided that each of us TV announcers would do a daily hour-long radio program, so we resorted to being disk jockeys again. These double media personality shows did not last, but I continued doing a sportscast and play-by-play of out-of-town Pensacola High games on radio.

Channel 3 had no network affiliation for probably at least the first year on the air, so we ran a lot of old movies, half-hour shows like "My Little Margie," and filler films such as "Industry on Parade". Finally, arrangements were made for us to carry selected programs from CBS such as the "Ed Sullivan Show" on Sunday nights and Edward R. Murrow's "See It Now" on a weekday evening.

The glamor and newness of television, and the fact that Channel 3 was the only station around, apparently made us a very effective means of advertising, and we had no scarcity of commercials. Nearly all our spots then were 60 seconds, especially live ones. So, in order to hit the network right on time when we had a CBS show coming up, we would have to backtime to get all the spots in. This procedure often caused us to be as much as 30 minutes ahead of schedule.

As our air time increased, we hired new employees. Not long after I started working at the station, Jack Kenney came over from Panama City after his stint in the Air Force. Jack started as a booth announcer and also did live spots. He was quite versatile and at various times did news and weather, and later was program director.

Fred Murray and Ed Chapman also joined the staff as announcers during that time frame.

Somehow, I continued to be the regular booth announcer on the night shift. I suppose I could flatter myself by thinking they wanted their best in prime time, but I hardly think that was the reason. Anyway, my schedule was from 4:00 p.m. to midnight, or later if the late movie went long. When I came in at four I began gathering information for my sportscast by checking the newswire, making telephone calls about local sports events, and lining up interviews.

When sports celebrities came to town, I nabbed them for my sports show. Among those I interviewed were three of the Four Horsemen of Notre Dame as well as Mel Ott, Arnold Palmer, and a whole host of notables. I closed my sports with the saying, "Remember, fans, in the game of life, as in any game of ball, play it clean, play it fair, or not at all." One night I had as my guest Sam Huff, star linebacker for the Giants and later the Redskins. He was on the set with me when I closed with that motto. Big Sam turned to me, and with a broad grin, said, "You mean I should quit, huh?"

Supreme Ice Cream was one of my biggest sponsors. Headquartered in Dothan, owner Woodfin Parkman, Jr. and general manager J. C. Adkinson knew me from my time with WDIG and liked my work. My cousin, Verbon Mathis, who had been with Supreme since high school, was working his way up and eventually became the general manager. Supreme sponsored my evening sportscasts five nights a week.. It was a popular program, maybe because of my rapid-fire staccato delivery, or perhaps because I made every effort to have the latest scores and news from the world of sports. One nice thing about having Supreme as sponsor was that Rose, in our station snack bar, had plenty of ice cream to serve the staff.

I felt very humble and grateful for the way people received me. The Channel 3 signal covered a large area and people from around Dothan and Ozark were picking me up. Unfortunately, my folks at Ewell did not have a TV set, but they were very proud when other people told them that they had seen me on television. I was still learning, and I knew I could always improve. For one thing, one of the young ladies, who worked with me, said that I should smile more. She was right. Maybe it was the intensity with which I performed that kept me from smiling. I worked on that, but it took a long time before I could easily smile on camera.

The second year I was with the station my parents became grandparents for the first time and I became an uncle. A baby girl, Wanda, was born to my sister, Merle, and husband, Bob, in Ozark. Wanda, who was a beautiful child whom I love dearly, is now the mother of two boys and a girl.

Supreme was happy with my performance on TV and in addition to my sports, they also sponsored a weekly syndicated half-hour show called "Rocky Jones, Space Ranger." They made me Captain Supreme, a likely rank for someone advertising Supreme Ice Cream. I wore a space-type suit that looked more like an airline captain, and did the three commercials inside each show. The appeal, of course, was to the kids. It was a merchandised program and I would tell them to send in their Supreme labels for tee shirts and other prizes. When the Rocky Jones series ran out, I still continued as Captain Supreme on Jet Jackson, another syndicated series.

I was beginning to be known as Captain Supreme about as much as Earl Hutto. I went to schools in my uniform and spoke to boys and girls, and made quite a few personal appearances. I rode on a special Supreme float in parades, including the Fiesta of Five Flags Parade in Pensacola and the National Peanut Festival Parade in Dothan. It would have been far-fetched, however, to believe that one day Captain Supreme would become a Congressman!

At one point in my employment at WEAR-TV, I lost my sports show, but of my own volition. The program was sold to a beer company and I declined to advertise alcoholic beverages. I do not condemn others for drinking, but I was not brought up that way and have always had a strong conviction that I should not drink. I have never found it necessary to drink to have a good time or enjoy life and I would like young people, especially, to know this fact because there is so much peer pressure on them. I have seen first hand how someone with a few beers can wipe out an innocent family because of alcohol in their system.

Anyway, I did not get fired. One of the announcers did sports for the duration of the 13-week contract with the beer company. I did lose the $5.00 per night talent fee, which was a big help in those days. After the 13-week period ended, I went back on sports.

Although receiving acclaim as a TV performer, I have to admit there still were times when I was lonely. I worked nights except Sunday and had little opportunity to have any social life. Although people knew me, I didn't know many people in those days. So, about every month or so I would go home to see my folks for a short while. On one visit, I took them a used TV set which I had bought, and they were pleased to get it so they could see me on the tube each day.

After boarding out and living in a small room, I became a home owner for the first time when I bought a three-bedroom house in Mayfair, a new subdivision that was built only a mile away from the TV station. The price was $11,475, which required a small down payment and monthly payments of less than $100 a month. I worked out a deal with White's Furniture to get the house furnished at low cost by agreeing to have it as a model home with open house for a few days. I enjoyed living at 703 S. Madison Drive for several years and was pleased to have a place where my relatives could come visit.

Homer Singletary, an engineer, came to work with the station about three months after I did. He and I were about the only single guys there, so occasionally we double dated together. Homer bought an old shrimp boat and fixed it up to a state of seaworthiness, he thought. I remember we took our dates for a ride in his boat one time. Later on, I read in the newspaper that Homer's boat had sunk in the gulf, but he and Gene Sudduth had been rescued. I chuckled, but was thankful they were safe and that this didn't happen with our dates.

Gene Sudduth was another of those versatile fellows who was very valuable to WEAR-TV. Gene was an engineer who helped put the station on the air. He was also its first weatherman and a good announcer. Gene kept a coat and tie handy so that, after performing engineering duties, he could quickly change for air work. One night he had forgotten to bring a coat and I gladly let him use mine. Gene is a tall, raw-boned sort of fellow and I am sure the TV audience laughed like we did when, during his on-the-air weather report, he reached up to point out temperatures in the northeast and it showed the sleeve of my coat reaching no further on his arm than his elbow.

Leroy Morris was a much loved announcer in Pensacola. After performing on radio for many years, Leroy came on TV with his live "RFD #3" program. Leroy, who liked to poke fun at his sponsors, weighed 395 pounds. Mel encouraged him to lose weight by asking him to weigh on the air each day and, for each pound he lost, he would get five dollars. It succeeded only to a point, but Leroy was a funny fellow who knew how to entertain an audience. One of his sponsors was Jarrard Motors and Leroy would say "Go on down and see them crooks at Jarhead Motors."

Lynn Toney was the key performer for WPFA-TV, Channel 15, which had gone on the air some time before Channel 3. But they had a weak signal and went out of business shortly after Channel 3 hit the airwaves. Our station hired Lynn Toney and he became a smash hit with his kids program, the Lynn Toney Show, which was on from 4:00 to 5:00 each afternoon. Lynn wore a leopard skin suit and picked on a bass fiddle. He knew how to make kids have fun. I introduced his show, off camera, by screaming, "....and now, the only unrehearsed, unscheduled, uncalled for program on television, the Lynn Toney Show." Then, the kids would go wild as Lynn came dashing in.

Television was more fun back then. We goofed right in your living rooms. With today's technology, everything is so perfected. We did not have video tape for a long time and ad-libbed most of our spots live. They were generally 60 seconds in length and sometimes we did not stop at that. The salespeople, like Ruth Fillingim, sold the sponsors, then would bring us the props and information and we would go on the air and sell whatever it was. One night I advertised a gas range for Charlie Wilkerson Gas Company and took it apart to show how easy it was to clean. I must have taken five minutes and I thought I would never get it back together.

Two of my best sponsors were Supreme, already alluded to, and Coca Cola. I have done as many as 20 or 25 live 60-second spots in a day. By the end of the day one begins to get a bit careless in what is said. In doing Supreme Ice Cream spots I dipped up a cone of ice cream, licked it and said "..mmm..good!" One night, as I scooped the cone, licked it, and held it out toward the camera I said, "Be sure to get it in the six-bottle carton." Did I ever hear about that!

I suppose I could be excused for goofing up when I first started out in television. My first commercials were for Danley Furniture who was sponsoring "Jimmy Dean's Town and Country Time" on Saturday nights. That afternoon, the refrigerator I was to advertise had already been put in place as my prop. The studio was clear and no one was around, so I practiced for hours on how I was going to open up the door of the refrigerator and tell 'em about all the features. When the show came on there I was waiting to do my very first TV spot. I opened up the refrigerator, talked about the roominess, the shelves for the butter and other things. Then I opened the crisper drawer down at the bottom, but got it off track and couldn't get it closed to save my life. I rammed..and I rammed...and finally said, with great embarrassment, "it sure does keep those fruits and vegetables cool and fresh."

White and White, a clothing store in downtown Pensacola, sponsored my Saturday College Football Scoreboard. On one show I was to advertise sweaters and jackets. Everything was going splendidly until midway in the program I paused in giving the scores to advertise jackets. I put one on and zipped it up, was supposed to pull that one off and put on another, but the zipper got stuck. I tried and tried to get it unzipped, but could not do it. So, I finished the show wearing the jacket. It was the talk of the town, but White and White liked it because they sold out of those jackets.

Lynn Toney, advertising for Toney's Pizza, held a real pizza on camera. About the time he hit the air the pizza slipped off the platter and Lynn, laughing all the time, spent the rest of the minute picking the pizza up off the floor.

Lynn advertised for the Old Firehouse Drive-In Restaurant and did their commercials when they bought my pre-game show before each of the NFL games, which we started carrying when we got the network. Lynn brought chicken and fish boxes which he would sample on the air. After we finished the show we would both help ourselves to the food. We only got paid a talent fee of $2.50 for each spot, so getting to eat the props was a little perk we enjoyed.

Viewers at home must have really broken up when they saw Dick Darby advertising Hotshot Bug Spray one time. Dick held out the spray can and pushed the button. One problem: he had the can facing the wrong way and sprayed the Hotshot right in his face. It was hilarious as Dick laughed and strangled the rest of the commercial.

Station management wanted to curtail expenses where they could. Once they bought a small remotely operated camera which could be operated by the engineer from the control room. He had a foot pedal with which to depress or elevate or to pan right or left. Mel decided the best time to try it out was on some of our Sunday daytime programming. We had a program called Pastor's Fireside with Father Terminello. As the program was introduced this particular day from the booth, Tom Lowery, the engineer on duty, turned on the new camera. But there was a problem, Tom could not find Father Terminello. He panned right...left...up...down...all over the walls and the ceiling, but he couldn't find his subject. He finally picked someone up, but it was one of Father Terminello's off-camera helpers and the poor man was terrified. Suffice it to say, the robot camera was taken out of service rather quickly after that.

In the early days of Channel 3 we did a lot of live programs. In addition to those already mentioned, Millie Long had a program called "Millie"s Guest Book," which featured local talent and was very popular. I did a lot of sports shows, including a weekly half-hour hunting and fishing program, and after we got regular network programs, I had a pre-game show before every game that we carried. Management and sales people were always looking for shows they could sell to sponsors. Before each World Series game I had a show featuring well-known baseball people living in the area.This started out as a 15-minute show, but eventually increased to an hour. I would rehash the game of the previous day and preview the upcoming game. Some of my guests with whom I had good discussions were Lance Richburg, who had played with Babe Ruth and had the record for the shortest hit in a World Series, Wally Dashiell and Monte Barrow.

Campaign season was always a time of good business for the station. A slew of candidates--local, state and federal-- purchased advertising. Usually the station would open up segments of time to sell in five minute blocks to local candidates, and there were state candidates who would purchase a full half hour. The first year I was with the station Acting Governor Charlie Johns was opposed by Leroy Collins for governor. Johns had a half-hour slot on Saturday afternoon. He had a number of supporters in the studio and they would applaud his every remark. As soon as he finished, we quickly ushered him and his people out because we had local candidates to put on. The next candidate was running for county commissioner and when he concluded his five minutes there was heard from the studio a single person clapping. Before his mike could be cut, the candidate exclaimed, with much embarrassment, "Mother!"

During those long hours I had to sit in the booth and make the announcements between programs, I had a lot of time to read and think. I read about FM radio, which had been tried back in the 40's but did not catch on, making a comeback. In addition to putting out a quality signal on the main channel, FM had two subchannels which could be utilized in what was called multiplexing. This was intriguing. I thought this could be a good business, so I wrote for information to some of the stations who were doing this.

I got deeper and deeper into this subject and before I hardly realized it, I was organizing a corporation to file an application for an FM Station. I had a mere $4,000 saved up and knew that would not go far, but I tried to line up people who could be of benefit to the cause. The only lawyer in town I knew, but not very well, was Reubin O'D. Askew. I knew him because he had been out to the station to do his political ads for state representive, a position he now held. Reubin agreed to do the legal work and buy $1,500 worth of stock. My good friend, Homer, who would help with the engineering, invested $1,500. So did Don Langford, who was a music man and could help with the programming. Another I enticed into buying $1,500 worth of stock was my brother, Rex, who worked with the Bank of Ozark.

I made arrangements with Bert Mead of Radio & Electronics Service Company to rent space on his tower for our antenna and to use a plot of ground next to his building to erect a small facility for our station. I was able to get a trade-out with businesses which provided building supplies in exchange for advertising once we would get on the air. My dad came down and spent a few days with me and dug footing and did other hard work on our little building. In this way, we were able to get our building done and use most of the money we had for a down payment on the transmitter.

I worked relentlessly on the application, with help from Reubin and consulting engineers, LJN Dutreil and Associates of New Orleans. It was a good feeling when, on behalf of Mellotone, Inc., I filed an application with the FCC for an FM station in Pensacola.

Because of my night-time schedule on WEAR-TV, I was able to devote a lot of daylight hours to getting the FM going. I kept watching the news wire at the TV station hoping to see that the FCC had issued our construction permit. After several months it came.

We ordered a Gates transmitter and when it arrived Homer, with some help from Chief Nasser who was stationed at Naval Air Station, and from Gene Sudduth, got it ready to go on the air. All these folks had other jobs and were donating their time due to their fascination with FM and because of their friendship with me. They called me at home about 2:00 a.m. one morning and told me to turn on my FM radio. When I turned it on I thought it was the clearest sound I ever heard. Whoopee! It worked and we would, after a few more tests, be ready to go on the air full-time.

I was the chief owner, president, manager, announcer,

salesman, custodian, and everything else that pertains to a radio station. It was a glorious day when we began official broadcasting on November 11, 1960, the first FM station in Northwest Florida and for miles around. The problem we faced was that we were pioneering frequency modulation radio and there were very few people who had FM sets. I tried to help that situation by going door-to-door selling small Granco FM sets for $30, which I had arranged to get from a distributor in New Orleans.

I wanted to keep my job at Channel 3, but Milt DeReyna, who had by now succeeded Mel Wheeler as manager, felt it was a conflict of interest. I understood that, but I really doubt we would have caused the TV station to lose money. Anyway, I was forced to put full-time to the FM.

The call letters I requested of the FCC at first were WPEN for Pensacola, but those were in use somewhere else. I then asked for WPEX-FM, which I thought had a good sound, and those call letters were approved by the FCC. Everybody who heard our new station at 94.1 on the FM dial raved about the great sound and beautiful music.

The main thing that prompted me to get into FM radio was the prospect of a good business providing background music to offices and stores by transmitting it on one of the subchannels, through the use of multiplexing. We had not been on the air very long when we determined that it would take a major investment to really get into the background music business. So, we had to work hard in promoting our main channel and making it go.

Although not top of the line in everything, we had the necessities to run a radio station, such as the transmitter, control board, turntables, and so on. We contracted for AP News. The big thing we did not have was money. We were able to sell a few ads all along and, as people heard about the station, more and more were purchasing FM sets. Joel Swanson, an executive with Delchamps Supermarkets headquartered in Mobile, had tuned us in and liked it very much. Delchamps became one of our best sponsors. But, it was tough sledding. Although we got some business from firms that sold electronic equipment, I felt those selling FM radios, and they were selling very well, should have been more supportive of the station.

We had a format of popular and popular concert type music, a lot of it instrumental, but with a few vocals mixed in. At night, we ran Concert Time, a classical music program from 7:00 to 10:00 p.m.

The theme was Tchaikovsky's Piano Concerto #1 in E Flat Minor. It became a very familiar piece of music. WPEX-FM had a dedicated audience, but obviously the listenership was not sufficient to convince advertisers to do a lot of business with us. We mimeographed, and later had printed, a monthly WPEX-FM program guide which we sold to listeners and that brought in a tidbit of money.

We taped most of our commercial spots and public service announcements. Our only fulltime employee was a young lady by the name of Linda Livingston. She would answer the phone, do typing, and operate the turntables to play music and turn on the taped announcements at the scheduled times while I was out trying to sell advertising. At various times we had Larry Williamson, Danny Treanor, and Rusty Minshew, all students at Pensacola High School, to do part-time announcing for us. We had also hired Max Holland, who came into town from Ohio looking for work, and he did a good job of announcing for the few hours we could pay him.

John Harris, who I had known as a high school student back at Dothan when he did some school programs on WDIG, was now grown up, married and looking for a job. I hired him to help me with WPEX-FM, the Golden Sound of the Gulf Coast. There was no instant success. We both toiled and sweated. Surely, sooner or later we would be rewarded for bringing good quality music to Pensacola.

I was under tremendous pressure, having practically no income and with bills to pay. I was working myself ragged and subsisting mostly on cereal to try to make a go of this thing. Mama kept telling me that I was working too hard and needed to get rid of the station. As so often is the case, the good Lord intervened, I believe. I received a telephone call from Bob Villar, with WSFA-TV, Montgomery who previously worked with me at Channel 3, telling me I should come to Montgomery to talk about being Sports director of that station and doing the Sunday statewide telecasts of Auburn Football with Coach Ralph "Shug" Jordan.

Had WPEX-FM been going well financially I would not have considered going to Montgomery, but it was an opportunity for me to make some money to plow back into our station. I accepted the challenge, left John Harris as manager in Pensacola and was Alabama bound!

Captain Supreme (Earl Hutto) was popular on TV and made appearances at schools and community events. He is shown here riding on his space-ship float in the Fiesta of Five Flags Parade in downtown Pensacola.

Sportscaster Earl Hutto is shown giving college football scores on his Saturday afternoon Football Scoreboard on television.

8

ON THE TUBE AGAIN

My television career had been revived! I did not plan on ever being a TV performer again. Since I had to give up my job at Channel 3, due to the conflict of interest with WPEX-FM, I had been off television for close to a year. Now I was hired for a television job bigger than anything I had done. I was now the sports director of one of the better operations in the country. It was first class and for me a pleasure to work at WSFA-TV, Channel 12.

This was the station that launched Frank McGee to a network career with NBC where he became one of their topnotch anchors. WSFA-TV did a lot of feeds to the network and McGee's coverage of the Montgomery bus boycotts in the late fifties propelled him to a New York job..

Racial tensions were still high when I went to Montgomery. I remember when George Wallace was inaugurated as governor and made his throw-down-the-gauntlet stand on segregation. Despite posturing this way, Governor Wallace became a booster for working people and minorities. His support by African Americans helped elect him to the governorship in later campaigns.

It was my responsibility at Channel 12 to be in charge of all sports under the news department. I had resources to draw on, including film cameramen who could accompany me when I went out to cover sports in the Montgomery area. I had not been used to having a full-time news department with its own dedicated employees.

This job was not without pressure to succeed. Channel 12 had been on the air about four or five years and Leroy Paul had been its sports director. Leroy had been lured away with a lucrative job in industry and Carl Stephens, already an announcer on staff, was chosen as his replacement. However, Carl, a member of the Air National Guard in Montgomery, had been called to active duty because of the Berlin crisis. Thus, the call to me and my hiring for the position.

The ultimate consideration for this sports job was finding someone who would do a good job with Auburn Football which is carried on a statewide network of TV stations throughout the state of Alabama. Leroy Paul had established an outstanding reputation for the way he handled this show. That's why there was pressure. But I was confident. I had done play-by-play of football, so narration of the action film and interview of the coach was something I felt I was well qualified to do. I prayed that I would do my very best.

Alabama is a football-mad state. They are as rabid as they come in supporting their pigskin teams. These folks are really serious about the game. In fact, I am quite surprised that the Auburn fans did not raise a stink about Leroy, an Alabama grad, doing the Auburn show. I would have no trouble with the fans, in this respect, since I am a Trojan from Troy State. My allegiance in this state rivalry between Alabama and Auburn had switched back and forth, depending on the kind of season each was having. But, now, with this job, there was no question about it. I had become, automatically, a dyed-in-the-wool booster of the Auburn Tigers.

My mettle would be tested soon. It was only a few days hence that I was thrust into the middle of all this. I took a trip to Auburn to get reacquainted with Coach Shug Jordan. I had met the coach several years before and interviewed him when he came to Dothan while I was working with WDIG, but I suspected he would not remember that. I found out, however, that Shug Jordan had a great memory and I would see evidence of this over the next several years.

.   One of the great things about my new job was attending a major college football game every Saturday during the season. I carried a three-man crew, sometimes four-man crew, to cover the games. I was assigned a seat in the press box with other scribes and I wrote down every play that I would later transcribe into my written script for the show.

The main camera in our coverage was on the photo deck of the press box and the photographer there shot every play. Our second man, with a hand held camera, worked the sidelines and took close up shots of action at a faster speed so that when it was played back at normal speed, it would be in slow motion. All of this was shot with 16-millimeter cameras.

When the Tigers were playing home games in Auburn or playing in Birmingham, we would drive the Channel 12 station wagon to the games. On the away games, we flew charter with Montgomery Aviation. Whether home or away, we rushed back after the game so that we could get the film processed and I could begin putting it together. Stan Tarilton was chief photographer and he was on the main camera at the game and oversaw the processing when we got back to the studio. Frank Adams and Charles Jones were also photographers who worked many of the games. Gene Jacobsen and Johnny Johnson, from the programming and production departments, often took their turns at sideline shooting. They would volunteer just to get in on the game.

I personally edited the film. While the film was being processed, I wrote my script. When Stan finished processing, I would put the main reel on one bench and the sideline footage on another. Working with a viewer I would wind the film from one reel to another. I had to splice every play and take out excess footage. On many of the outstanding plays, I spliced in slow motion footage from the second reel. It took a long time to put this show together, and I often got home and got to bed in the wee hours of the morning.

On Sunday afternoon I think most Alabamians settled in for two hours of watching their favorite and unfavorite football teams. Alabama Football with Coach Paul "Bear" Bryant came on from 4:00 to 5:00, originating from Birmingham. This program, in which Coach Bryant did the narration, with his sports information director, Charlie Thornton, as his straight man, so to speak, throwing in a comment every now and then. The Bear's sponsors were Golden Flake Potato Chips and Coca-Cola. It was a colorful program with the Bear crunching potato chips and occasionally lamenting, when an opposing player made a 10-yard run, "Holy cow, I thought he was gonna run out the end of the stadium."

Auburn Football with Coach Ralph "Shug" Jordan then came on from 5:00 to 6:00 on the same lineup of stations, but originating from studios at WSFA-TV in Montgomery. Although we did not have the Bear and his colorful comments, I really believe we had a better-looking show. The production on the pre-produced opening and closing were professionally done. Our well-edited film with cutaway shots and natural exciting sound from the crowd made the viewers feel like they were at the game. I hope that my narration and Coach Jordan's comments were also instrumental in making it a topnotch production. We certainly got a lot of compliments.

Coach Jordan was not only a good football coach, but an outstanding gentleman. He possessed a good personality, was friendly, kind, and patient. He made me feel comfortable and at ease when we were on the air together. I am sure that I was a little nervous as I faced the cameras for the first time on Auburn Football that late September Sunday in 1961. After all, this was the biggest audience I ever appeared before. The telecast was carried by TV stations all over the state and maybe a few in border states.

Thankfully, my debut on the Auburn show started with success. I say that because the Tigers won their season opener by beating the Tennessee Volunteers in a thriller 24-21. That meant the Coach was in good spirits, although I can honestly say that Shug was even-tempered and nice even after losing, as I would find out later. This first show was successful, also, because it went off without a hitch. Coach Jordan and I clicked as a team, like clockwork. I sensed the right times to pause for his comments or to ask him a question. His favorite saying, which people liked to mimic, was "You're so right, Earl."

Though the Auburn Football show was a big part of my job, it was seasonal. However, we provided quite a bit of Auburn and Alabama coverage in other sports of baseball, basketball,and track by running film in our regular sportscasts.

The emphasis was definitely on football and I would take a film crew to Auburn and Tuscaloosa to do interviews of coaches and players for a pre-season show each year. I understand that my predecessor, Leroy Paul, despite being an Alabama alumnus, had difficulty interviewing the Bear because of his abrasive personality. But I hit it off good with Coach Bryant. He saw me at a football banquet and made a point of complimenting me on the way I handled the Auburn show.

Let me relate to you a true story about Coach Bryant. For Alabama fans the Bear was like deity. There were stories about him walking on water and other such tales. But this one is definitely true. One pre-season when we went to Tuscaloosa to shoot footage of the team and do interviews with the coaches, it was raining like everything. We took shelter because we could not let our equipment get wet and we could not get this filming done in the rain. But, would you believe it? As soon as Coach Paul "Bear" Bryant walked onto the practice field the rain ceased. Honest!

The 6:00 to 6:30 Monday-Friday block at Channel 12 was formatted with separate news, sports, and weather segments. News Director Charles Cox did the news, I did sports, and Ralph Williams did weather. My sponsor on sports for a long run was Fannin Men's

Store. I stood beside a rear screen, where slides and pictures were shown, while I gave the sports as well as the live commercial. I would go down to Fannin's and get outfitted in new clothes which I would wear and advertise on the air. They did not give me suits, but I did get a discount when I bought.

The format at 10:00 p.m.on Nightbeat was different. Carl Stephens, though he had been activated for duty with the Air National Guard, did not leave Montgomery and continued to work at the station. He did the Nightbeat News, I did the sports, and Ralph did the weather. Carl and I had podiums side-by-side and Ralph the weather map next to us. Carl had about three segments of news and Ralph and I each had two segments of weather and sports, but there was flexibility on various nights, depending on what was happening.

We had a neat open and close to Nightbeat that was pre-recorded. The engineer would run the opening and closing tapes from the control room. The show opened with a wide shot of all three of us live on camera. There would be a drum roll, and then the introduction would go, "This is Nightbeat... (drumbeat) News with Carl Stephens (closeup of Carl,who smiles and nods)...(drumbeat) Sports with Earl Hutto (closeup of Earl, who smiles and nods)...(drumbeat) and Weather with Ralph Williams (closeup of Ralph, who smiles and nods). Then the scene switched back to a closeup of Carl who gave a headline, and then I and Ralph followed likewise. Then, Carl kicked off with the news.

A classic foul-up occurred one night and I would give anything to have a tape of it. As Nightbeat began and we were introduced and gave our nod and were about to begin our headlines we could hear through the glass of the control room that the engineer had forgotten to stop the tape and it went into the close. We heard "this has been Nightbeat with Carl Stephens News, Earl Hutto Sports, and Ralph Williams Weather". We all three broke up laughing and murdered our headlines. For example my sports headline was to be "The Dothan High Tigers defeated Lanier's Poets tonight", but in our hilarity I said "Figers" instead of Tigers.

The night of the big mix-up just happened to have been the time that our manager, Carter Hardwick, had asked that Nightbeat be taped to send to our sister station, WIS-TV in Columbia, South Carolina. Of course, the tape was not sent. But how wonderful that this hilarious episode was captured on tape. It would have been great on the World's Funniest Videos. But some people have no sense of humor. The first thing the next morning, Mr. Hardwick had it erased. What a shame. We wanted to get copies so that through the years we could look back and laugh at our shenanigans on Nightbeat.

Meanwhile, what had happened to my FM station, WPEX-FM? I was making pretty good money at Channel 12, about $150 a week, plus $75 each game when I did Auburn Football, and smaller talent fees for live appearances on sports and commercials. Most of this was going into more stock I bought in Mellotone, Inc. to pay bills for our FM operation. John apparently was having little success in selling advertising.

After the football season, I drove back to Pensacola on weekends, in my little VW beetle, as often as I could to check on the station. I slept at the station while there. Eventually, John left WPEX and Jim Young, a longtime Pensacola radio announcer, was placed in charge. It was still a worry for me.

Another plus for me being in Montgomery was the fact I was less than 90 miles from my hometown of Ozark, or more specifically, Ewell, and I could zip down to see my folks in less than two hours. In March of 1963, my brother Rex got married and I was his best man. You will recall I was 11 years older, but I was happy to see Rex marry Sara York, an attractive young lady from Pinckard, another town in Dale County. I think my folks were beginning to wonder if I would ever take the step that Rex had taken.

Early in my second year at WSFA-TV I ran into the same bugaboo with my six o'clock sports. It was sold to a national beer sponsor. I thought I had an understanding with the station that I would not be associated with alcoholic beverages, but there was nothing in writing and apparently someone in sales did not understand. Anyway, as in Pensacola, I gave up that sportscast until the 13-week contract ran out, although I continued to do my Nightbeat Sports.

As in Pensacola, I would interview sports celebrities who came into town. Montgomery was the hometown of Bart Starr, who played at Lanier High in Montgomery before going on to Alabama and to the Green Bay Packers, and Bart was home to see his folks pretty often. Dizzy Dean, Moose Skowron, and Billy Hitchcock, along with many Alabama and Auburn stars, were just a few of those I had on the air.

We did a few live sports events, including a Ladies Professional Golf Association tournament at Montgomery Country Club. Most of the name stars on the ladies tour were there and it was fascinating to watch people like the great Patti Berg play the game and to be able to interview her, Mary Lena Faulk, Cathy Whitworth, and other stars.

The Alabama legislature was in session and on one particular date they were running overtime and working into the night. After our Nightbeat telecast, Carl Stephens and I decided to go watch the lawmakers. It was an interesting experience and, as we sat in the gallery and watched them, I said to Carl, "I wouldn't mind being a legislator someday." Years later, he would remind me of that remark.

My role was to announce sports, but I got into the social realm one time. It was the one and only time I announced an engagement on the air. Carl had been dating a fine young lady by the name of Mary, a Huntingdon College coed, and I knew they were getting quite serious. One night when Carl came in to do Nightbeat he told Ralph and me he had just gotten engaged. I asked him if I could announce it on the air. He said okay, but I don't believe he thought I would do it. On my last segment of sports that night, I closed by saying, "..and finally, a social note, it is with much pleasure that I announce the engagement of Carl Stephens to Mary McKinley." Carl is still with WSFA and we still talk about this. Carl and Mary are still married, with two fine children.

The annual Blue-Gray game pitting the North and South college all-stars against each other is played in Cramton Bowl in Montgomery. I enjoyed covering the squads each of the two years I was in Montgomery. Some of the top coaches and players from around the nation are in Alabama's capitol city for a week as they practice for this game. It was my pleasure to be asked by Allyn McKeen, who headed up the Blue-Gray, to do the public address system during the Blue-Gray game. I was able, also, to meet some of the network announcers who came into town to cover the contest.

I was deeply humble and grateful to the thousands of people in the Channel 12 viewing area who had such glowing remarks about the work I was doing. It was especially good to hear from people I had grown up with in Dale County and many I had gone to school with at Troy State. I cannot understand how some performers disrespect or have little use for their fans. As far as I am concerned, we owe our success to those who tune in and I am always pleased and thankful for the good response I have received through the years.

It is always great to see Auburn football and the school spirit that is prevalent at Tiger games. The cry of "War Eagle" can be heard anywhere there are Auburn fans. Our crew arrived before noon and we enjoyed lunch in the press box before those afternoon contests at Cliff Hare Stadium. The two years I did the Auburn telecasts the Tigers had winning seasons, but not great seasons. In 1961, Auburn finished 6-4 and in 1962, the record was 6-3-1. Unfortunately, that final game which counts most for Auburn and Alabama fans was bad both years for Auburn University. In 1961, the Crimson Tide won 34-0 and, in 1962 the Tigers were blanked 38-0.

The losers in this big game suffer for the next year. The fans can sometimes be quite brutal if their team does not come out a winner. I really felt for Coach Jordan in those season-ending losses to Alabama. He shared with me how he had received very nasty phone calls and letters.   But, as I stated earlier, Coach Jordan was a gentleman in victory and in defeat. He was gracious as a winner and complimentary of the opponent when he lost. It was good to see that Cliff Hare Stadium was renamed Jordan-Hare Stadium in honor of Coach Jordan. That stadium now seats 85,000 fans.

My desire always has been to do the best job I can for my employer. In doing Auburn football, I put a lot of time and effort into making it a good production. It would have been much easier for me to simply take the master reel of film, clip out the excess footage on each play, and add just a few cut-ins, and be done with it. I could have done that in an hour or two. But, instead of having a play end and then immediately seeing the team back on the line of scrimmage, which I think makes it look like a scouting film, I would splice in slow-motion and closeup shots very frequently, and splice in cutaway shots after every play. I think it made the fans feel like they were there at the stadium in the thick of the action.

Because of this extra attention to detail, I was spending more and more time putting the show together when we returned from the game. It was getting to the point that I worked all night long, and in fact there were times I worked all the way through to noon or after on Sunday. I would get home and only sleep an hour or two before I had to get back to the station for the 5:00 p.m. airing of the show.

I have only asked an employer for a raise about once or twice in my life, but I was not getting paid enough for all the work I was putting in on the Auburn Football show, so I asked Mr. Hardwick about a raise. I am sure the station was doing well financially on this program with Southern Bell as the network sponsor, but Mr. Hardwick turned down my request for a raise. I was only getting $75 per week for all I was doing on this program. I felt so strongly about the issue that I turned in my resignation. My thought was to go back to Pensacola and make a go of WPEX-FM.

My folks couldn't believe it when I went home and told them I had quit my job. I explained that I gave it up because I was getting paid too little for the job I was doing on the Auburn Football show, and that I planned to go to Pensacola and get the FM station moving.

Mama and Daddy urged me not to go back to the FM station. They knew how I was struggling two years before that when I got the call to go to Montgomery. They convinced me that going back to Pensacola now was not the right thing. Okay, I would look elsewhere for work. This was really the only time in my life, including the days of teenage work at Camp Rucker, that I had been unemployed. What was I going to do?

I had confidence in my ability and knew someone could use me. Although I did not have an abundance of money, I decided on heading to Atlanta and north from there. I felt that maybe I should take a shot at New York and the bigtime. What better time to give it a try than when I am not working? Nothing ventured, nothing gained.

I had gotten to know Billy Hitchcock, from Opelika, whom I had interviewed several times. Billy was then Manager of the Baltimore Orioles. I decided to go see Billy and ask if he would help me get an appointment with Bill McPhail, Vice President of CBS Sports in New York. Mr. McPhail was the brother of the General Manager of the Orioles.

So, I headed north in my VW beetle. I arrived early for an Orioles home game and was able to see Billy during the team warmups. He graciously consented to call Mr. McPhail and arrange for me to have an appointment the next day. I had been in New York once before on liberty when I was in the Navy, but this was the first time I had driven in the city. I managed to handle the New York traffic without much difficulty. The low-cost hotel where I spent the night was nothing to write home about, but it was a place to sleep for the one night I was in the Big Apple.

The interview with Mr. McPhail went very well. He was a pleasant person, but as one might surmise he did not immediately offer me a job doing NFL games. In fact, he did not offer me a job. But, he did try to be helpful. He suggested I try to get a sports director's job in one of the large markets, and mentioned Seattle specifically. I did not tell him, but I was not ready to go that far away. Anyway, I left him an audition tape and thanked him for seeing me.

On the way home, I had no specific plan, but I was driving into the night and decided to pull into a rest stop on I-85 outside Greensboro, North Carolina, and spend the night in my car. I slept pretty good and in the morning shaved with cold water at the rest stop and headed into town.. WFMY, Channel 2 in Greensboro gave me an audition which seemed to click. It was my understanding that they were going to need a sports man right away and would call me.

In Atlanta, I was able to get an interview and have my tape viewed at WSB-TV. Then, I was given a further audition. In both Greensboro and Atlanta, they seemed to be impressed with my eye contact, which had been one of my trademarks, even in an era when teleprompters had not come into prominence. Hal Suit, news director of WSB-TV, offered me a job in news. A lot of people would give their eye teeth for a job at one of the nation's premier stations in a big market like Atlanta. But, I really did not want a job as a newscaster. I felt deeply that sports was my thing and if I were going to continue in television, that should be my field.

So, back to Ewell I went to stay with my folks until I could hear from Greensboro or find a job elsewhere. I did not know what an ordeal this was going to be. In the ensuing days, I called a number of stations and wrote letters, but there were no openings or encouragement. After all, there were only an FCC limited number of TV stations and then, as now, only limited positions available for many who seek them.

The station in Greensboro did not fulfill its promise to call me. I was getting nowhere. I was beginning to have feelings of despair. Mama and Daddy suggested I go to Fort Rucker (changed from Camp Rucker several years earlier when the base became permanent) and seek a civil service job, but I did not believe that was my kind of calling and if I took such a position, I would never have the opportunity to return to broadcasting, which was more to my liking.

Days turned into weeks, weeks turned into a couple of

months, and I was getting desperate for a job. My confidence was beginning to wane. My parents gave me encouragement, but I was in a situation in which I had never been.

Finally, I decided to call Ray Carow. Remember, he was the assistant program director when I started my TV career in Pensacola and was the one who said he did not know what to do in his job? Ray was now vice president and general manager of Gray Communications which owns WALB-TV in Albany, Georgia, and WJHG-TV in Panama City, Florida.

I explained to Ray my situation and that I needed a job. At this point I was willing to take most anything. Ray, who was headquartered in Albany, said he would check with Jim Tighe, manager of the Panama City station to see if he could use me. It wasn't long until he called back and said they would hire me at WJHG-TV. I would do their 11:00 p.m. news and commercial announcements, but they would only be able to pay me $90 a week to start. Beggars can't be choosers. I took it.

Thank the Lord, a job at last! This would be a comedown for me. It would be the smallest TV market I had worked in after Montgomery and Pensacola. It would be a lot less in salary than in Montgomery. But another way to look at it is that I would be making a lot more than not working at all and having no pay coming in. I was indeed thankful to be going back to work. Also, I would be closer to Pensacola and have a better chance of checking on the FM station.

This had been a tough two months, but in all things give thanks. I truly believe that this period of unemployment made me a better person. It gave me a deep appreciation of being employed and earning a living. It provided me with a deep feeling of compassion for those who do not have a job or the ability to make a living for themselves or their families. Also, I believe, of necessity, I learned to be a little more patient. I had learned, perhaps the hard way, several lessons in life. There was a silver lining to those storm clouds.

I immediately packed my bags, loaded the beetle, and headed down U. S. Highway 231 bound for Panama City. I was feeling much better and looking forward to what the future held for me. It was my return to Florida.

9

RETURN TO FLORIDA

I was proud of my home state of Alabama. That was where I was born and raised. That is where my family lives. I have many fond memories of the state, and a few memories not so pleasant. This I know: There are some of the finest people in the world living in Alabama and I will always appreciate and hold in my heart the wonderful friends who have meant so much to me throughout the years. But, now I was back in my adopted state of Florida.

I was back in Florida, all right, but I have to admit that I did not plan to work a long time in Panama City. In my mind, employment with WJHG-TV, Channel 7, was going to be short term until I could get employment in a bigger market.

Realizing the traumatic two months I had spent without employment, I was certainly going to maintain a positive attitude, which is my nature, but all the while I would be looking for opportunities to move on to greener pastures.

I was not impressed with WJHG-TV, but I was impressed with the staff. These people were so nice to me. In fact, some of them looked up to me, knowing of my work at Channel 3 in Pensacola and then in Montgomery, as someone who could help their operation. I had known of this station, which was formerly WJDM-TV, when I was in Pensacola.

WJDM-TV was originally owned by Mr. J. D. Manley, from South Florida and although, officially, call letters of a station do not stand for anything, applicants for the construction permit can petition the FCC for letters they would like to have and, if there are no stations currently on the air with those call letters, the requested letters are granted. Thus, WJDM-TV for J. D. Manley. Mr. Manley, so the story goes, knew nothing about broadcasting, so he had contracted with Gulfport Broadcasting Corporation, owners of WEAR-TV in Pensacola, to run Channel 7.

WEAR-TV fed a lot of programs to WJDM-TV in those early days, and it was a fiasco for the folks in Panama City. A weak microwave signal from Pensacola to Panama City often caused Channel 7 to have technical difficulties and lose programing. When

Channel 3 ran film programs, like movies, Channel 7 would often not know when Pensacola was going to cut out for a commercial, and oftentimes Channel 7 would have Channel 3 commercials on the air before they were able to cut away. It was a nightmare for Panama City, as those who worked there at that time will attest.

When I joined Channel 7 Gray Communications had already bought the station and changed the call letters to WJHG-TV (James H. Gray). I could not have blamed the folks at Channel 7 if they had ridden me out of town on a rail for the transgressions when I was with Channel 3. But they were forgiving and accepted me with kindness.

I found a little one bedroom upstairs apartment when I got to Panama City that was barebones to say the least, but it had a good bed. I did not have to work until afternoon and found myself sleeping until late morning. I must have been tired from my work in Montgomery and the trauma of not having a job for two months. Anyway, I got plenty of rest.

Three weeks had gone by since my arrival in Panama City and at noontime I was watching my colleague, Donnell Brookins, on his farm program which Donnell himself would tell you was not a very exciting show. He generally read farm market reports and a few local announcements. But, on this particular day, he had world shattering news. Donnell came dashing onto the set and said, "Ladies and Gentlemen, I have some terrible news! This Associated Press News Flash reports that President Kennedy has been shot in Dallas....Again, AP reports that President Kennedy has been shot." Shocking News! Donnell went on to say that he would keep reporting the information as it came in. Momentarily, Channel 7 joined the NBC television network....and of course, the news that President Kennedy had been shot to death by Lee Harvey Oswald was heard around the world.

This was such a mournful time for America and the free world. That afternoon Donnell and I, with our photographer Louie Walker, were assigned to go out onto the streets of Panama City and do interviews with people about the President's assassination. Among those we interviewed was head football coach Len Register of Bay High School who was bringing his team out of a movie prior to their football game that night. Our interviewees were heart broken and grieved at this tragic turn of events. For many years after, Channel 7 news director Earl Hadaway ran these filmed interviews on the anniversary of President Kennedy's assassination in Dallas.

The assassination was such a shocking event that the football game that night in Panama City between Bay and crosstown rival Rutherford High School was almost canceled. But, the decision was finally made to go ahead with the contest. This was a most significant game because Rutherford was a new school that had not been open long and their Rams were playing the Bay High Tornadoes for the first time in a much ballyhooed contest at Tommy Oliver Stadium. The game ended in a 0-0 deadlock and will be remembered always by those in attendance on a day that our president was slain.

It was a dreary time for me, especially because I was concerned not only about our country, but about my future. In the ensuing weeks I did get a call from Bill McPhail, the vice president of CBS Sports, telling me that he had viewed my audition tape and liked it, but there was no opening for me. I never expected a response, much less a job, but thought it was quite nice of him to call.

Would you believe I also received a call from Ralph Williams, my old colleague with whom I had done Nightbeat in Montgomery? Ralph, as chief announcer, called to offer me a job to come back to work at WSFA-TV. The job offer was not as sports director because Carl Stephens had assumed that position, but as announcer. Monetarily, I could have done better, but I did not want to backtrack, especially in a lower position. I did appreciate Ralph thinking of me.

A couple of days later, Phil Snow, of WKRG-TV in Mobile, called to ask me what it was like working at WSFA-TV. He had been offered the job. I told Phil that it was a good station and I enjoyed working there. Phil took the job, later began doing Auburn Football, and has continued doing it for many years.

My eyes were certainly open for new opportunities, although any thought I had of leaving , of course, was not known by the people at the station. In the absence of any immediate offers, I had an idea for a program which I felt I could successfully produce and sell for syndication. I had made arrangements with sports information directors at all the Southeastern Conference schools to get two or three minutes of filmed highlights of each of their football games. These highlights were used on my regular sportscasts, but I thought if I could put these clips together and tape a half-hour Southeastern Football show each week of the season, it would be saleable.

At Channel 7, we had old Dage studio cameras that did not produce a sharp picture, so I decided to do a pilot program at

WKRG-TV in Mobile since they were capable of doing the best production. Wes Diamond, production manager, worked with me and we spent a lot of time one night getting this pilot program produced and kinescoped to film.

Now that I had my pilot, the next task was to sell it. I managed to get three or four days off from work, went by Ewell and got Daddy to go with me, and headed out once again in my VW beetle to points north. My destination was New York, with stops in Atlanta and Philadelphia. In each city I had appointments with advertising agencies, hoping that they would buy the show for one of their clients and syndicate it to stations throughout the southeast.

This was the furtherest my father had been away from home and I was pleased he could go with me to see some of the big cities. In Washington, we spent only a short time, but did visit President Kennedy's gravesite to see the eternal flame, and drove by the U.S.Capitol. We spent a night in Philadelphia, but having little money we stayed in an old hotel where we had to go down the hall to use the restroom. In New York City, Daddy got a big kick out of going to the top of the Empire State Building, and seeing other sights.

The meetings I had were somewhat encouraging, but no one was ready to buy. Their hesitancy seemed to be mostly concern over my ability to produce this show and get it to the stations in a timely manner each week. I felt that I could do it. The most interest appeared to come from the Tucker Wayne Agency in Atlanta for their client, Southern Bell Telephone. We communicated by phone over the next few weeks, but nothing was worked out.

I would not be defeated on this project, even if I had to peddle it myself. A few years later that is exactly what I did. Ron Jones, Jack Crusan and the production crew at Channel 7, where we now had good color equipment, helped me produce it.. I did not have a long list of stations lined up, but Southeastern Football was a pretty slick show which I sold for an average of about $75 per program. I left slots for three commercials inside each program and the show was well received in such cities as Orlando, Florida; Jackson, Mississippi; Huntsville, Alabama; and Albany, Georgia.

It seemed predestined that I was to stay in Panama City because my desire to further my broadcast career in a larger market was not being fulfilled. As the second year in PC passed and then my third year came, I felt that I was stuck in a place I did not want to be.

But I made the best of it. Jim Tighe made me production manager. My background was not in production, but I gained some knowledge during my time in TV and I took this assignment on as a challenge.

Channel 7 had originally been located at Panama City Beach in a rather small facility, but one which had been built especially for television. When I got to Panama City, however, the station had been relocated downtown on Harrison Avenue, the main drag, in an old bank building. I couldn't believe it when I first saw the studio. It had old burlap bags hanging from the ceiling. Apparently someone had thought the bags were necessary for proper acoustics.

One of my first acts as production manager was to remove the burlap bags. Also, we improved the looks of our sets and camera angles. With a small staff, the engineer on duty had been doing the directing, or switching from one camera to another, during live programs. So, there was not much imagination or creativity in how the programs looked on the air. One thing we began to do was cross shoot when two or more people were involved in on-air conversation.

During campaign years the station did well in selling time to candidates. In addition to spot announcements, we blocked out a half-hour or hour of time and sold it in five-minute segments. Some candidates, mostly statewide office seekers, bought half-hour slots.

I remember a rather humorous incident when Miami Mayor Robert King High was going against Haydon Burns for Governor of Florida. Mr. High had purchased a half-hour in late afternoon and his supporters had set up a flatbed truck just outside our studios where he would speak. The man was about to be late. I waited out front to hurriedly escort him to the platform. As he was being introduced by a supporter and we approached the platform Mr. High mistakenly handed me his speech and mounted the platform with a newspaper instead. Somehow, he managed to wing it without his script.

Ira Jenkins was a colorful individual running for sheriff of Bay County against incumbent Doc Daffin. Mr. Jenkins, at the time, was an alcoholic and his performance on his five-minute telecasts was good enough to command a sizeable audience. Other candidates wanted to purchase time next to Ira's because they knew he would have a lot of people watching. One quote from Ira Jenkins that folks will probably not forget was, "Friends, elect me your next high sheriff. I know what it's like to be in that jail, because I've been there."

My television career had always been marked by my having to

work at night. Panama City was no different. Instead of having three people doing the news, weather, and sports at 11:00 p.m. I did it all in a 15-minute program. However, on the weather part there were no weather maps or visuals. I simply read the area forecast in about 15 seconds, and if I could not put my hands on the latest forecast during the summertime, I would be safe in saying, "Clear to partly cloudy with the possibility of scattered mostly afternoon and evening thundershowers." I could not go wrong with that forecast.

The preceding adlib forecast was not something I used often, but remember Jack Ridner who gave me my break by getting fired for saying something he shouldn't over the air in Pensacola? Well, Jack was not completely fired. He was just banished to Channel 7, which in those days must have been like being exiled to Siberia. When Jack got to Panama City he was assigned to do the weather. Not having a news machine or any way to get weather information except out of the newspaper, I am told that Jack faked it all the way. He had a weather map framed in glass and, with a grease pen, he just indiscriminately drew weather fronts everywhere, making up temperatures and forecasts as he saw fit.

I managed to meet some people and have a few dates, but these would either have to end early or I would have to bring my date by the station with me to do the Late News. A friend of mine told a school teacher about me in such manner that, after tuning me in, she expressed an interest in meeting me. So, I called Nancy Myers and made a date with her. When I came to her door, she was surprised to see that I was not nearly as big as I looked on TV.

Nancy and I dated off and on for several months and I enjoyed being with her. One night, shortly after meeting her, we decided to play tennis. Knowing that I had to do the Late News, she kept wondering, as the time approached 10 o'clock, when I was going to leave for the station. When we did get to the TV station, about 10:30, I cleared the newswire, made my calls to the sheriff's Department, police department, and fire department to see if anything was happening locally. Nancy, afraid to ask since we had not known each other very long, kept wondering when I was going to change from tennis clothes into a suit for the newscast.

This first grade teacher I was dating that night could not believe it when, at about five minutes before 11:00 p.m., I got dressed. I put on an old shirt, with a rip on one shoulder, over the tee shirt I was wearing, slipped on a tie and coat and headed into the studio. Nancy was completely amazed that I was doing the news with a shirt, coat and tie slapped over my shorts and tennis apparel. After all, it was black and white TV then and to the people looking in, I appeared to be dressed like a Philadelphia lawyer.

In time my bare legs would be revealed to the television audience. Later on, the station adhered to my earlier suggestion to make the Late News a half hour block of news, weather, and sports from 10:00 to 10:30 p.m. to be done with three people. The ratings went up exponentially, as a lot of people who did not stay up until 11:00 p.m. were now tuned in to WJHG-TV's Late News.

Buddy Wilkes was a young man the station hired to do the weather and handle other assignments. Buddy, despite his youth, did a good job and had a lot of fun in the process. He was a practical joker and one night, as the program was signed off, we were still visible on the TV screen with the credits superimposed over us when Buddy decided to pull the desk from in front of me. There I was, shorts and all, being viewed by thousands of people.

The six o'clock news block was done by Earl Hadaway with news, Donnell Brookins with weather, and me with sports. Our theme music was the Guadalcanal March. One night as we closed the show, with credits superimposed, I nonchalantly called the three of us to attention, military style, commanded a left face, and the viewing audience saw the three of us marching off the set. What fun it was to work in television in small town America!

One nice perk I had in Panama City was golfing privileges at Panama Country Club. I reported regularly on golf events there, including the women's matches each week, and the PCC folks felt justified in allowing me to play gratis. I oftentimes played in the morning, at times by myself, when other people were working. I made friends with a couple of educators, Pete Holman and Warren Sasnett, and we played together on Saturday in the "dog fights"at the club.

Gardner Dickinson, Jr. was a successful touring golf pro at that time. Dickinson had grown up in nearby Dothan, Alabama and his family, including his father, Gardner Dickinson, Sr., were now living in Panama City. The senior was known as "Pop" Dickinson and he worked with his son to get a Little Tournament of Champions for Panama City. Gardner, Jr. was able to get about a dozen of the top PGA players to Panama City, including such greats as Sam Snead. It was a plum for the Gulf Coast area and we taped the action to run on TV at night during the event. The tournament, which folded after a few years, was not well run and there were no scoreboards or communications for the fans to know who was leading the event.

We worked to improve our local sports presentations. Once or twice we did a delayed telecast of the Bay-Rutherford football game in their rivalry for the city championship. Joe Johnson, an educator who had done sports work at Channel 7, did color and I did play-by-play. Also, we did a pre-season football show featuring the Florida Gators and Florida State Seminoles. Photographer Louie Walker and I went to Gainesville and Tallahassee and filmed the players and coaches about the forthcoming season. I asked the coaches to get their players to run a few drills or plays while I interviewed the coach and let him tell about each of the prospects. One year, FSU Head Coach Bill Peterson was naming the linemen we were watching knock heads as he talked a little about each one. When he got to number 66 he drew a complete blank and could not remember his name. He said something like, "Number 66 is, uh...is, uh.., he's just a big ole boy."

In many ways the year 1965 was not a good one for me. Vocationally, I did not feel I was making progress. I was still stuck in a small market. My mother was ill quite a bit that year. To add to it, I think any person who wants to get married and have a family and has not achieved that goal, is lonely. I was also living in a small house I had rented which apparently was rat-infested. It was a pretty neat little house in some ways, but I needed a better place to live. My folks, after visiting me there, wanted me to move out.

Another thing that weighed into my anxiety was the situation with WPEX-FM in Pensacola. While I was in Montgomery I had continued to buy stock in Mellotone, Inc.to keep the station afloat. At one time, I owned something like 80 per cent or more of the corporation. Though FM was gradually coming into vogue, it still was a tough go in Pensacola and we did not have anyone who could promote it enough to break even. We were offered an advertising contract by a beer company but, even though we needed the money, I could not in good conscience accept it.

Mr. L. T. France, a fine old gentleman who owned Bonded Transportation, a moving and storage company, was a big fan of the station and agreed to buy stock and become one of the owners. As time went on, he eventually bought enough stock to attain controlling interest. I was in agreement with this. Finally, after having been on the air for five years, we sold WPEX-FM to Fred Brewer, who was in the background music business and had talked to me many times about using one of our subchannels to transmit his background music. Though it was necessary to sell, I have always taken pride in the fact that we had kept it on the air for all that time.

Would you believe that we sold WPEX-FM, the Golden Sound of the Gulf Coast, at 94.1 in Pensacola, Florida, for a measly $25,000. Even in those days, that was like peanuts for a radio station. But what could we do? It was losing money, I was 100 miles away in Panama City, and Mr. France had no knowledge of broadcasting. I am convinced that Mr. France was being a good Samaritan in wanting to keep the station on the air and to help me. Anyway, we were able to take some loss on our income taxes and be thankful we were able to keep it going and pay the bills.

Just a few years later, I heard that Mr. Brewer had turned down an offer of a million dollars for WPEX. Even so, we could take pleasure in the fact we were ahead of our time. We pioneered FM on the Gulf Coast and brought a good sound and good music to the area. But there was another blessing in our selling I will discuss later.

There was, however, a bright spot in '65, because that is the year I met Nancy. Nancy was a first grade teacher at Cherry Street Elementary School. She was from Oviedo, near Orlando in central Florida, though her Dad was born and raised in the Panhandle at Chipley, Florida. She was a bright young lady and we enjoyed each other's company. Through the years, I had dated some very fine girls, but to me marriage was for a lifetime and I was too particular. Several times, if I felt the girl I was dating was getting serious, I would back off, because I was not sure she was the right one.

I would tend to find something wrong with each girl I dated, such as being too tall, too short, or this or that. One weekend, I asked Nancy to go with me to an Auburn football game. On the way, we went to Ewell to get Rex and Sara, who had agreed to go with us to the game, and I introduced Nancy to my parents. They liked her. She had so many good qualities it was hard for me to find fault with her, but when I talked to my mother about her, later, I managed to find a few things wrong. Mama shot down all my nitpicking and told me I should marry this fine young lady.

Nancy and I dated infrequently for about a year. I was really unfair to her because I knew that I certainly had faults of my own. Faults notwithstanding, I was still not sure that I was in love and that I was ready to marry.

I had always been careful in trying to avoid hurting any of the young ladies I dated, but I am not sure I succeeded because of my laid-back, non-committal style. I believed Nancy was in love with me and it bothered me that I still had some anxieties about my own feelings. Nancy, in the absence of any interest on my part, decided to leave Panama City and teach in Ocala, some 300 miles away.

About that time I decided to buy a house trailer and get out of the little house I was renting. The trailer was located further away from the station, but at least I had made a small investment in a one-bedroom mobile home in Parker, just outside Panama City.

Nancy and I continued to stay in touch through letter writing and an occasional telephone call. One weekend that Fall of 1966 I went down to see her and we took in a University of Florida football game. A few months later, in early Spring, I called Nancy and suggested we meet on Sunday for lunch at Wakulla Springs, roughly half way between Panama City and Ocala. She agreed and we had a nice little picnic there. I returned to Panama City with the same hesitancy toward a commitment.

I had prayed fervently for years about finding the right life's partner. It was perhaps several weeks after our date at Wakulla that I awoke from a sound sleep about 2:00 a.m. one morning and it was as if God was telling me, "Nancy is definitely the one!" I was euphoric and completely relieved. There was no doubt whatsoever in my mind. That was on a Saturday and a few hours later I was on the telephone asking Nancy if she would meet me the next day in Wakulla Springs again. I dared not reveal my excitement to Nancy on the phone, but I could not wait to see her!

Our meeting this time was not the mere picnic that we enjoyed the first time at this lovely resort. I was a man on a mission. Nancy was already there in the parking lot as I arrived. I took her by the hand and we took a stroll through the wooded grounds surrounded by beautiful springtime flowers. It did not take very long for me to share my mission. Probably less than a hundred yards into the walk I faced Nancy and said, "I have something to tell you. I love you!" Her eyes sparkled and she replied, "I love you, too."

What a glorious day in May! Nancy agreed to marry me and we spent hours making plans for a wedding. There were a lot of things to do, but we wanted to arrange it as soon as possible. Could we have it in early July? In looking at the calendar, we analyzed all the preparations that had to be made and settled on July 8th.

Our families both rejoiced with us in this decision. The next day, my good friends at Channel 7 also were happy about learning of my intent to bring Nancy back to Panama City. The next weekend, we went to Oviedo for me to visit her parents and grandparents on her mother's side. I officially asked for Nancy's hand in marriage and was pleased when that request was not vetoed. Apparently, I passed muster and everyone was excited about the forthcoming wedding.

An interesting sidelight to my visit with Nancy's folks is that the two of us were going out to have Sunday dinner in Orlando with her parents. When we went next door for me to see her grandfather, who was 92, and her grandmother, about 89, they were all dressed and ready to go out with us, although they were not invited. To ourselves, we had a good chuckle about that. Of course, we took them with us and we all had a wonderful time together.

On Friday, July 7, I was late for my wedding rehearsal. I had trouble finding my way from the motel in Orlando, where my folks and I had stayed the night before, to the First Baptist Church in Oviedo. But I was not late for my wedding, the real thing, the next afternoon. Nancy's good friend, Patricia Williams, of Panama City, was her matron of honor; and Mimi Wheeler and Anne Martin of Oviedo, were bridesmaids. My brother, Rex, was my best man, and ushers were Nancy's brother, Albert Myers and my good friend from Pensacola, Homer Singletary.

It was a beautiful wedding, if I do say so, and the Reverend Flournoy Jernigan, pastor of the church, tied the knot good. I was calmer than I thought I would be and when I said "I do" it carried throughout the church. Nancy obviously was a little nervous because when the preacher asked, "Do you take this man to be your lawfully wedded husband?", she responded, "Yessir," instead of the traditional "I do". I joked later that since she did not respond correctly I could get out of this arrangement anytime because it was not legal.

I had made reservations for our honeymoon at Little Switzerland in the mountains of North Carolina, but we took three nights and two days to get there after stopovers in Gainesville,

Florida, Callaway Gardens, and Dillard, Georgia. On arrival at Little Switzerland, I had a telegram from Donnell Brookins and the gang at Channel 7 stating that I should cut my honeymoon short and report back to the station where I was badly needed. The Western Union operator cooperated and I refused the telegram, but instead sent one telling them we had changed our honeymoon location to the Bahamas.

The first residence of Mr. and Mrs. Earl Hutto was at 3904 West 16th Street in Panama City. When it came to rental houses in Panama City at that time there was not much to choose from, and Nancy referred to our first home as a "shack." It was a small 2-bedroom house owned by an older couple, Frank and Crystal Huebscher, who lived next door. Oftentimes, Mr. Huebscher would work out in the yard in his bathing suit and Nancy referred to him as the "fat hairy man." Nancy was able to get employment again with the Bay County school system, but this time she taught second grade at Cove Elementary instead of first grade at Cherry Street Elementary. Unfortunately, it was a very unsettling year for Bay County teachers, and indeed for all Florida public school teachers, as a couple of strikes took place that year. Nancy joined the first walk-out, which was a Bay County strike over pay, because she felt the county had broken her contract. But she was one of those who did not go out on strike during the statewide walk-out, and continued teaching along with a number of colleagues and other fill-ins from the community.

Married life was wonderful! I was barely 41 when I took the nuptial vows and my bride was 29. It was one of the greatest things that ever happened to me. Now my searching and loneliness had ended and I was settling down.

Nancy rejoined Cove Baptist Church and I joined for the first time and was baptized. In fact, this was the very first time I had joined a church, though I had been a Christian since childhood. My father had been a Methodist in early life and my mother a Baptist. At some point after they were married they became members of the Assembly of God Church. That is where I was brought up and where I had attended Sunday school. Though I had a deep faith and commitment to God, I somehow had not felt led to join their church.

We became very active in church. In a year or so I was elected a deacon and then served as chairman of the board of deacons. Nancy and I worked with the high school youth in Sunday school, and I later taught a young marrieds' class.

We were happily married, but Nancy shared my ambitions for improving myself in broadcasting by landing a job in a larger market. Early in 1968, Buddy Rutledge, the play-by-play man for the Auburn Tigers football radio network died suddenly. Buddy's responsibilities also included that of sports director of WAPI-TV in Birmingham. I applied for the job as did scores of others across the nation.

The applicants for the Auburn job were asked to submit a tape of play-by-play of a football broadcast. I did not have one available, but I simulated a game, complete with sound noise, and submitted it. I was chosen as one of the four finalists for this position. The four of us had our expenses paid to go to Auburn for the A-Day spring practice game on a Saturday afternoon in May.

Others participating were from Milwaukee, Chattanooga, and Louisville. Each of us would do a quarter of play-by-play of the game and this, apparently, would figure heavily in the final selection. Nancy was pregnant with our first child, so we decided that she would stay in the car outside the stadium and listen to the game. The four of us prospects drew for the quarter we would call and I got the third. I came away pleased with my performance.

After the game we were taken to Birmingham and treated to a fine dinner at one of the better restaurants in town. Following our night at a motel, we headed back to Panama City with a good feeling. Nancy felt, as I did, that we had a good performance on which to be judged. Apparently the station manager did not see it, or should I say " hear" it that way. I was notified several days later of his choice. I did not get the job. Someone was looking after us, as you will find out later. Not getting this job was a tremendous blessing.

After about 13 months in the "shack" we moved into a nicer house, with three bedrooms, at 1201 Lindenwood Drive. There we began assembling more of our own furniture. We did not have much furniture to move, but in the process of moving it I knocked off one of Nancy's toenails with a dolly. It hurt and she hobbled for several days, but we would speak of it fondly as it related to our moving into a better house. Now, every time we start to move anything, even for just a few feet, she stands clear if I have anything to do with it.

Luckily, about that time, I sold my house at 703 South Madison Drive in Pensacola, which I had bought when I worked with Channel 3. Charlie Wooten, a tenth grader I had hired as a part-time cameraman at Channel 7 and who later went on to become a brilliant engineer, went with me to Pensacola and we loaded a U-Haul trailer with furniture that had been in the house there. We had some excitement on the way back to Panama City when clothes in the trailer caught fire. We were able to put it out before it did too much damage and only lost a few clothes and a couple of nice quilts which had been given to me by my mother.

It was in 1968 that WJHG-TV moved into brand new quarters near Panama City Beach at the site of the original station. This was quite uplifting and everybody was proud of this very fine facility. We also received better cameras and equipment, most of it as hand-me-down from our sister station, WALB-TV in Albany.

In that year our colleague, Donnell Brookins, threw his hat into the political ring and ran for tax collector. In a landmark case, his Republican opponent, George Logue, requested time on the air to compensate for all the years that Brookins's face had been seen on the tube. The FCC granted Mr. Logue time and he was seen in half hour shows morning, noon, and night. He was on the air so much till apparently he wore out his welcome. Donnell, a very popular performer on radio before he was on TV, won the race in a landslide.

The unprecedented granting of this kind of free air time by the FCC brought out the national media and both of the candidates were on network TV. A funny sidelight was when a friend of mine, on his way home from Vietnam, woke up after an afternoon nap during a layover in San Francisco and saw Donnell Brookins on the television screen. He thought he was already home until he listened further and found out Panama City was in the national news.

Married life, a new TV station, satisfaction with my church, and a number of things helped me like Panama City more and more. From the outset, I had great friends in PC and now I was settling down to be a part of the community. I took the lead in organizing a Civitan Club. Collectively, members of the club could do a lot more for the community than we could as individuals. For example, we bought a van for the Mary Mackin School for Retarded Citizens.

The Civitan motto is "Builders of Good Citizenship" and we sent a group of high school students each summer to Harding College in Arkansas for a week to participate in seminars on patriotism and good citizenship. Civitan's major fund-raising is done through sale of Claxton fruitcakes at Christmas time, but we also sponsored college freshmen football games between FSU and Southern Mississippi, and

FSU and Memphis State.

The crown jewel of 1968 for Nancy and me was the birth of our first child. One night, when Nancy was getting close to delivering, she thought I might need to take her to the hospital soon. So I called and asked Donnell Brookins, or as we called him, DB, to do the news for me so that I could be home and ready to fulfill my duty. We were watching the news when DB explained that he was substituting for me because the stork was fluttering over the Hutto house.

It was close to midnight when I took Nancy to Bay Memorial Hospital. Shortly after nine the next morning, the 27th of September, 1968, our little bundle of joy was born. I was looking for a boy, but it was the cutest little girl I had ever seen. Lori Keeffe Hutto was the new addition to our family. What a proud daddy I was! I wouldn't trade her for any ole boy. I took a Polaroid photo of Lori and Channel 7 showed it on the air.

DB, of course, had to give up his job on TV after his election as Bay County Tax Collector. Tom Hipps, a fine musician as well as announcer, took DB's place as the host of Daybusters, an early morning program from 6:00 to 7:00 on Channel 7. Occasionally I had to host it. When I got home from doing the late news each night about 11:30, I would feed Lori a full bottle of milk and she would sleep the rest of the night. One night as I was feeding her, I was called and told that Tom was sick and I was asked to take his place the next morning. Well, during the night I got sick, too, and when I tried to get up to go to the station I simply couldn't make it. So, Tax Collector Brookins was called back for Daybusters. During the course of the show, DB mentioned that I might have Hong Kong Flu, which was going around.

Someone who worked with my sister, Merle, up at Fort Rucker, Alabama had heard the telecast and told her about it. Merle, who usually touched base with our parents, called and told them about hearing I was sick. Pretty soon Mama was calling Nancy to find out how bad that Hungarian Flu was that I had. She apparently thought she heard Hungarian instead of Hong Kong. Anyway, I have never been as sick. I could hardly move for about two months.

After being in the Lindenwood house for less than a year we had an opportunity to buy a house up the street, on the corner of Lindenwood and Brenau Terrace. The address was 1100 Brenau Terrace and we were pleased to own our first house since our marriage. It had beautiful trees, a nice front yard, and a fenced back yard where Lori could play.

Our family was growing. In early May of 1970, Nancy's mother came up from Oviedo to help me with Lori when Nancy had to go to the hospital for the delivery of our second baby. Again, I was waiting outside the delivery room to hear about the birth of a son. For the second time it did not happen that way. Our precious Amelia Ann was born on May 5, exactly a week before my birthday. Like her sister, she was a beauty and I would not trade her for any boy either. We were just pleased that she was a fine healthy baby like her sister. Naturally, her picture was shown on Channel 7.

When Lori started to talk, we taught her to call Nancy's parents Nana and Pappy, which is what they wanted, and they called my parents Granddaddy and Grandmommy. After Amy was born, Nana came to the hospital and, of course, brought Lori. Dr. Si Mathison, a Methodist minister, was visiting in the hospital and he dropped in on Nancy while there. When Brother Si, as he is called, saw Nana and Lori in the downstairs lobby he realized that Nana would like to go up to see Nancy and the baby so he asked Lori, who was 19 months old, if she would like to have a tea party? While Nana went to see Nancy and the baby, he took her to the snack bar and bought her a softdrink and a cookie to eat. Since then, when we take a break, we refer to it as a "tea party."

My parents, needless to say, were thrilled when Lori came and I was glad that Mama got to hold her and know her, but unfortunately Mama had a series of small strokes and then a big stroke which had her in a nursing home at the time of Amy's birth. A few months later we would take Amy into the nursing home and she held Amy briefly, but we are not completely sure she understood who Amy was.

Our girls lit up our lives. They continued to grow and bring joy to our home. When Lori was four, she fell off the swing in our back yard. We heard her crying and knew she was hurt. We took her to the emergency room and sure enough her leg was broken. Lori wore a cast on her right leg for a long time and I can still see her scooting on the floor or dragging that right leg as she walked.

After the initial shock of seeing Amy get a lot of attention right after she was born, Lori got over her little jealousy and the sisters loved each other dearly, and are still close today. Amy made

Lori, and all of us, laugh a lot. She was into everything. When Amy was less than a year old Lori came running out of Amy's room, shouting, "Mommy, Daddy, come look at Amy." I rushed into her room to find her jumping up and down in her crib completely covered from head to feet with Vaseline. She had been able to reach a big jar of vaseline on a shelf near her crib and had put it all over herself and the bed. It took Nancy a long time to get her cleaned up, but the baby lotion she applied afterwards made Amy look and smell a lot better.

My mother had suffered a major stroke as she was coming down the front steps of church after a Sunday service. After a period of time in Dale County Hospital, the doctors said there was nothing further they could do for her and that we would need to put her into a nursing home. This was a difficult thing for us to do because Mama had always said she never wanted to go a nursing home. But, there was no choice since Daddy could not take care of her in that condition.

Mama was confined to the Ozark Nursing Home for 19 months. Just past midnight on February 13, 1971, we were all gathered there when she passed away. Though she had rarely known us for the time she had been in the home, it was still a big loss. It was the first break in our immediate family. She was also the first person I ever saw die.

Throughout my childhood, I remembered praying "Dear Lord, please let Mama and Daddy live until Merle, Rex, and I are grown." I was the oldest and I had a fear of being left with my little sister and brother. Another prayer answered. Now, we were all grown and I was 44 years old. Mama passed away so peacefully. We knew she was ready to go and were comforted with the knowledge of her dedicated Christian life and the fact that our loss was Heaven's gain. This was reflected in the beautiful music and words of good friend, the Rev.LutherTadlock, who conducted the service on Valentine's Day before a church full of people who loved her so deeply.

Daddy had been to the nursing home everyday she had been there--and now he was without his life's partner. But he kept on the go and was very busy with the church. He worked with the youth, who loved him. He joined the youth minister in helping with the activities of the young people and I know he made a difference in many of their lives.

Earl Hutto as he appeared on the Late News on Channel 7 in Panama City
in 1964.

Earl, in his position as Production Manager of WJHG-TV, is shown supervising
the telecast of a parade in downtown Panama City, Florida.

10

A HAT IN THE RING

It was a slow day on a January afternoon in 1972 as we were just beginning to put together our news and sports for the Six O'clock News at WJHG-TV, Channel 7, in Panama City. The idle chatter turned to politics and someone noted that, in addition to the parade of presidential candidates now frequenting Florida, including Panama City, it also was an election year of state and local interest. Speculation immediately began on who, among the local pols, might have a hard time winning re-election or who might be challenging.

Out of the blue I flippantly stated that "I am tempted to run for the Florida Legislature." One of my cohorts chimed in and said "Hutto, I'll bet you could win that state representative's race." Others agreed. That was intriguing. It was not something premeditated by me, although I had long had an interest in politics. But I had never given thought before to actually running for political office. The comment by others that they thought I could win egged me on in my thought process. My flippant remark had turned serious. I got to telling myself, "I'm gonna run! I'm gonna run!"

I have already mentioned that at Channel 7, in a smaller market, I not only did sports, but doubled as the state news editor. In the latter capacity I had prevailed on the station to allow me to go to Tallahassee during the legislative session and film interviews with state senators and representatives. Photographer Louie Walker and I would go over to Tallahassee two or three times during the 60-day legislative sessions and do interviews which were spread out over a period of time in our newscasts. This, without a doubt, had whetted my appetite for keeping up with state politics.

There was another thing, though perhaps subliminally, that might have played into my overall inclination toward the political arena. Remember Reubin Askew, my former partner in WPEX-FM? You may recall that, when I talked him into putting some money into Mellotone, Inc. and doing the legal work for us to build the station, he was state representative from Pensacola. Well, now he was Florida Governor Reubin O'D Askew and I supported him when he was elected two years earlier, in 1970. I was on his advisory committee for Bay County. Prominent attorney-businessman Charles Hilton, an activist in promoting Panama City beaches, was also on that committee. Keep that latter name in mind for a little while.

Why would I want to run for the Florida House of Representatives? Was it an ego trip? No, that was not the reason. I had all the recognition and acclaim I needed from my TV work. I did have ambition. However, as down to earth as it might seem, I ran because I had a strong desire to serve the people, hopefully to do the right things for our state and community, and maybe make life better for our citizens. I had found a great deal of satisfaction in helping to organize the Panama City Civitan Club, in serving as its president and as deputy governor of the Alabama-West Florida District of Civitan International. It was gratifying to know that through our club's hard work, we were able to help the retarded citizens at Mary Mackin School as well as others.

When I went home for supper on the day of my rather tenuous newsroom decision to run for office, as I did each evening for a couple of hours between the six and ten o'clock news segments, I broke the news to Nancy about my grand political aspirations. I expected her to say something like "Are you crazy?," but instead, she surprised me by saying "When do we start?" My wife was a complete novice on politics, although her grandfather Albert A. Myers served one term in the Florida House of Representatives in 1917 from Washington County. His one mission was to get a law passed that would require all cattle to be stock dipped. Mission completed, he ended his political career.

The incumbent state representative for Panama City in 1972 was an enterprising young lawyer, Joe Chapman. Joe came from a political family. His mother was supervisor of elections of Bay County. Joe, right out of law school, became legal counsel to Florida Governor Haydon Burns. Some were speculating, after his election to the Florida House four years earlier, that he had high political ambitions and perhaps would one day succeed Bob Sikes in Congress.

My decision to run was not based on whether or not I would be facing an incumbent, but I was not naive enough not to know that it would be better to run for an open seat if possible. Representative Chapman, despite his presumably bright political future, might just want to step down. It appeared there were reasons why he might not run. One was that the legislature had reapportioned the districts and Bay County was now in the 8th District which included portions of Washington and Walton Counties, new territory for the incumbent.

By this time, Joe also appeared to be going great guns with Royal American Construction Company, a business he had formed primarily to build government housing.

I was grateful that my TV exposure had made me well known in several Northwest Florida counties and this could only help in my political venture. Whether this would have any bearing on Representative Chapman's decision to run, or not to run in the new 8th District, I had no idea. He had not yet announced his intentions about running for re-election, so I decided to call him to let him know my plans and ask if he would be running. He had heard that I was going to run, but said he had not yet made up his mind.He informed me he expected to decide soon and would let me know. He was as good as his word and in a few days called to let me know he would not run and to wish me luck. Hey, that was good news!

There were still a few stumbling blocks that had to be removed, however, before I would be off and running. How about your job, Hutto? Would I be able to continue with it? Would I be fired or have to take a leave of absence? Some of these matters I had been working on simultaneously. There was at least some precedent in the Gray Communications organization for employees running for public office. At our sister station, WALB-TV in Albany, Georgia, newsman Dawson Mathis had run for and been elected to Congress.

I talked with our Channel 7 manager Ray Holloway about my intentions to run. Ray, incidentally, was an old-timer with the station, having served as an account executive (salesman) in the early days and then as sales manager. When Jim Tighe was transferred to a new Gray acquisition in El Dorado, Arkansas in 1968, Holloway had been named to succeed him as manager of Channel 7. He initially appeared not to like the idea of my desire to run, but then came around to being more understanding of my position. Of course, he would have to get permission from higher authority.

Let me bring up another name from the past. It is again Ray Carow. He's the fellow at Channel 3 in Pensacola who admitted that he did not know what to do. Now, Ray was executive vice president of Gray Communications, so he was our big boss in Albany, Georgia who hired me for the job at Channel 7. It was Ray Carow who would make the decision on whether or not I would have to take an unpaid leave of absence and if so, when would it begin. I wrote to Ray explaining my desire to run, and also mentioned the years of service

I had given to the station.

The Gray organization was still smarting from the FCC decision to grant all that time to Donnell Brookins's opponent back in 1968. It had been pretty much understood that I would not be fired, so in Ray Carow's response to me, he acknowledged my contributions and my value to the station. He also gave me news that I pretty much expected and that was that I would have to come off the air at some point. But he threw in a caveat to make it a little more palatable. I would be able to continue working, but would not be able to continue my on-the-air work after other candidates had announced for the same office. I breathed a small sigh of relief. I would still get a paycheck, for a while, at least! I was informed I would have to take a leave of absence after I qualified to become a candidate.

Qualifying for state and local offices did not take place until July, 1972, so I had several months before I would make my official announcement for state representative. In the meantime I continued my TV work with a major assignment being to interview the presidential candidates who were really making Florida a battleground. I enjoyed doing the interviews, most of them filmed at locations where the presidential aspirants would speak, but a few of them just made stopovers at the station and I interviewed them for our newscasts. The Democratic candidates I interviewed included Hubert Humphrey, John Lindsey, Ed Muskie, Shirley Chisholm, Henry "Scoop" Jackson, and George Wallace. I interviewed Senator Muskie in his motel room and a minute or so into the interview I heard the film run out in the camera. I was embarrassed because I knew that was the last roll of film we had with us, so I just did not let on and kept asking questions. Joe Chapman was Muskie's state campaign manager and afterwards he whispered to me, with a grin, "I heard that film run out." But we at least had enough footage to make a story for our newscasts. Another sidelight to the presidential primary, ABC Newsman Sam Donaldson, in a speech at the Marina Auditorium in Panama City, predicted that Congressman Mo Udall would win the nomination.

In preparation for my big race, I realized I would need to have some funds to run any semblance of a campaign. Frankly, at that time I did not personally know many of the business people, which I figured would be my best source for contributions. Nancy did have a cousin, Sonny Myers, who was co-owner of Kendrick-Myers

Oldsmobile, so she and I paid a visit to Sonny to see if he would help me raise funds. His partner, Wallace Kendrick, whom I had hardly met, was there and seemed to be real interested in my campaign. He took the bull by the horns and assumed the task of raising money for me. Wallace got on the phone with business people and others. During the course of the campaign he assisted me in raising some $3,700, which was exactly enough.

Two candidates qualified to run against me, Wayne Brown and Joe Patterson. My work was cut out for me. I did not know much about my opponents. Wayne was from the eastern part of the Panama City area and Joe from Panama City Beach. Wayne appeared to be a blue-collar type and Joe represented the tourist-oriented beaches area. It was my intention to have rapport with all segments of the district.

Shortly after qualifying in July there were two rallies scheduled on a Friday afternoon. This would be the first time I would have an opportunity to publicly present myself to the voters. One rally was sponsored by each of the parties, though I do not believe any Republican was running in Bay County. Nonetheless, there were a few people trying to build the party. The Republican rally was scheduled for 4:00 p.m. at Frank Nelson Park and the Democratic rally for 6:00 p.m. in Southport. All candidates were invited.

Nancy's parents were visiting us that weekend from Central Florida. Pappy and I decided it might be a good idea for us to go to Southport early to put up some posters in the area of where the Democratic rally would be held and then come back and go speak at the Republican rally. While we were at Southport, Nancy, Nana, Lori, and Amy decided to go shopping. When we got back home from Southport, we waited for them to return so we could all go to the first rally. As time for the rally approached, we were getting anxious. Finally, as it was time for the rally to begin, we decided that we would leave them a note that we were going on to the rally and they could meet us there.

As we approached the rally site we could see that a pretty good crowd was gathered close to the flatbed truck where the candidates were speaking. As we got out of the car and headed to the scene we saw Nancy coming toward us. I said, "Where have you been?" She caustically replied, "What do you mean where have I been? Where have you been? I have been up there speaking for you!" My family and Nana had figured we had plenty of time to get back from Southport and maybe we had gone on to the other rally, so they had proceeded to the site of that first rally. There, Nancy had made my first political speech for me!

Nancy related that, before the rally started, candidates were milling through the crowd and my opponent, Joe Patterson, whom she did not know, shook hands with Nana and asked for her vote. She explained that she was from Central Florida and could not vote in Bay County, but that her daughter lived here. Nancy stuck out her hand and said, "Hello, I'm Nancy Hutto, it is a pleasure to meet you, but I will be voting for Earl Hutto for State Representative." Joe seemed a bit embarrassed, but was very cordial. Later, when the candidates for state representative, District 8, were called and I did not respond, Joe spotted Nancy in the crowd and asked her to come up and speak for me. She was not prepared for that, but went to the platform anyhow. She said her speech did not last more than about 30 seconds, in which she said something like, "He's a good husband and a good father and will make a good state representative." She later was kidded by some lady who said to her that she forgot to mention her husband's name. Anyway, Nancy will always have the distinction of having made my first political speech.

Rallies were held on Friday and Saturday nights and often were preceded by a fish fry or food sales to help the local Democratic committee defray expenses. Nancy and the girls accompanied me to all the rallies in Bay, Washington, and Walton Counties. In my speeches, I did not make great promises, but told of my background and my desire to serve and work hard for them in Tallahassee.

My theme was more or less embodied in this statement from some of my speeches: "Our state government is getting too big and administrative costs are bleeding the taxpayers. I pledge to work for wiser use of the taxpayer's money. I am opposed to a state income tax. I feel that there should be no need of further taxes for years with the natural growth of Florida taking care of additional needs."

One morning during the campaign Nancy asked me to go to the convenience store to get some milk before breakfast. Lori and Amy went with me. As we headed to the store we met a fellow in a pickup truck. I threw up my hand and waved to him. Lori asked, "Daddy, why did you wave to that man?" I said, "Oh, just being friendly." She responded with another question, "Were you trying to get some votes?" I laughed and acknowledged that I was indeed trying to get votes and that I had to be friendly with everyone if I wanted to win.

Out of the mouths of babes! Another incident that lingers in my memory was a question posed by our youngest daughter, Amy, during that first campaign. She was not even three years old.. One night when I was tucking her in bed she asked, "Daddy, what is politics?" Try explaining that to a two and a half-year old. Try explaining that to anyone!

The first primary election day of September 12 finally arrived. We had done all we could do. We had worked hard. I had shaken many hands. My message had been totally positive, a trait I would adhere to in all my future campaigns. The reception by the people was wonderful. Folks had kind words for me and pledged their support. We were ready and felt good about the situation. But this was the first election in which Earl Hutto was a candidate and we did not know what to expect.

Nancy and I voted early and people at the polls were wishing us luck. That first election night we gathered at our home, 1100 Brenau Terrace, to await the returns. Our Sunday school class, the young marrieds from Cove Baptist Church which Nancy and I taught, brought covered dishes and we enjoyed ourselves before, during, and after the election tally. The results were outstanding, even better than we anticipated. We had hoped to win the election without a runoff-- and that we did! We had a lot of well-wishers come by the house that night to congratulate us and I was constantly busy on the phone for several days receiving joyful and pleasing words of encouragement.

What a victory we had won! The final results showed: Hutto 8,590, Brown 1,372, and Patterson 1,321. That was a smashing 85.1 per cent of the vote for our first campaign. It was a little difficult to take in. There would be no runoff. I had no general election opponent. I was elected state representative! What a mandate from the people! I could not and did not gloat over this tremendous vote. I was deeply humble and grateful to the people for electing me.

Almost immediately I began getting mail addressed to the Honorable Earl Hutto. Honorable!? That sure is a high-sounding monicker. But it is an attachment to my name that I would carry for years to come. To most people, however, I would remain just "Earl."

I set out to learn as much as I could about state government. Fortunately, since I had no further opposition I had some time to become more educated before being sworn in November. I talked by phone with some of my future colleagues. I received a considerable amount of information from the clerk's office. I had met Representative Billy Joe Rish, of Port St. Joe, several times since he was elected two years before and we got to know him, his wife Carol, and their family, and formed a friendship which we maintain today.

Shortly after the general election, Speaker-electTerrell Sessums, of Tampa, hosted a weekend there so new members could meet their colleagues and hear the speaker talk about some of the issues we would face once the session got underway. On the drive down we went by Oviedo and left the girls with Nana and Pappy.

Billy Joe and Carol flew down to Orlando where we picked them up, took them to Tampa and then brought them back to Port St. Joe after the enlightening weekend. On the drive back, I kept asking Billy Joe "What are y'all going to do about this? What are y'all gonna do about that?" Finally, he said, "Hutto, what do you mean 'y'all? The question is, what are 'we' going to do about these things?" How funny!

Indeed, I was going to be part of 'them'... hopefully a part of the solution! I was ready to assume the challenge ahead!

Earl and Nancy Hutto with Lori, four, and Amy, two, climb the steps of the Capitol on the day Earl was sworn in as Florida State Representative.

The Hutto family rides on watermelons aboard Mr. Farrell Nelson's pick-up truck in the Watermelon Festival Parade in Chipley, Florida.

Earl's 1963 VW Beetle was utilized in the re-election campaign for State Representative in 1974. In this photo the Huttos are about to leave for church.

11

LEGISLATING IN FLORIDA

What a great feeling to know that the people have chosen you to represent them in state government! If only my mother could have lived to see me attain such stature. She would have been so proud! But, she probably would have had a few words of advice. I can hear her now, "Son, just remember where you came from, trust in the Lord, and do your very best." Thankfully, my Dad was right there with us, along with my sister, Merle, and brother, Rex on the night of our big victory!

In Florida, state legislators take the oath of office in late November following the election of that year. So, it was exciting when Nancy and I, along with four-year old Lori and two-year old Amy, climbed the capitol steps in Tallahassee on the day I was sworn in as a state representative from District 8 in Northwest Florida.

At that time Florida House members were allowed only one staff person. I hired Bobby Branning as my first administrative assistant. Bobby and family were good friends of ours. We were members of the same church and Bobby and I were fellow deacons. He was qualified for the job, having just received his master's degree in political science from FSU. Bobby was politically wise and had a good personality that bode well for me. He was a Bay County native who knew the ropes. Bobby did an excellent job of getting me prepared for my work in Tallahassee with all the supplies I needed.

Tallahassee was buzzing, as it always is when the legislature is in session, at the beginning of the organizational session in 1972. The House chamber was gaily bedecked with beautiful flowers from well-wishers on nearly every desk. Before the opening day session got underway, spouses and children were allowed on the floor to take pictures. We got some nice shots of the family and, though Nancy could not be on the floor during the swearing in, Lori and Amy remained at my desk as I strode forward to the podium to be sworn in by Justice B. K. Roberts of the Florida Supreme Court.

The procedure was to swear in a group of legislators from a common area until all had taken the oath. Taking the oath with me were Rish of Port St. Joe, Mixson of Marianna, Donald Tucker and Carroll Webb, both of Tallahassee, and Pat Thomas of Quincy. "I do solemnly swear to......," as we repeated after the Justice I spoke with clarity the oath of office because it was a big moment in my life. I was now officially a public official, a responsibility I did not take lightly.

Terrell Sessums, of Tampa, was elected speaker. Of course, as always, this had been predetermined at least a couple of years before. Those wishing to be speaker start lining up support several years in advance. Barring big surprises in the election the winner is decided earlier, but officially the vote that counts is the one after the swearing-in. At that point, the nominee of the majority party and leader of the minority party are in the race with the outcome pre-ordained. Then, especially if the mood is right, the minority leader will ask that the vote be made unanimous, a gesture that acknowledges that the winner is the speaker of all.

I requested and received assignment to three committees I felt would be good ones--Governmental Operations, Education, and Health and Rehabilitative Services I was also assigned to several subcommittees on each of these committees. This, in my opinion, is too many committees for a member to sit on. After my first term, I dropped the HRS Committee, not that it was not a good committee, but I could better apply myself with my work on the two other committees. Now in Tallahassee each member has even more committees. I believe they should be limited to two full committees.

The organizational session is usually just that as the legislature gets organized, adjourns and then returns for the regular session in the Spring. However, there were a few bills, mainly of local nature, that were passed in my initial session. My bill was one of them. Walton County, in my district, had a local bill that needed to be passed in a timely manner or it would cost the taxpayers money. So, I got an agreement from the speaker that it would be taken up.

This was my time to shine. The speaker, after the clerk had read the title of the bill, said, "The gentleman, Mr. Hutto, is recognized to explain his bill." I picked up my microphone from my desk and addressed the House of Representatives for the very first time. I do not remember the details of the bill and likely did not know that much about it then. I do not know if I did a good job of explaining it to my colleagues, but I think I impressed upon them the urgency of getting this bill into law. I moved that it be passed, the speaker intoned, "the vote is on the motion of the gentleman, Mr. Hutto, to pass the bill. The clerk will open the machine. Those for it will vote yea and those opposed will vote no."

I felt pretty good about the chances of the bill passing, but I had never even seen a bill voted on in the legislature. I did not know what to expect. Suddenly, I looked up at the electronic board where the votes of all the members were lighted up. Fear gripped my heart! I could not believe what I was seeing. All the lights were red except two or three, meaning all were voting no except my deskmate Billy Joe, and Wayne Mixson and Pat Thomas who sat right ahead of us. These three guys made it look like, as my good friends, they were with me. Oh no, I thought, this cannot be happening. My first bill in the legislature was going down to defeat by almost unanimous vote. I am sure I must have had the most embarrassed look on my face I ever had. Then, the chamber broke out in laughter and all switched votes from no to yea.

This little trick is known as "redlighting" and is often pulled on new members when their first bill is brought up. Those rascals Rish and Mixson had conspired with the members to do that to me. They passed word around that when the vote was taken to vote no, but change votes to yea before the tally was announced. Believe me, I gave a sigh of relief to see the bill finally passing unanimously.

Local bills would not be the only business we would take up in late November 1972. A special session was called to reinstate capital punishment following a U. S. Supreme Court decision to throw out the death penalty. So, after a rather lengthy day's debate, Florida became the first state to reinstate the death penalty. This was the first substantive bill that I ever voted on. I believe capital punishment is necessary and a deterrent to crime. Thus, I voted, along with a majority of my colleagues, to reinstate the death penalty.

Back in Panama City, I was reinstated as a full-time employee with Channel 7 and was back on the air doing state news and my sportscasts. Ray Holloway had been a bit hesitant about my return to the air, but it was worked out with Ray Carow in Albany that I would be allowed to return to full-time activity with the station.

About the time I started my first regular session in the legislature was the time that construction started on our new house on a lot we purchased in a new section of Forest Park. In September of 1973 we moved into this new home, roughly a mile from the old one. Plans for the home, at 3015 State Avenue, were drawn by Nancy, with little help from me. The 2244 square foot, 3-bedroom house, was built by J. C. Scalf and would be our home for many years.

At Channel 7 I worked with a fine bunch of people. Earl Hadaway was program director; Joe Moore, news director; Tom Hipps, announcer and musician; Ron Jones, Jack Crusan, David Atchison, and Tim Steele were in the Production Department. Salesmen included Hugh Roche and Joe Pijot; Cathie Ray did the weather; Billy Carpenter, Wendell Holley and Jim Bates were engineers; Jack Reinhart managed the film room; and Betty Wright and Helen Schuh did women's and childrens' shows. These are some of the people I worked with through the years at Channel Seven.

Tom Hipps was another of those guys who likes to break people up on the air. His antics off camera often succeeded. But, I was wise to Tom and he had a hard time getting me tickled while on camera. Conversely, I was the only one who could break Tom. I could get near where he was talking and whisper in a low tone audible to him but not picked up on the air. Often, Tom would laugh. I think it was due to the fact this was an extension of the duty he and I had in "taping the book" each day. This was a notebook with announcer's copy for the next day. We alternated announcements to give a change of voice and sometimes it was a riot trying to get through because we frequently burst out laughing and had to start over.

The Snapper Bowl game at Pete Edwards Field, Panama City Beach, each year was great for young football players. Teams from out of state came to compete with the local midget teams and I tried to publicize the event as much as possible. One year, when I had another commitment, I asked Hipps if he would go film the Snapper Bowl for me. He did it all right. Everything except the game. He got the cheerleaders, the band, and a lot of crowd shots, but Tom had difficulty explaining why he did not shoot the actual game. This Snapper Bowl episode became a big joke. Tom played another practical joke on me later on when he spliced some of the Snapper Bowl film footage he had shot to one of my sports stories. I did have to laugh, this time, when I saw that come up, out of place, on the screen during my sportscast.

Tom Hipps also pulled the Buddy Wilkes trick on me by pulling the desk from in front of me at the end of one of our programs, exposing the fact that below that well groomed tie and coat above the desk I was wearing walking shorts below the desk. This time my bare legs came across in living color, as the station had gone to color by then.

I found out that handling my full-time job with Channel 7 and performing my duties as a state legislator was a tough proposition. I had to take a two months leave of absence during the 60-day legislative session in April and May and at other times the station had to cover for me when I had to attend committee meetings in Tallahassee or other events in my district. It was just too much to handle if one was going to do justice to either job. Toward the end of 1973, I realized I had to make a change. I lined up a few accounts which I could handle as an advertising agency and formed the Earl Hutto Agency. I gave the station notice that I would be resigning at the end of the year. The temporary job I took in 1963 had lasted ten years. Anyway, with the agency, I had more flexibility in setting my own agenda and the commission I made, while not great, was a good supplement to my $12,000 legislative salary.

I did not realize how tired I was until I left Channel 7. I had been working at night for years. Now, if I did not have a commitment to speak or be away from home, Nancy and I usually hit the sack by 10 p.m. and were asleep pronto. My routine of getting in bed at midnight or later for such a long time apparently had built up some sort of residual tiredness.

During the regular session of the legislature I left home Monday morning, drove to Tallahassee and returned early Friday afternoon to Panama City. Nancy and I felt it was not worth uprooting our young family by moving to Tallahassee two months out of the year. Monday through Thursday nights of each week I stayed at the Quality Inn Motel for $10 a night. All I needed was a place to sleep and I was appreciative to Mr. Belch, the motel owner, for giving me such a good deal.

Frankly, I did not like being away from my family and when I got home Friday afternoon I was very glad to see them. We were so close and had so much love for each other. Although I talked to them by phone everyday of the week, I looked forward to being with them on the weekend.

One Monday morning while driving to Tallahassee, I happened to have WPAP-FM, Panama City, on the radio and a lady called in saying she had puppies to give away. I wrote down her number and when I got to Tallahassee, I phoned Nancy. To make a long story short we got a little puppy which the girls named Zach, short for Zaccheus about whom they had recently studied in Sunday

School. Zach became a much loved pet in our family.

One of my first bills of statewide significance which I got passed in the legislature and the governor signed into law was at the behest of Bay County Sheriff Tullis Easterling. It provided that shoplifters could be arrested on or off the premises with reasonable cause. Previously, they could only be arrested on the premises, so this was a big help to businesses in apprehending shoplifters.

Perhaps the most significant bill passed in my first term was the Florida Education Funding Program I co-sponsored as a member of the Education Committee. This resulted from a Governor's Management and Efficiency Study Commission report. The FEFP equalized education for all the state and was landmark legislation.

Another measure considered was the ERA, Equal Rights Amendment to the U. S. Constitution. I spoke against this bill, telling my colleagues that "I have a wonderful wife and two beautiful daughters that I love dearly and, although I want them to have every opportunity, I do not believe we should erase the legal difference between male and female. I support equality of the sexes, but this measure, if passed, will cause further deterioration of the family unit." It passed in the House by about three votes, but did not pass the Senate. It still has not passed.

I think the most emotional issue for me in that first session was the lowering of the drinking age to 18. With the able leadership of Representative Jim Redman, of Plant City, we were able to defeat this move by a single vote. But Speaker Don Tucker was pushing this bill and through a parliamentary maneuver brought it up again and passed it. It has been proven conclusively that the lower drinking age has caused more deaths and more problems. Now, due to federal legislation to withhold highway funds to states not complying, the drinking age has returned to 21 in most states.

Unfortunately, I lost Bobby Branning who received a good offer to return to Gulf Power Company, his employer before he went back to FSU for his Masters degree. After interviewing several prospects, I hired Dan Dobbins, an idealistic young man from Gainesville, to be my administrative assistant. Dan was quite concerned about the environment and particularly the erosion of the beautiful white sand beaches along Northwest Florida's gulf coast.

For years these sugary white beaches were Florida's "Best Kept Secret," as proclaimed in beach promotions. There is a strip of about 100 miles stretching from Mexico Beach westward to Pensacola called "The Miracle Strip" and "The World's Most Beautiful Beaches," the latter referring to Panama City beaches.

Where 20 years before or even more recently these beaches were unspoiled, they had now been discovered by developers, and condominiums were going up all over the place. Dan Dobbins and I went out to look at the site where one big project was about to begin. Many of these high-rise buildings were often built too close to the water. It concerned me greatly that this close proximity, plus the sealing off of the beaches to the public in places, was hurting our beaches. It did not seem right to build these buildings close to the water, causing wave action to erode the beaches, and then ask the government for millions of dollars to restore the beaches.

I took a public stand in favor of a setback line for building on the beach. You can imagine what a furor this ignited! Suddenly I became a very controversial public official. I issued a news release asking developers to voluntarily move new construction further away from the water. I knew I was going against the establishment, especially motel owners, but never thought of political consequences.

My stand caught a great deal of attention, even in other parts of the state, in my criticism of some specific projects. I soon found out that some of our advertisers on Channel 7, particularly a developer in Destin, were up in arms about my position. Manager Ray Holloway had a talk with me about it. Though philosophically he agreed with me, he let me know my position could cost the station. My stand also brought to the forefront the fact that there were some lawyers and local investors involved in these projects. Nonetheless, it was a matter of principle and I had to stick to my guns.

A year or so before I entered the legislature, a bill had been passed to provide that Florida's beach areas should have a scientifically established setback line. But the program was not being implemented very speedily. This was to be done through the Bureau of Beaches and Shores in the Florida Department of Natural Resources. Panama Citian Harmon Shields was DNR Director. This put Harmon in an awkward position because his good friend, Senator Dempsey Barron, had motel interests on the beaches.

Bill Carlton headed up the Bureau of Beaches and Shores and was very understanding about the need to establish the setback lines and spoke in favor of it, both before the legislature and publicly. I worked closely with Mr. Carlton on moving forward with the lines.

It was evident as soon as I took my position that the public was highly in favor of what I was doing. I received a lot of phone calls and mail supporting the setback line. Many pointed out, and rightly so, that a lot of these big developers were big firms from out of state that were out to make money and had little or no concern about the protection of the beaches. Several citizens behind me on this matter organized SOS, for Save Our Shores. A number of meetings were held and there were a lot of people who joined the effort.

I was not at all against development, but felt strongly that taxpayers should not pay out money to rebuild beaches because some developers did not respect the dune system, the natural beach protection, and built too close to the water. I believed then, and still do, that government should not preclude a citizen's right to his property without just compensation. This was my philosophy throughout my political career. I support property rights. But, in many cases along our shores the construction could very well be moved landward to protect the integrity of the environment.

My buddy, Representative Billy Joe Rish, who lived in Port St. Joe, but who had a small part of Bay County in his district, and I issued a statement asking the builders to stop their construction until the setback line was established. Billy Joe later pulled back on the issue and I couldn't blame him as most of this concerned my district.

As the 1974 session of the legislature got underway, the furor over the beaches still raged. I introduced a bill that would speed up the process for getting setback lines established 150 yards landward of the mean high water mark throughout the state. It came before the Natural Resources Committee. I was there to speak in support and Elliot Messer, a prominent lawyer in Tallahassee, was there to speak against it. Two of my friends, Representative Jere Tolton of Fort Walton Beach and Grover Robinson of Pensacola, were members of the committee. They knew the bill was controversial and sheepishly hid their heads and grinned. Later, they kidded me about introducing a "communist" bill. We still joke about that today.

The bill passed the committee and later went to the floor. It stirred some pretty interesting debate. It would have passed, but stiff opposition from some key members resulted in the bill being pulled on a point of order, much to the relief of those who did not want to vote on it. Had it passed the House, I do not think there is any way it could have passed the Senate. But we were keeping this subject in the public eye and working toward getting the lines established.

A number of hearings were held in Bay County and finally, with the University of Florida's oceanographers scientifically proposing a plan, the Florida cabinet scheduled a vote on the setback line in late Summer. An angry crowd filled the meeting room in Tallahassee with intense emotions expressed late into the night. In Florida's unique cabinet system there are certain matters over which both the governor and the cabinet have jurisdiction and equal votes. When the vote was finally taken, the setback line for Bay County passed. It was clearly the thing to do.

John Johnson, the young man who was president of Save Our Shores in Bay County, stated that the setback line would increase the property value in the beaches area. He was right. In all fairness, there were some beach property owners who realized that the establishment of the setback line was in the long-range interest of the beaches as a tourist area. There were, indeed, strong feelings on both sides of the issue. In fact, there was some fear on the part of my neighbor, Ernest Gladstone, who had driven me to Tallahassee for the cabinet meeting, about our safety in driving home. We stayed clear of any confrontation with those so adamant in their position.

It should be pointed out that beachfront owners could still seek variances from the line. In reality, it has proven over the years not to be as strong a commitment to protecting the beaches as might be needed. Numerous variances have been voted by the governor and cabinet since the establishment of the setback line in Bay County.

In our personal lives, our girls were growing and were no longer babies. Lori started first grade at Northside Elementary School in 1974. Northside, a mile from where we lived in the Forest Park area, was a very nice school, the newest in Bay County. Lori was an excellent student under her first grade teacher, Mrs. Sue Hall.

My strong support in taking action to get the setback line in Bay County assured me of one thing--an opponent for the 1974 campaign. Remember Charlie Hilton, with whom I sat on the Reubin Askew Bay County Advisory Committee? Well, Charlie, with his motels, sand and gravel company and law practice, was the most vigorous opponent of the setback line. Despite his previous support of the governor, he called it the Hutto-Askew confiscation line.

Charlie, an active player in Bay County and area politics,

decided this time he would get in the fray himself. He announced his candidacy for District 8 Representative. Charlie had plenty of money, so it would be a hard fought race. There was no question I was going against powerful interests in my second run for office.

Wallace Kendrick continued to help me raise funds and for the '74 election we raised a total of $7,000, a small amount, but twice as much as the first race, and again, it was just the right amount to carry me through the campaign. Harold Phillips, a hard worker who had built his meat and seafood company into a good business, was a good supporter. Though he and Wallace had not met before, they became good friends and provided dedicated support to me.

In addition to the usual fish fries, rallies, and speeches, there were also special events that were a must on the campaign trail, such as Fun Day in Wausau, the Watermelon Festival in Chipley, and later the Chautauqua Festival in DeFuniak Springs. In the Watermelon Festival Parade in June, our family rode on a pickup truck full of watermelons driven by Mr. Farrell Nelson, a Washington county school board member and farmer, who had grown them. I think the girls enjoyed the parade and waving to the crowd, but would not admit it. At the end of the parade, we all enjoyed eating the melons.

One year my good friend, State Representative Wayne Mixson, who would later become Lieutenant Governor for eight years and then Governor of Florida for three days when Bob Graham resigned to take his seat in the U. S. Senate, decided to walk in the Watermelon Festival Parade carrying a watermelon on his shoulder. The melon must have weighed 40 or 50 pounds and at the end of the parade, Wayne vowed never to tote another watermelon anywhere.

At Wausau, a small place south of Chipley with wonderful people, their Fun Day was scheduled the first Saturday in August. It was just about always quite hot and humid. Lori and Amy did not call it Fun Day. They called it HOT DAY! But folks came from miles around to enjoy the parade and the country and gospel music. Possum Day was another title applied to the Wausau event. Dalton Carter, the founder and emcee, made the opossum, or simply possum, the theme of the festivities. During auctioning of the possums, with politicians bidding, such names as "Sand Hill Sam" or "Choctawhatchee Broadsmile" pedigree were tagged on the marsupials. I did not bid because I did not have that kind of money, but the year Charlie ran he bought one for $200.

In one session of the legislature I joined with Wayne Mixson, Chairman of the Agriculture Committee, in proposing an amendment providing for a possum canning factory in Wausau. It was all in jest at a time when levity relieved some anxiety about more serious legislation. It was a good promotion, though, for Wausau's Fun Day.

Another feature of Fun Day was the National Hog Calling Contest. It was a lot of fun to hear some of the old-timers sound off with "coooaaaa...piiiig....coaaa," and other such sounds that delighted the crowd. A local fellow named Jamie won for several years.

During the '74 campaign one of the SOS members had bumper stickers made which said "Sorry Charlie," a takeoff on the TV ads of Charlie the Tuna. Although Charlie did not make the setback line his central issue, everyone knew that was why he was opposing me. Charlie referred to me as having an "Ipana Toothpaste smile." I stuck to my usual positive campaign and stressed my record.

On September 10, the date of the first primary in Florida, I faced my first re-election vote. Again, I had campaigned hard and enjoyed it. About the only change in our election return plans was that the covered dish party was in our new house and we had room to accommodate more people. As we listened to the radio and caught the breaks on TV, it appeared things were going our way from the outset. The final tally showed me getting 78 per cent of the vote and defeating Charlie Hilton 9,130 to 2,584. Having no further opposition, I was elected for a second term.

The Associated Press ran a rather lengthy article equating my big victory with my pushing the cabinet to establish the beach setback line. The article quoted me as saying, "You would have thought the cabinet was doing the worst thing in the world. The opponents had all the lawyers in Panama City and much of the monied interests there, but I knew I had felt the pulse of the people and I think my support of the setback line has been vindicated."

Natural Resources Director Harmon Shields stated he thought approval of the Bay County line cleared the way for establishing others around the state with few problems. "When we got over the Bay County hump, we got over the setback line hump," he said. The article pointed out that Shields was a hometown friend of both Hilton and me. Charlie Hilton did become a future supporter of mine.

Before the convening of the 1974 organizational session of the Florida Legislature, Billy Joe Rish and other Northwest Florida legislators had been lobbying me to support Don Tucker, of Tallahassee, for Speaker of the House. They portrayed Tucker as being more conservative than Representative Buddy MacKay, of Ocala, the other candidate for Speaker. Tucker, being from the Big Bend area, nearest to the Panhandle, was more in tune with our philosophy, they averred. I took their word for it since I had not followed their voting records and voted for Tucker

Perhaps my friends did not know Tucker quite that well, either, because as time went on Rish and I, along with Marianna's Wayne Mixson, probably voted with MacKay more than Tucker, after he was elected. Tucker was liberal in his agenda, but quite fair to me.

Dan Dobbins resigned as my staffer to go to law school and I hired Richard Foreman to be my third AA. Going into the 1975 session, I was named Vice Chairman of the Governmental Operations Committee. I continued to serve on the Education Committee, but dropped the Health and Rehabilitative Services Committee.

One night during the session the Port St. Joe Chamber of Commerce invited me to their annual dinner meeting and Billy Joe invited me to be their house guest overnight in Port St. Joe. The next morning, Jay Rish, their young son who was probably five or six years old at the time, bragged to his friends that a "real representative" spent the night at their house last night. Billy Joe still likes to tell that.

In September of '75 Hurricane Eloise was bearing down on the gulf coast. We monitored the media to keep tabs on the location where the storm might come ashore. As Nancy and I went to bed around 11 o'clock, we left the TV on so we could monitor its progress. Before 2 a.m., Eloise was predicted to hit Panama City. We quickly bundled up the girls and headed for Daddy's house in Alabama. On the road, we found that just about everyone else was evacuating, too. It was bumper to bumper all the way to Dothan.

As we traveled north we kept monitoring WPAP-FM, which had the strongest signal of the Panama City stations, to see what Eloise was doing. We arrived at Daddy's house in Ewell around daylight. We found out in just a few short hours that these storms can also be severe inland. We were about 100 miles from Panama City, where Eloise had come ashore, but we sure felt her wrath in Ewell. The fierce winds blew down Daddy's carport as well as his pump house and some trees. We were surprised when we got back to Panama City that our electricity had not even gone off at home.

There had been little damage in Panama City itself, but the 21 miles of beaches west of the city suffered about $100 million damage. Florida Director of Natural Resources Harmon Shields commented that "God showed them the setback line." Indeed, there is no question Eloise's fury caused a change in the way beach buildings are constructed.

In 1976, I ran what I call the best campaign that anyone can run and that is "a campaign without an opponent." This was the first time I had absolutely no opposition. In Florida, when there is no opponent, the qualifying candidate is not even listed on the ballot. What a blessing not to campaign! This gave me an opportunity to do work with my agency and spend time with family. I was grateful.

At the organizational session in November, Don Tucker had lined up his support and became the first speaker, at least in modern times, to be re-elected to a second term. It is difficult to oppose a sitting Speaker and risk being in the doghouse for two years, but my friend Jim Redman, a very popular man, made a brave challenge.

In December of that year we had planned, as usual, separate celebrations at Christmas time with Nancy's folks and my folks. On Sunday, December 19th, we had a wonderful time with Daddy, Merle, Wanda, and Rex and Sara and their two children, Alan and Kristi, at our home in Panama City. They had left to return to Ozark about two or three o'clock that afternoon because Daddy had to sing in the Christmas cantata at his church that night.

I was supposed to do the narration of the Christmas pageant in our church in Panama City. But as we prepared to depart for church, I received a call from Rex telling me that Daddy had been taken to the hospital with a bad stroke. I immediately called to ask that someone do the narration for me and I headed for Ozark.

It was a severe stroke. Though Daddy tried to talk to us, and we could understand a few words, we knew his condition was serious. He had been rehearsing with the choir and they had just donned their robes and were taking a little break before the performance when he was stricken. Very quickly an ambulance arrived and took him to Dale County Hospital. We were by his bedside for 12 days before he passed away on the last night of 1976 at age 78. As it was with Mama, I watched him die peacefully.

Also, as with Mama, Daddy's funeral was on a Sunday afternoon. He had passed away in one year and was buried in another. It was a beautiful service at First Assembly of God in Ozark on January 2, 1977. Pastor Billy Johnson, Associate Pastor Henry Morrow, and the Rev. Luther Tadlock, a close personal friend, delivered the eulogies. The choir sang "Because He Lives" and "I'll Meet You In The Rapture." The church, again as with Mama, was overflowing. Rex commented that it was the biggest funeral he had seen in Ozark. Hundreds of folks were there to pay tribute to a common man with a gentle spirit they loved. He was laid to rest beside Mama in Ewell Cemetery. We would miss him greatly, but how could we be sad? He was with God in peace.

In Washington in early 1977, Bob Sikes took the oath for the 19th time as Congressman for the First Congressional District. Jimmy Carter became president. In Florida we were continuing to grapple with problems of being the fastest growing state and having to accommodate the more than 300,000 each year--nearly 1,000 per day--who were coming into the sunshine state to live.

I worked hard to try to achieve greater efficiency in government. Each session I had introduced legislation to put the state on biennial budgeting. It was obvious to me that every agency of government worked hard to spend every dollar appropriated by the end of the fiscal year so that they could get more for the next year. I contended that, like a pig, the more times you go to the trough, the more you get. Fewer times to the trough by state agencies would mean they would have to plan for better use of their funding and the legislature would have more oversight of their spending.

I continued to push multi-year budgeting the next two years. The Policy and Procedures Subcommittee, which I chaired, held hearings on the issue. Representative Herb Morgan, of Tallahassee, a member of the subcommittee was an opponent of biennial budgeting, but after our hearings he became convinced it was the right thing to do. Appropriations Chairman Ed Fortune, of Pace, had spoken favorably for a longer budget cycle, and Governor Reubin Askew, as well as State Senator Bob Graham, supported it. Senate President Dempsey Barron and Speaker Don Tucker also came on board. In the '78 session biennial budgeting finally passed.

My subcommittee, under the Government Operations Committee, had jurisdiction over a number of issues that had been studied by a Florida Management and Efficiency Study Commission. I was pleased to bring a number of commission recommendations to the floor and get them passed to save millions of dollars to taxpayers.

I was appointed Chairman of a Select Subcommittee on the Reduction of Paper Work. We did our best to reduce the level of state government paperwork, but anything that was done seemed to be a stop-gap effort and I will have to say that we found ourselves rather helpless in stopping the endless flow of paper. Someone wisecracked that all we did was create a little more paper work.

Once in a while a serious bill can bring a little levity. Such was the case when Billy Joe's bee bill came up. BJ had an excused absence the day it came up, but I was not going to let his bill be postponed and took the floor to move it myself. The following AP story tells the rest:

The House was abuzz with humor Monday before it approved a bill aimed at helping farmers with diseased honey bees. After a large number of legislators flashed no votes and then switched to yes, Rep. Earl Hutto, D-Panama City, the floor manager of the bill, said, "I thought I had been stung." The final vote was 104-3.

Rep. John Forbes, D-Jacksonville, noted that the farmers had given legislators jars of honey the past two years while the bill was being considered and suggested the bill be left pending until the honey is received. "We're being taken for granted," he said.

"The Speaker's office received its honey," Speaker Don Tucker, D-Tallahassee, replied. Hutto said the farmers were just being considerate by making sure the legislators didn't receive any diseased honey because the bees had been sick for three years. The measure died in the Senate in the previous two sessions.

Rep. Richard Langley, R-Clermont, interjected, "The reason we didn't get any honey was because the queen bee had a headache."

In all six years I spent in the legislature, I was the only member of the House Education Committee from Northwest Florida. In that capacity I felt an obligation to make sure that we properly provided for the rural counties in our area. Jim Redman was Chairman of the Education Committee my last two years and appointed me as Chairman of the Subcommittee on Post-Secondary Education, which meant I had jurisdiction over the universities and community colleges.

In 1976, Amy entered first grade at Northside School. That meant we had two young'ns in school. Both were good students and we were naturally very proud of them. The school system did not furnish transportation for students living within two miles of the school. So, we had to take them to school. When the weather was good, they enjoyed riding their bikes. Nancy and I visited in the school regularly and often had lunch with the girls in the lunchroom.

Since I was not restricted to a set schedule at the TV station, I had a lot of flexibility in running the Earl Hutto Agency. For the most part it was a one-man operation, but I did hire a couple of young men, Steve Slaughter and Ronnie Ingram, at different times. Both were quite creative and did a good job, but they were not with me for a long span of time because it was a part-time thing with me and I did not have enough accounts to afford a staff. But the agency did allow me flexibility and I was happy to spend more time with my family.

I enjoyed making speeches to civic clubs, school and community groups, and holding town hall meetings. I always had plenty to do, but at least I could better set my own agenda than when I had to be ever present to do the news and sports on TV.

Some people did not understand that my authority was limited to state matters and often we got calls from people who wanted the road fixed in front of their house, or someone to fix their stopped-up sewer, or their neighbors were making too much noise. I would patiently listen to their stories, then advise them I had no jurisdiction over these matters and directed them to some agency or person.

One woman wanted me to stop her neighbor's cats from coming into her backyard. Another one, who ran a country store, wanted me to make the bread truck deliver bread to her store.

Still another lady, who lived up in Walton County, had a habit of calling me collect in the middle of the night. She ran a country store and she apparently liked to imbibe. I listened to her spout off for long periods of time. Like many people, I think she was kind of lonely. One morning the phone woke me up ringing at 2:00 a.m. The operator said, "Mrs. (Blank) is calling Rep. Earl Hutto collect. Will you accept the charges?" Normally, I would say yes, but this night I was so tired, I told the operator, "Tell her if she will call back about 7:30 in the morning I'll be glad to talk to her." I heard the woman demand, "I wanna talk to him now!" I quickly said, "Yes, mam, I'll talk to her." Yes, it was an awful hour, but this was my constituent and I did not want her telling everybody who came into her store that Representative Hutto would not even talk to her on the phone.

When the police in Springfield, a suburb of Panama City, received complaints from neighbors that Vietnamese who had settled there were killing and eating dogs, they asked me to determine if there was a state law against it. It is not unusual that dogs are eaten in Vietnam. I had staff research the matter and they found no law against it, per se, in Florida, but found a law that provides a one year sentence for unnecessarily killing an animal. The Associated Press quoted me as saying, "I have one dog. My wife says he is a Heinz 57 breed, but he's a nice dog. I wouldn't want him eaten."

During my upbringing in Alabama and since I had been in Florida I had seen very few Republicans in my life. In fact, we joked that we did not know what a Republican looked like. There were few in Bay County, but in the legislature I saw more Republicans than I had ever seen. There were about forty in the 120-member House and eight or ten in the 40-member Senate. I found out that they are real people, just like we are, and I agreed oftentimes with their positions.

One thing I did not like was partisan bickering that sometimes broke out. In the Florida legislature at that time there was a lot of working together in a bipartisan spirit. In later years I found out what real partisan bickering and deadlock was all about. Even now in the Florida legislature it is a lot worse than when I was there.

Serving in the legislature entails much more than making laws. In fact, that may be one of the lesser aspects of the job. Riding herd on state agencies and working with them on problems, some of which come as a result of constituent complaints, occupies a considerable amount of time. Due to the close proximity of Alabama to my district, it was necessary sometimes to work on common problems. Alabama authorities were tentatively planning a turnpike from Northwest to Southeast Alabama. I urged Governor Askew and Florida highway officials to work with Alabama toward continuing this turnpike into Northwest Florida. The plan died for lack of money.

Specific problems in our area required me and others to prevail on the Department of Transportation to address these needs, such as completion of U.S. Highway 231 from the Alabama line to Panama City. At another time, I worked to get DOT not to remove traffic lights in downtown DeFuniak Springs as they had planned.

One night during the time the legislature was in session, I flipped on the TV and could not believe my eyes and ears when I saw the program that was being done locally on the public television channel. Some of the most vulgar four-letter words I had ever heard were coming out of the mouths of some half dozen people who supposedly were in a drug therapy session. This was in prime time.

I blasted the telecast and my colleagues in the House agreed if these kinds of sessions are necessary for drug addicts, they should not be telecast. I think it was the next day that the public television bill was on the floor and I amended it. The amendment forbade "obscene or profane four-letter words describing the sexual act or body excrement." Rep. Alan Becker asked me what words I meant. "I would not dare use those words in this chamber. I would probably get thrown out and I know I would not get re-elected," I replied.

Rep. Barry Kutun, of Miami, argued that the amendment would put the legislature in the position of censoring public broadcasts. I responded, "If Mr. Kutun wants to allow four-letter words to come into his living room in Miami maybe he could make a tape and play them all he wants to." The bill, with the amendment, passed the House 105-2. It isn't hard to identify the two nay votes.

At another time, I assailed the Department of Corrections for removing chapels from the state prisons. They had done this in several and were about to close the chapel at the road camp in Panama City. In a strongly-worded letter, I called on Director Louie Wainwright not to neglect the spiritual aspects of prisoners' rehabilitation. A lot of people supported my efforts, particularly Sonny Myers, a volunteer chaplain at the road camp.

For many years north Florida legislators, often called "pork choppers" had dominated state government because the largely rural areas tended to re-elect their legislators on a greater basis than South Florida, thus giving the rural areas more experience and seniority. Although some of the more outstanding legislators still come from Northwest Florida, it has become more equalized due to several things, such as the U. S. Supreme Court's one man, one vote mandate, the new constitution approved in 1968, and the news media.

It was incumbent upon us to work together to counteract greater numbers of legislators from Miami and South Florida. For example, we amended a bill on water management to levy only .05 of a mill on our area, much less than the rest of the state, due to our not having water problems like central and south Florida.

Once a Constitution Revision Commission was considering a unicameral legislature and at another time reducing the size of the

House from 120 members to 80 members. I testified against these proposals. Certainly the urban problems need to be addressed, but not at the expense of the rural areas. In Northwest Florida and other rural areas, an 80-Member House would mean that the representatives and senators would have such large land areas their constituents would have little chance of ever seeing them.

Back then, as now, there was a great concern about our youth. I was able to get through the legislature a bill that provided for the publishing of the names of juvenile lawbreakers. The bill passed the House 92-7 and later passed the Senate. In my arguments for the bill I said, "We need to identify the bad kid on the block so he won't reflect adversely on the great majority of our fine young people. We need to take the stigma off about 95 per cent of our youth who are good, law-abiding citizens".

In other efforts to help youngsters, I worked with Senator Pat Thomas, of Quincy, in getting a bill passed, amending child labor laws allowing young people to work more hours, lowered to 14 the age at which minors could participate in cooperative education programs, and authorized 14 and 15-year olds to operate farm tractors in the course of work on a family-operated farm if they had completed a recognized training course in tractor operation.

Still on this subject, Chris Gilmore, Director of Operation Involvement, commended me for my successful efforts on the floor to keep the program alive in Florida. Gilmore stated that the program, through the University of West Florida, worked with 800 juvenile delinquents and their families and that Operation Involvement was a success in reducing juvenile crime.

I was particularly proud of being able to get enacted into law a bill providing for registration for those wishing to donate organs, upon their death, at state drivers license offices. The anatomical gift program was designed to save lives. It was a pilot program at a limited number of offices, but later I sponsored HB 667 which expanded the program.

Litter along public streets and highways is so unsightly. At the behest of Jerry Gerde, a lawyer and a Republican from Panama City, I introduced and got passed a litter law which I thought would be a big help in controlling litter. The previous law provided a fine of up to $500. My bill reduced littering to a non-criminal offense with a fine of $25. A good provision was that monies from the fines would go for litter control. This law is one that, if enforced by state and local authorities, could be very effective. Its passage, however, did not make Gerde one of my lifetime supporters. I think he did support me earlier on because of my work on the setback line, but later when he became Bay County Republican Chairman he did all he could to defeat me. Oh well, so it goes.

Some family-related legislation I got passed included a grandparents' visitation bill, which allows a court to approve such visits if in the best interest of the child; bills that provided for a continuing writ of garnishment for child support and alimony rather than allowing deadbeat dads and husbands to get by without paying their obligations; and a bill I got through the House, but the Senate didn't pass requiring children to help support destitute parents if able.

All of my bills did not escape the wrath of the governor's pen. My HB 3121, which would prohibit state agencies from suing one another was vetoed by Governor Reubin Askew. This legislation was provoked following a lawsuit between the Department of Natural Resources and the Game and Fresh Water Fish Commission over the stocking of weed-eating fish in Deer Point Lake in Bay County. Although the measure passed the House 100-7 and the Senate by a lopsided margin, I could understand the governor vetoing it because it provided that the cabinet had to approve lawsuits being filed. Some agencies are under the governor and cabinet, so the governor felt he should have a voice in the matter. I worked with Senator Phil Lewis to make needed changes. My comment on the issue was "These disputes should be settled within the family. It is ridiculous to go to court against each other and use taxpayers' money for this purpose."

I was one of five members named to a select committee to rewrite Florida's Administrative Procedures Act. The chairman was Bob Hector (D-Miami) and others on the committee were Representatives Marshall Harris (D-Miami), Charles Boyd (D-Pembroke Pines), and Curt Kiser (R-Dunedin). Harris was the most dominant person in the legislature, a brilliant lawyer of liberal persuasion but one who was respected by all. With Marshall Harris, it was difficult for the rest of us to have that much input, but we all contributed and brought to the floor a bill that was hailed by some as a model for dealing with the bureaucracy. It sought to get a grip on what Sen. Dempsey Barron (D-Panama City) had often referred to as "phantom government" It passed both bodies overwhelmingly. It may have helped, but there are still bureaucratic problems in Tallahassee.

In looking back at the record, it would appear that I was much more of an activist than I thought I was. I was for the most part low-key. But I spoke out for what I thought was right. If I introduced a bill, I felt it addressed a matter of importance, worked it through the committees of jurisdiction, prevailed on the Rules Committee to put it on the calendar, and got it to the floor for action. Somewhat unobtrusively I got a lot of legislation passed. My colleagues began to notice and commented about all the bills I had passed.

I asked a few of them if they would put those comments on paper. They did, and one of my ads in my first campaign for Congress included the following: "I suspect Earl Hutto has had more bills to pass the House than any other member"-- Rep. Ralph Haben (D-Palmetto); "Rep. Hutto has provided great leadership and I am sure this will continue if he is sent to Washington"-- Rep. Lee Moffit (D-Tampa); "I am sure Rep. Hutto must have gotten more legislation passed than anyone during the years we served together"-- Rep. Mary E. Hawkins (R-Naples).These were kind comments, indeed. Both Haben and Moffit went on to become Speakers of the House.

I was honored by receiving a number of statewide awards during my legislative career. Included were Legislator of the Year from the Florida Association of Retarded Citizens, from the Florida Community College Association, and from the Sunshine State Association for the Blind. I also received environmental awards from Woodmen of the World and the Bay County Audubon Society.

In early June of 1978, at the end of the legislative session, I ended my career in the Florida legislature. What a deep and meaningful experience it had been for me. Never in my wildest dreams would I have thought that I would serve in such a position. It was gratifying to have done well. Sure, there were some tough issues and a few rocky times, but I had a good feeling of having served the folks back home in a way that pleased them. Through prayer and hard work, my six-year tenure had been a success. Above all, it was really heartwarming to have made so many good friends, in and out of the legislature, and to know that I had the respect of my colleagues.

Representative Earl Hutto debates a bill in the Florida House of Representatives.

Governor Reubin Askew signs a bill as its sponsors, Representative Earl Hutto and Senator Don Childers, look on. Although good friends and former business partners, Askew vetoed some of Hutto's bills.

12

CAPTAIN SUPREME GOES TO WASHINGTON

My first campaign for Congress was covered in Chapter I. What a sweet victory it was in getting elected to the Congress of the United States! Now, it was time to prepare for the big transition.

"I do not want to go to Washington." Remember those words? They were uttered three or four years earlier by me when I first broached the subject of Congress to my dear wife, Nancy. You will remember that she quickly responded, "No way!" Yet, here we were preparing to do just that. That, indeed, was our feeling back then. But once we decided that running for Congress was the right thing to do, we had set our hearts on it. Now, we looked forward with much anticipation to the great adventure ahead. There was enormous gratification within us about being chosen by the people to go to Washington to represent them.

What would it be like? Where would we live? Where would Lori and Amy go to school? Where would the family attend church? Would we like living in such a metropolitan area? Could we drive in the Washington traffic?

Even before we headed for the nation's capital, there was much to be done. Naturally, I had to think ahead about committee assignments, office selection, and hiring a staff. I made lots of phone calls--to the Clerk of the House, to Members of Congress, especially those on the Democratic Steering and Policy Committee with whom I lobbied for membership on the House Armed Services Committee. I asked for information from every source and, in turn, was flooded with more than I could digest in a timely manner.

There was one thing for sure. There was no shortage of people who wanted to go to work with me. Well before the campaign was over, I was getting bombarded with resumes. Not long after the election, the applications were so numerous that Nancy started putting them in grocery bags. Most of those seeking employment were young people just out of college, but there was an assortment of others, including some who had worked with other members of the House or Senate. I tried to, at least, look at all of them. But, my more immediate move was to hire those who would be working on my staff in the First District in Northwest Florida. I had in mind those I wanted, but I needed to nail it down.

It was no surprise that the "whiz kids" all wanted jobs with me in Washington. I was deeply appreciative of the help they gave me in the campaign, but they were not the ones I had in mind for my staff. Not that they could not perform well. It was just that I felt very strongly that each of them should finish their college education before entering the work force. I scheduled an interview with each of them the next day or two following the election. It wasn't easy for me to break the news to them that I would not be hiring them.

I am confident that I made the right decision not to hire these young men. Two of them, however, later were employed by me. Steve Strickland went back to Beloit College in Wisconsin for his senior year. After graduation I hired him and he did good work in my Washington office for a year before running for state representative back in Panama City, a big mistake. He was walloped by incumbent Representative Leonard Hall. I made no endorsement in this race.

Tommy Todd, the only one of the three who was married, had graduated from the University of Florida and was planning to go to law school. I urged him to do that. He eventually did go to law school at the University of Alabama. Congressman Richard Shelby (D-Alabama) a native of Tuscaloosa, home of the university, upon my recommendation, hired Tommy for part-time work. At last report, Tommy was practicing law in the Tampa area.

Robert Higdon, who I believe at that time had graduated from Gulf Coast Community College, attended college in the northeast for a year or so and decided to come to Washington to continue his education. During that time, I hired him as an intern. Later he got a full-time job with Senator Lawton Chiles in the mail room. In succeeding years he would become, I understand, the chief fundraiser for President Reagan's library in California and at last report was doing the same for former British Prime Minister Margaret Thatcher.

One resume I received surprised me. It was from Randy Knepper, the young banker from Fort Walton who helped me in that area during the campaign. It surprised me because I thought Randy had a bright future in banking. I was pleased to know this young fellow at least had some interest in joining my team. I was certainly interested in talking with him, so I called him up and asked him to come over to Panama City to meet with Nancy and me in our home.

After chatting with Randy, I shocked him by offering him the top job of administrative assistant. Though he had no governmental experience, Nancy and I were confident that Randy was the right choice. His Christian and moral principles were the same as ours and he was a fun person to be around. Randy, understandably, needed a little time to think and pray about this awesome responsibility. He soon advised me that he would be honored to work with me in this capacity. There is no question that it was an opportunity for this young man of 28 years. He gave his notice at the bank and we stayed in close touch because there was a lot of planning that we needed to do.

It was my thinking from the beginning that I needed offices in Pensacola, Fort Walton Beach, and Panama City, the three most populated cities in the district. There was no question who I wanted to run the Pensacola office and represent me in Escambia and Santa Rosa counties in the western part of the district--and that was Carol Biven. Carol did such a good job for me in the primary runoff and general election that she was a natural for district administrator.

I called Carol and asked her to come to Panama City to talk about her future in government. She really wanted to be on my Washington team, but agreed it made sense for her to handle the area where her good work had borne fruit. Carol was greatly loved by our volunteers and was someone who could meet the public as well as handle the administrative chores of a district office. She accepted and when I rehired Dick Foreman, my AA from the state legislature, as a district administrator for the Panama City and Fort Walton offices, my district staff was set except for secretarial help to be hired later.

Smart realtors in the Washington area follow the election returns in congressional races throughout the nation. Some were calling us even before the general election. We thought they were being a bit presumptuous and told them to wait until after the votes were counted. Nancy did have one requirement as to where we would settle. She wanted us to live as far south as we could. I would not argue with that. We knew very little about the Washington area and Woodbridge, Virginia had a nice ring to Nancy. As we read some of the material that was mailed to us and heard more from a certain realtor we began to think in terms of Springfield as being a possibility.

Some Members of Congress choose not to take their families to Washington. They commute from Washington to their home districts every weekend. That may be good for some, but not for me. I wanted to be with my wife and our two daughters more than that. In fact, had I not had them with me during the week I would have little time to be with them when I was back in Florida due to all the speeches and meetings around the congressional district.

It was a foregone conclusion when I started running for Congress that when elected we would, of necessity, have to maintain two homes--the one we were in and one in the Washington, D. C. area. As Nancy points out, in notes she prepared for this book, changes for a family cause a lot of anxiety. There's excitement, yes, but a lot of unknowns with which to contend. Who would take care of the house? Who would cut the grass? What about Zach, our dog?

The freshmen of the 96th Congress had an orientation the first week of December 1978. Not only was it important for Nancy to be with me during this time, we also felt strongly that Lori and Amy needed to be with us. We took them out of school and the teachers cooperated by giving them the homework they needed in order to keep up. It was necessary for all of us to survey the situation, so off to Washington we went, driving through the night.

After a 19-hour drive, in which Nancy and I alternated at the wheel we arrived at the Hunter Motel in Springfield, Virginia. The next day I picked up my AA, Randy Knepper, at National Airport. Not only was Randy shivering from the cold, he was in awe of flying into the big city. He also took a room at the Hunter. The orientation provided some helpful meetings for me and the other new members.

There were also a few meetings for the spouses. This was an opportunity for us to begin the process of getting acquainted with our leaders and colleagues with whom we would be serving. The majority leader, Jim Wright, gave a dinner in the Cannon Caucus Room for the freshmen and Speaker Tip O'Neill gave a beautiful dinner party in Statuary Hall of the Capitol one night. The highlight of the social gatherings, of course, was the dinner given by President and Mrs. Jimmy Carter in the State Room of the White House.

Nancy likes to tell about that first White House gathering as it relates to the china used. Practically everyone at our table was curious as to who made it, was it the Carter china or that of another president? Finally, good manners notwithstanding, curiosity got the best of all. As if on cue, two or three, including my wife, turned over a piece of the china to find it was the Lyndon Johnson china.

A most important part of that first trip was finding a place to live. Bill Seiffert, a realtor who had called us, helped us find a townhouse to rent at Rhygate which backed up to the golf course at

Springfield Country Club. Oddly, I never played that golf course until some 10 years later.

Nancy and the girls flew back to Panama City on Thursday of that week. This was exciting for Lori and Amy because they had never flown before. They enjoyed it, but their apprehension of the move chilled their reaction. Randy and I stayed in Washington another week to begin the process of hiring and staffing an office.

What office? I did not even have one at that point. But Congressman Sikes was kind enough to let me work from his office. My office desk is not always the cleanest, but Mr. Sikes's desk was so stacked with papers it was hard to even find a place to write. At least it was a place where I could interview people and make phone calls, and his longtime administrative assistant, Alma Butler, a native of Chipley, was most helpful.

The procedure for choosing offices is by lottery. Since there were some 72 new members in the 96th Congress, numbers from one through 72 were put into a box. Members would draw by name alphabetically for the order of selection. There were charts showing the available offices from which to choose and each person, after drawing, had 15 minutes to run and take a second look at offices, which most had already inspected, before making a selection. Some spouses and some staff did the drawing for the member, but I did my own drawing and got number 43.

My high draw in the process caused me to get a less desirable office, number 508, on the fifth floor of the Cannon Building. The Pensacola News Journal carried a headline the next day that said, HUTTO IN OLD ATTIC. Well, it was not all that bad. It was small, all the elevators in the building did not go all the way to the fifth floor, and it was a long way from the House Chamber. Other than that, I guess it was okay. It would have to be for the next two years, at which time I would let Nancy do the drawing. But, gee whiz, if fifth floor Cannon was good enough for John F. Kennedy and Richard M. Nixon in their early congressional years, it ought to be okay for me. Nancy, incidentally, did do better drawing for me two years later. She drew number 17 and we moved downstairs to a larger office at 330 Cannon where I would stay for six years before getting into Rayburn.

Because of the preponderance of military facilities in Northwest Florida I felt it was essential for me to find the right person with military experience to serve on my staff. Congressman Bill

Chappell, a member of the Florida delegation who was on the Defense Appropriations Subcommittee, had three retired military guys on his staff. One was a retired rear admiral and the other two were retired Navy captains. The admiral wanted me to hire one of the captains. Personally, I think he wanted to get rid of him because there was some squabbling among the three. I interviewed the captain as well as a number of other prospects. They all had good credentials and I was especially impressed with a retired commander, Jack Davis, but he smoked and that bothers me greatly, so he did not get the job. In later years, Jack would become a good friend and I enjoyed playing golf with him on several occasions. We would laugh about his not getting the job because of his smoking.

I was still without a military staffer. In the midst of all the papers on Mr. Sikes's desk I had found a little corner where I had laid several resumes. Alma Butler told me that Nancy Smathers, then wife of Florida Secretary of State Bruce Smathers, had come by the office while I was out and highly recommended a young man by the name of Tom Culligan. I had scanned his resume and stacked it on the others, giving no thought about this young fellow of 28 years of age being a candidate as a military staffer. Somehow, while I was on the telephone, my eyes glanced over to the part of Culligan's resume which showed that he was an officer in the U. S. Air Force for three years. This discovery of military service by Culligan did not excite me all that much, but I figured I ought to, at least, grant him an interview. So, I called him in and was much impressed with Tom, who had gone to high school in Jacksonville, graduated from Florida State University, and had managed Bruce Smathers's losing race for governor. I was convinced that Tom Culligan, despite his youthfulness, possessed the kind of personality, depth of knowledge, and commitment for the job. He also was willing to start at a very modest salary, so I hired him as my Legislative Director.

Al Frith, who had worked part-time with Congressman Flowers, from his native state of Alabama, was hired on as a legislative aide. Al's sister, Sharon Penton, had taught with Nancy in Panama City, but we had not met him before.

I thought it would be wise to hire some of the Sikes staff to have some continuity. Alma Butler,coming from Chipley and having faithfully served Congressman Sikes for 36 years, would have been a great asset to my staff, but Alma was ready to retire. I hired Jeanne

Timmins, who had worked on the Hill for a number of years in the Sikes office and prior to that with a couple of other congressmen, along with case workers Mary Ahlfeld, Betts Spracher, and Jessica Wright. They all smoked, but not in my office. We did not allow it.

Gwen Martin, from DeFuniak Springs, came to Washington as one of my case workers and Mary Anne Williams, of Pensacola, joined me in the early days. The hiring of Diane Deville in Pensacola and Barbara Bennett in Panama City pretty well completed our staff at this early time. Members of the House are allowed 18 full-time employees and four part-time. In all my years I never had the authorized number and turned back millions of dollars allocated to my office. We had a sufficient number of staff to do our work.

There was a matter of great importance I dealt with during this period, even before I was sworn in. Southwest Forest Industries, operator of the paper mill in Panama City was talking about closing the plant. The Bay County folks were upset and worried. I met with company officials, and with the assistance of incoming lieutenant governor and good friend, Wayne Mixson, we were able to get them to hold off on closing the plant, which would have meant the loss of several hundred jobs and a blow to the Bay County economy. Later, SFI sold to Stone Container Corporation.

Randy had worked on administrative matters and we had consulted about staff during that week in Washington and, of course, we were trying to find our way around Capitol Hill as well as the Washington and Northern Virginia area. It was time well spent and we felt good about how things were shaping up as we flew back to Northwest Florida for the Christmas holidays.

After a wonderful period of time with loved ones over the Christmas period, we got busy preparing to head north. Randy rented a truck in Fort Walton Beach, loaded his possessions, then came by Panama City where we loaded on a few things that Nancy described as early marriage furniture that was excess to our needs in Panama City, along with sheets, towels, toys, stuffed animals, and bicycles for each of us. Most of our furniture, including our beds, were left intact at 3015 State Avenue, Panama City, because we would be back home often. When I was back in the district, I would sleep in my own bed if possible and during holidays and summer the family would be there.

Randy headed out with our furnishings, along with Steve Strickland and Robert Higdon who were going up to help us get settled before going on to college. I flew to Washington the next day in time to help them get the stuff in our rented townhouse. We also bought a couple of beds from a family in Springfield related to friends in Pensacola. One was a three-quarters bed and the other a single. Despite some discomfort, these fellows and I slept in beds we had and on the floor. I flew back to Panama City at week's end.

While I was in Washington, Nancy took the girls and went shopping for cold weather clothes. She checked Lori and Amy out of the Bay County School system which she described as very sad because of leaving long-time friends and heading for the unknown.

When I got back to PC and we started loading the car, we found this to be quite a trick. We had thought we could get everything in the vehicle. Wrong. I had to dash out and buy a car top luggage carrier. It turned out to be a great purchase as we have been using it ever since. We stuffed the trunk of the car, the top container, and inside the car to the point of putting a few plants in the back window and warm coats resting over the front seat.

As we got ready to leave our house, I saw a touching scene I will never forget. There was Lori hugging our dog, Zach, and sobbing "Bye, Zach...Bye Zach!" Zach was a pretty dog and one that we loved. He was an outside dog and there was no way we could take him to Washington. So, I had made arrangements with a young fellow, Randy Williams, who had helped with our yard work to come by each day and feed Zach and we would keep him in his own environment. Two weeks later when I was back in Panama City, Zach appeared to be okay. But the next time I came he was nowhere to be found and we never saw him again. We often wonder if someone stole him. Our girls still accuse us of neglect in our treatment of Zach.

Anyway, packed to the hilt, we pulled away from Panama City in late afternoon that day and headed for a new world. After a brief stopover for dinner at a restaurant in Dothan , Alabama where I saw a few old friends who wished us good luck, Nancy and I alternated in driving through the night while the girls slept soundly. It was very cold along the eastern seaboard and as we stopped for breakfast in Concord, North Carolina one of our girls, seeing icicles hanging off buildings, shouted, "Mommy, Daddy, look at the ice nails!" They had never seen ice like that.

It was bitter cold weather with a lot of ice as we arrived at our new abode in Springfield. Having only the three-quarter and one twin bed, we went straight to a shopping center and purchased a king sized bed for Nancy and me and double beds for Lori and Amy. But guess what? They would not be delivered for two weeks. So, Nancy and I slept in the three-quarter and Lori and Amy traded turns from night to night sleeping on the twin bed and box springs.

Our girls were enrolled at West Springfield Elementary School. Fairfax County has a good school system and we were pleased with Lori's fifth grade teacher and Amy's third grade teacher. They did well in school despite the fact that Amy had not had multiplication in Panama City and her class in Springfield had finished it. Amy buckled down and learned her multiplication tables. She also entered a word contest promoted by a Washington television station and heard her name announced on the air as the winner of a tee shirt.

It made good sense to buy a house instead of renting so that we could build up some equity. But we thought it best to rent for a while until we could learn more about the area. In the Spring of '79, we purchased a home at 7404 Gambrill Road in Springfield and moved into it May first. Nancy went to work painting and putting up wallpaper. Wasn't it nice that my job kept me so busy that I could be of very little help to her? We put in some carpet and upgraded most of the early marriage furniture. I appreciated our home because I did not like the up and down living of a three-story townhouse. This would be our home for the duration of our time in Congress except for the last year and a half when Nancy and I lived in a cramped two-bedroom condo after selling our home.

On that momentous day in January, 1979, when I raised my right hand and was sworn in as a Member of the Congress of the United States, it was another mountain-top experience. Lori and Amy were allowed on the floor and, during the election of the speaker when members yelled out their votes, it was funny when they asked me why so many people were named O'Neill. Again, it would have been wonderful if my father and mother had been able to witness their son in such an exalted position, one of only 535 people representing the entire population of the nation. Another American success story!

We had briefly discussed bringing busloads of our volunteers from Northwest Florida to see me sworn in. However, most of those folks were either retired on a small fixed income or could not get off work. They could not afford to pay for their trip and we had no funds for it. However, a few home folks came for the big event, including

Wallace and Edith Kendrick and Harold and Shirley Phillips.

A few weeks after that, we had Billy Joe and Carol Rish as our house guests. It was always good to see home folks and through the years we would have a lot of our constituents come by my capitol office, which I always revered as "their office." If I were in, I tried to take as much time as I could to welcome them and tell them about how Congress operates. My staff made them feel welcome and we provided information on the many attractions around Washington.

For approximately my first year in congress I used public transportation to and from work rather than bucking all the traffic on Shirley Highway leading into and out of the city. I would catch a bus in Springfield, ride to a central loading zone at the Pentagon, and take the Metro subway into the capitol. Occasionally, in the morning, I would catch a ride from Springfield to the Pentagon or to D. C.

Many people would park their cars in designated parking lots in Springfield, line up next to Long John Silver's and catch a ride to work. From about 6:30 to 9:00 a.m. each weekday morning two single file lines waited for drivers, who wanted four people in their car in order to get in the express lane, to come by and pick them up. One line was for those going to the Pentagon and the other for downtown.

Several times Nancy drove me the two or three miles to Long John Silver's. I stood in line and usually in a short time I would have a ride, sometimes to the Capitol, and at other times to the Pentagon, where I would get the subway on in. Oftentimes, I did not have much to say to these strangers with whom I was riding. At times I got an earful about what they thought about Congress. I enjoyed their conversations, but I would not let on that I was a member. Sometimes it took all I could do to keep from snickering.

Soon, the irregular hours of the House sessions and my tremendous workload that caused me to work later hours led to my driving. Though there were times when I got into horrendous traffic jams to and from the Capitol, it was quite convenient to drive right to my parking place in the members' garage underneath the House office buildings. I went from the warmth of our garage to the warmth of the building I worked in without even wearing a coat. But I did have an overcoat in the car just in case of an accident or a breakdown.

After I started driving to and from work I did a turnabout regarding the carrying of passengers. If I were going in during rush hours, which was often, I would swing into the parking lot at Long

John Silver's, roll my window down, and shout, "Capitol Hill...L'Enfant Plaza?" If no one stepped out of line to get into the car, I added another destination, "Seventh and Independence?" It was not hard to get riders, although sometimes I might have to wait a few minutes for someone to show up headed my way. I would then get right into the express lane and zip into Washington.

Now that I was the driver, instead of passenger, I still heard some interesting talk. Often the passengers noticed I had a Florida license plate on my car and would ask, "Are you from Florida? What do you do?" Generally, my first response was that I worked for the government. But, if they pushed it, I would say something like, "I hope you do not have a Social Security problem because I am a Member of Congress." This was hard for them to comprehend. They could not believe they were being chauffeured by a congressman.

In all the years I drove to and from work in the Washington area, I am thankful for one thing--I did not have a single accident or a breakdown. There was one accident, however, that happened in the first month we were in Washington, before I started driving regularly.

Admiral Tom Kilcline and wife, Dornell, invited us to their residence on board the Washington Navy Yard for dinner. Dornell is a native of Pensacola like many other Navy wives. That is why Pensacola is known by many as "the mother-in-law of the Navy". Anyway, it was a lovely evening. Nancy had driven into the office and we left my car in the garage while we went to the dinner.

Afterwards, I got a wake up call about driving in Yankee weather. We went by the garage to get my car and I followed Nancy down Shirley Highway. It was beginning to snow and as we were going over the Potomac River bridge, traffic slowed down ahead. I applied my brakes. When I did my car went uncontrollably into a skid. How frightening! In those split seconds I was trying my best to keep that vehicle in the road. But it sent me into the left guard rail and almost immediately my car was hit on the left side by another car. It happened so quickly. The gentleman driving the other vehicle was nice and apologetic. I learned that he was a brother-in-law of John Haney, a retired Navy captain with the University of West Florida in Pensacola. Every time I saw John afterwards he always quipped, "Has my brother-in-law run into you lately in Washington?"

Thankfully, neither of us was hurt. However, it did considerable damage to my car and flattened my rear left tire. It caused an embarrassing massive traffic jam until the D. C. police got the vehicle to the other side of the bridge where Nancy had wisely gone and pulled off the side of the road. I have nothing but praise for the D. C. policemen. Two of them worked to get the mangled tire off and put on the spare. They went beyond the call of duty in being helpful without the slightest inkling that I was a Member of Congress.

That snow did not amount to much, but was enough to make driving hazardous. A few weeks later, we experienced one of the biggest snowstorms the area ever had. In February, around George Washington's birthday, we were hit by 21 inches of the fluffy white stuff. How beautiful! But, oh how inconvenient and bothersome at times. The whole Washington area seemed to practically shut down.

I left my office a little early on the afternoon the big snow started to fall. As usual, I took the crowded Metro subway to the Pentagon. What a mob scene! Everybody was trying to get home. From the Pentagon I would always take a Metro bus to Springfield. But this day the crush of people caused the buses to run late and they were full. It would be a long wait in line. Suddenly a fellow came up and said, "I need riders to get in the express lanes to Springfield." How lucky, I thought! In those days it took four people per car to get in the express lanes to and from the city. I quickly volunteered.

I had never seen such a spectacle. I had never seen as much snow. We headed for Springfield. We did not get very far. Cars were spun out on the freeway, many were stuck, and we proceeded at a snail's pace. Finally, we reached Old Keene Mill Road in Springfield. But before we could get to West Springfield, where we lived, we came to a slippery hill and a complete halt. I thanked the kind driver for the ride, got out of the car and walked the last mile. Time from office to home: six and one half hours! How nice it was to be with my family in the warmth of that townhouse!

At our townhouse we had difficulty getting the front door open because the snowdrift was so high. I was home for several days while our offices were closed. The whole family did have a jolly good time playing in the snow. It was the first time Lori and Amy had experienced snow and getting out of school added to their pleasure.

Though we had some snow every year, there was only one other time to rival the 21-inch job of February 1979. That was January 1982 and I'll go ahead and tell about it now. This one caused a lot of trauma for my dear wife, Nancy. When the heavy snow began to fall, we allowed our staff to go home. I called Nancy and told her I was heading out. I was driving this time and I was stalled in traffic on Shirley Highway when I heard the shocking news about a Air Florida plane crash into the 14th Street Bridge. I had crossed that bridge probably an hour before.

It was a terrible day...snowing heavily and extremely cold, freezing weather. Believe me, after that one and only accident I ever had I was extremely careful. But, on this occasion there was not much need of applying the brakes because the traffic was moving so very, very slow.

Meanwhile Nancy was at home monitoring the radio and TV. It was announced that Fairfax County Schools had closed. A couple of hours went by and the buses had not delivered our girls. Nancy and Caroleen Rector, her friend who also had a child in school, commiserated with each other on the phone. Then, she heard about the plane crash and people being hit and killed on the bridge. That was my route and she couldn't help wondering if I could have been involved.

As my slow pace continued south I listened to reports of the tragedy. Finally, after more than four hours, I got to the Springfield exit. I stopped at a service station and called Nancy to let her know I was okay. By then, although I knew nothing about the school buses running so late, the girls were home. Nancy had really been worried, but now she began breathing easier. However, it took me a couple more hours to drive the remaining three miles to get home. The bottom line: six and a half hours from DC to home, the same amount of time as in the other big snow. As I drove down the hilly driveway of our home, Nancy and the girls ran out to greet me and hug my neck. Thank God, we were all safe and sound on a terrible day!

There was no question about it--this was not Northwest Florida and we had a tale to tell about a day the likes of which we hope never to see again!

Nancy Hutto shakes hands with Rosalyn Carter as she and Earl go through a receiving line at the White House. Also shown are President Jimmy Carter and Vice President Walter Mondale.

The Hutto family members--Earl, Nancy, Amy, and Lori--are shown on the east steps of the United States Capitol.

13

DAVID AND GOLIATH

Being able to get on the right committees is a very important matter for Members of Congress. Generally, most members want to be on committees that will relate best to their districts and their people. For me, that meant the Armed Services Committee. The Democratic Steering and Policy Committee and a similar committee for the Republicans make nominations for these assignments. Even before I arrived in Washington and after I got there, I lobbied the Steering and Policy Committee members very hard for Armed Services. Being nominated for these assignments is tantamount to election, although the full House perfunctorily votes on them.

The nominating committee has a number of members appointed by the leadership and the rest elected from regions. Florida is in a group with Alabama, Mississippi, and Louisiana. John Breaux, of Louisiana, had been elected our representative on Steering and Policy. He was the one who was supposed to carry the ball for me. Up until the day and right up until the actual time the committee met to make nominations, Breaux had assured me the freshman from his home state of Louisiana, Buddy Leach, was not seeking the Armed Services Committee and that it looked good for me.

Guess what? When John Breaux called me after the nominating session, he congratulated me, not for getting Armed Services, but on being assigned to the Public Works and Transportation Committee as my major committee and the Merchant Marine and Fisheries Committee as my non-major committee. And Buddy Leach of Louisiana? He got Armed Services. Enough said.

So, I had come up empty in my bid to get the committee most needed to serve my district and country. I believed from the depths of my heart that, to protect our precious freedoms and lead the free world, we needed to improve the strength of the U. S. military.

Not getting on the Armed Services Committee would not deter me from supporting the military generally, and the First District in particular. For a while, however, it looked like I might have another problem--that of having to contend with being undermined by my predecessor, Bob Sikes.

The Pensacola News-Journal, in late June 1979, ran a story with a front page banner headline, SENATE LAST HOPE FOR USS LEXINGTON. The article quoted Sikes as saying the House had passed an appropriations bill without funds for dredging in Pensacola to accommodate a replacement carrier for the Lexington, the aged training carrier that supposedly was headed for decommissioning. Sikes added that the Senate was the community's last hope for keeping a training carrier after the Lexington was scrapped.

Although I am known as someone who is cool, calm, and collected, I can tell you that this story burned me up. I can be tough when I have to be. What was the old guy up to? I had to call his hand on this. I phoned the News-Journal Editor, Earle Bowden, to set the record straight.

The next morning the paper carried a story with the headline: NAVY WANTS TO KEEP CARRIER HERE -- HUTTO. Carlton Proctor, PNJ Writer, correctly quoted me in saying Sikes's statement about the future of the Lexington contained "false and misleading" information which "unduly cause conern and worry" for Pensacolians.

The article quoted me as saying the bill that passed was the Energy and Water Resources bill and the Military Construction and Defense Appropriations bills had not been passed by the House and it would be possible to include the Pensacola project in one of these, "but, if this does not happen, we will be ready to go next year and it will still be timely." I also made it clear that the first step toward channel and turning basin deepening had been taken by the Navy and a $250,000 request for an environmental impact study, funded internally, had been forwarded to Chief of Naval Operations by Admiral Paul C. Gibbons, CNET in Pensacola.

Tom Culligan, my legislative assistant, also was quoted as saying that in recent conversations with Florida Senators Chiles and Stone I had been assured of their support in the Senate for the dredging project. He reiterated that I had also been working with the Military Affairs Committee of the Chamber of Commerce to keep carrier training in Pensacola.

Not surprisingly, Sikes took exception to my rebuttal. He called me in Washington and when I answered, he said, "Alright, you've called me a liar." I said, "No, Bob, those are not the words I used." I was firm with him and went on to tell him I welcomed his comments, but I did not want to be undermined in what I was doing.

A few days later on July 4, Independence Day 1979, the News-Journal carried a front page story with a banner headline SIKES' SHADOW DIMS HUTTO'S SPOTLIGHT. My picture was on the left with 'haunted' captioned underneath and Sikes photo on the right had 'still the star.' Here is the text of the article by Chris Collins, Gannett News Service:

Washington -- Rep. Earl Hutto may not believe in ghosts, but he's being haunted by one: Bob Sikes.

Like most ghosts, Sikes still roams the corridors he frequented in the past -- before he left Congress where he represented the Florida Panhandle for 38 years. His wails of distress, heard both here and in Florida, send shivers through Hutto, who replaced Sikes as the Panhandle's Democratic congressman only six months ago.

Unlike other ghosts, however, Sikes still is very much alive. In theory, the once-powerful subcommittee chairman, who was reprimanded by the House three years ago for some allegedly questionable business dealings, has retired to his hometown of Crestview, "to start living like a Floridian," as he said last year when he announced he would not run for a 20th term.

But when Hutto went to testify before a Senate subcommittee last week, there was Sikes, ostensibly in town to sell his house. At the subcommittee chairman's invitation, Sikes sat at the head table with all the senators still in office, staring at Hutto while he gave his testimony.

When Sen. Lawton Chiles, D-Fla., held a hearing in Crestview to probe a train accident, there was Sikes, showing up unannounced and expecting to testify. Although scheduled speakers usually testify first, Sikes was allowed the star position as leadoff witness.

And when a newspaper editor in Pensacola picks up his telephone, often it's Sikes on the other end, warning him of something awful going on in Congress. Here, politicians scratch their heads in bewilderment when told what Sikes is saying, because his story doesn't jibe with what they know.

It is hard to determine whether Sikes is trying to undermine Hutto or just can't stand sitting on the sidelines in Crestview, watching someone else representing "his" district and basking in the spotlight that was his for 38 years.

The two don't talk about it in public. Although he refused to endorse Hutto or any other candidate during last year's election, Sikes has had only the nicest things to say to reporters about Hutto and vice versa.

And, because Sikes is a living legend to many, in his district, it's virtually impossible to get Florida politicians or staffs to say anything but polite nothings about Sikes.

Privately, however, Floridians here speculate if the two Panhandle Democrats were to really speak their minds, Sikes would brag that Hutto will never fill his shoes and Hutto would ask Sikes to do him a big favor and go fishing.

Most doubt Sikes has anything personal against Hutto. Instead, they assume he finds it hard to exchange the hectic life he led here for a retired life in Crestview.

Others speculate that Sikes' ego never recovered from the battering it took when the House reprimanded him in 1976 for allegedly questionable financial dealings and stripped him of his long-time position as the powerful chairman of the military construction appropriations subcommittee. He's been trying ever since, they say, to prove he still is indispensable to the Panhandle.

"I just think the old boy...he just can't let go", a long-time aide to another Florida Democrat says. "He's got nothing left now except his monumental ego."

Others feed that ego. When a Panhandle TV crew came to Washington to interview Hutto, for example, they were taping a special broadcast on Sikes' life, not Hutto's. And Sikes is in demand as a speaker in his old district.

There's sympathy here for Hutto, who's generally considered a competent, earnest politician. While he may never set the world on fire, the consensus is that Hutto is learning the congressional ropes quickly and will develop into a good congressman -- if Sikes doesn't torpedo his chances for re-election by making him appear to be a duffer.

"From Hutto's position, it must be tougher than hell," one Florida staffer sympathizes. "He just can't afford to let the guy dig holes for him, but he can't say much against him. What Sikes is doing is not helping Hutto at all; there's no way you could put that face on it, unless you're a fool."

Ironically, the first to bring the issue up was Sikes.

"I'll be trying to help the district any way I can" Sikes said of his post-retirement plans in an interview a year ago. "Probably make a nuisance of myself with the person who succeeds me up here, tell him how to run his business. And I'm sure he'll want a reasonable amount of advice."

Wouldn't you know that very night as Nancy and I arrived in Crestview for a Fourth of July program at the stadium, the first people we saw were Bob and Inez Sikes. It was like there had never been any conflict. They were as friendly as could be and invited us to sit with them during the program, which we did. Afterwards, we took them up on their invitation to come by their house for ice cream and cake. We were dying to see the inside of their house, anyway. During our stay nothing was said about the flareup between Bob and me.

The visit at the Sikes Crestview mansion was indeed pleasant, and I do not recall another time in my 16 years in congress that Mr. Sikes tried to undermine me. I was aware, however, that each election he tried to get someone to run against me.   Outwardly, he was friendly and oftentimes in succeeding years he would make some comment, like "I don't think you have anything to worry about in the next election." Sikes even gave $100 to my campaigns a time or two.

I appreciated Mr. Sikes and his support of the military and, despite the fact that I knew of his behind-the-scenes support of my opponents, I always felt kindly toward the old gent.   Although he divorced Inez and married Joan, a younger woman, during the first few years of my tenure, Inez was always a good friend and supporter.

In the middle of September, 1979, Hurricane Frederick struck the Gulf Coast, inflicting some damage in the Pensacola area, but causing a lot more devastation around Mobile and the Mississippi coast. I responded quickly in trying to help through my office. The day after the storm, Congressmen Jack Edwards (R-Alabama) and Trent Lott (R-Mississippi), along with my administrative assistant, Randy Knepper, and I were flown by a Navy T-39 jet to our districts to inspect the damage and help coordinate recovery efforts.

Randy was seated in the back seat adjacent to Congressman Lott. Minutes before landing in Pensacola, we heard a commotion in the back seat. We turned to discover that Randy had thrown up all over the Congressman. Trent was a good sport and we all had a good laugh. When the plane landed in Pensacola to let Randy and me off, before going on to Alabama and Mississippi, Lott went to the restroom to try to clean up a bit before flying on.

Trent Lott always dressed immaculately, so it must have been hard to explain his appearance when he faced his waiting constituents in Mississippi that day. Trent went on to become elected to the U. S. Senate in 1988, and on June 12, 1996 was elected Majority Leader, following Bob Dole's resignation from the senate to run for president. Meanwhile, Randy Knepper can claim a distinction that probably no other American can claim. Is there anyone else who can say, "I once upchucked on the majority leader of the U. S. Senate?"

Florida Governor Bob Graham met me and other officials at the Emergency Operations Center in Pensacola and, after praising and encouraging the workers, we took a helicopter tour of damaged areas, mainly Pensacola Beach and around Perdido Bay to the west. The newspaper report stated that the governor lauded me for playing a key role in getting a disaster declaration for the affected Florida counties.

The next day I met President Jimmy Carter at NAS when he flew into Pensacola aboard Air Force One. Several helicopters took the president's entourage and Congressmen Lott, Edwards, and me on a flyover of coastal areas of the three states. On board my helicopter was White House Press Secretary Jody Powell.

This was a memorable time from another standpoint. It would be the only time I would ride with the President of the United States aboard Air Force One. President Carter invited me to fly back to Washington with him. An added bonus was that I also flew with him from Andrews Air Force Base to the White House aboard his helicopter, Marine One. The reason that both of us needed to get to the White House was to attend the swearing-in of new Trade Representative, Governor Reubin Askew of Florida. Nancy and other members of the Florida delegation met us there for the ceremony.

When I got to Congress, I faced a huge issue relating to my district. For four straight years, the House had voted to consolidate undergraduate helicopter pilot training from Whiting Naval Air Station in Milton with the Army program at Fort Rucker, Alabama. It had only been stopped by Florida Senator Lawton Chiles in the Senate and in conference committee. I had my work cut out for me. If Bob Sikes, with his nearly four decades of seniority and position on the Appropriations Committee, as well as his chairmanship of the

Milcon Subcommittee, could not defeat this move, how was I, as a lowly freshmen, going to do it?

It was a foregone conclusion that with a freshman representing the area where Whiting is located this was going to be the year that consolidation would be approved. Even the Navy had thrown in the towel. Navy Secretary Graham Claytor seemed to have this as his biggest mission. Even the White House was pushing it. The entire Alabama delegation was supporting the consolidation effort. Congressman Bill Dickinson (R-Ala), a senior member of the Armed Services Committee on the minority side, in whose district Fort Rucker is located, was the spearhead. He had successfully offered an amendment for four straight years to move the Navy training from Whiting to Fort Rucker, winning by big margins.

This was like David going up against Goliath! It appeared that everybody in powerful positions was against me. I started to work on this monster at the very outset of my first term. I began talking personally, one on one, with my colleagues and explaining that consolidating the Navy and Army programs was like mixing apples and oranges. Their missions are different. I also had information refuting GAO's contention that it would save $100 million.

These personal contacts provided a wonderful way for me to meet and know my colleagues on both sides of the aisle. Nearly all agreed this consolidation was not the right thing to do. I did not stop this quiet crusade with just the House. Tom Culligan and I worked the Senate which had been more inclined toward our position in the past.

Senator Sam Nunn, then Chairman of a Senate Armed Services subcommittee, held a hearing and I testified against consolidation. Former Congressman Sikes was present, but did not speak. Among those testifying for it was Brig. Gen. Carl McNair, a Pensacola native who was deputy commander at Fort Rucker. Carl, an energetic young flag officer who would later, as a two star, become commanding general at Rucker, was in essence going against his home area, and so was I in going against consolidation at Rucker, where I once worked and where a bunch of my kin folks still worked.

When the full Appropriations Committee marked up the defense bill, an amendment for consolidation of undergraduate helicopter pilot training from Whiting to Fort Rucker was offered. Primarily due to the efforts of my Florida colleague, Bill Chappell, this effort was defeated. It is doubtful this bothered Bill Dickinson, because it was on the floor where he had always won the amendment..

The date of September 27, 1979, will forever be etched in my memory, for two reasons--that is our daughter Lori's birthday and on this particular day I won an enormous victory in Congress. It was the date the bill came to the floor. The battle lines were drawn! However, my sense is that Bill Dickinson, who had won so easily in the past, really did not think there was going to be any battle. Why should there be? He had won so overwhelmingly in prior years against a powerhouse congressman and now, going against this little freshman just getting his feet wet, would be a snap.

Did we have news for him!

Nancy was in the gallery waiting to see what was going to happen. As a matter of fact, she quickly learned a lesson when she was called down for having papers and pen in hand while in the gallery. She did not know there was a rule against that and was sitting writing checks to pay our bills. Culligan was there with her.

As the amendatory process began, I saw Congressman Dickinson saunter into the back of the chamber. He seemed very loose and relaxed as he took a seat toward the rear of the chamber. It was not that way for me, or Nancy, or Tom Culligan, or the folks down home. There was a tenseness that I could feel. Could we pull it off? I honestly don't believe Dickinson knew I had been working so hard on this. Had he known, he might not have looked so relaxed.

Dickinson still appeared confident when he rose to seek recognition. The presiding chairman of the Committee of the Whole House: "For what purpose does the gentleman from Alabama rise?" Dickinson: "Mr. Chairman, I have an amendment." "The clerk will read the amendment." Dickinson: "I ask unanimous consent that the amendment be considered as read in full." Chairman: "Without objection.The gentleman is recognized for five minutes." At that point, Dickinson strode forward to the well to make his presentation.

He explained that the amendment would move the Navy helicopter pilot training from Whiting NAS, Florida, and consolidate it with the Army helicopter training at Fort Rucker, Alabama, saving the government $100 million. During his talk, I interrupted and asked him to yield. He did and I asked him some questions about the nature of Navy helicopter training and its need for flying over water, as well as the fact that the Navy primary training included flying in T34 fixed wing aircraft as well as the TH57 helicopter. I also pointed out that in the long run there would be no savings, but actual losses. It was obvious that we disagreed on the efficacy of this proposed move.

I had only spoken on the floor briefly a few times. Now was the time for me to speak out. I knew that the folks back home were watching on C-SPAN. Also, WCOA Radio in Pensacola had made arrangements to carry the debate. When legislation is debated in the House, the body resolves itself into what is called the Committee of the Whole House which means that it takes only 100 members for a quorum. The speaker appoints someone to preside, who is called chairman of the Committee of the Whole House.

When Congressman Dickinson concluded his speech, I rose for recognition. The Chairman: "For what purpose does the Gentleman, Mr. Hutto, rise?" "To Speak against the amendment." The chairman: "The gentleman is recognized for five minutes." I went to the well of the House and spoke sincerely on why the proposal to consolidate was not in the interest of the Navy or Army, or for our defense. Congressmen Bill Chappell (D-Fla) and Dick White (D-Tex) had fought this before and spoke again on the issue.

During my speech, I was pleasantly surprised at the number of members on both sides of the aisle who rose to ask me to yield and agreed with me. These included some liberal members with whom I was seldom in agreement, like Tom Downey (D-NY). Also supporting me against consolidation was Steve Symms (R-Idaho).

Perhaps the most important supporter in this debate, however, was Joe Addabbo, Chairman of the Defense Appropriations Subcommittee. Bob Sikes had not had kind remarks to say about Addabbo, but I had gone to his office to talk to him about this issue when I first arrived. I found Joe to be a warm, friendly, and decent person. Of course, he was liberal on many issues and he and I would not vote the same on a lot of measures. But from all I could gather, Joe Addabbo was a man of honesty and integrity. He would remain a friend who would help me on numerous military matters in the First Congressional District of Florida. In this fight, I am sure that, as the manager of the bill, his support helped me greatly.

In the gallery, Nancy and Tom hung on every word. I am sure it was the same with many back in Northwest Florida. I truly believed, and I feel this has been borne out, that this was not just a parochial issue. It would have been a drastic change in the way the Navy trains its pilots.

Debate concluded, the chairman put the question. On voice vote the chairman ruled that the nays had it. Good! But, I knew that would not stand without a recorded vote. I was right. Dickinson said "Mr. Chairman, I ask for a recorded vote." A sufficient number rising, the chairman advised the vote would be taken by electronic device. The machines were opened and members began to vote.

Oftentimes people visiting in the gallery and watching congress in session are surprised at the few people on the floor. The fact is that if all the members stayed on the floor during debate there would not be time to get other things done, such as meet with constituents, answer phone calls, and a multitude of other things. Usually, most of those on the floor during debate are on the committee that handled the legislation through the committee process. Other members stay abreast of what is happening by keeping up through the news media day by day as well as reading summaries and information on bills, and keeping an eye on the House proceedings by television in their offices.

As the vote was called on Dickinson's amendment, most of those then on the floor voted nay, and it always seems to help if the votes start going your way early. This was encouraging, but most of the members had not yet voted. As they flooded into the chamber, Congressman Dante Fascell, a member of the Florida delegation from Miami, was heard to say, "Help Hutto get re-reelected. Vote no." Well, I thought, this probably would be something that would help.

The vote followed the early trend and the number of nays on the electronic tally board continued to mount. The digital clock in the chamber was winding down and we still had a large lead. I think we all were beginning to feel a little relieved. I probably thought back to those days in the state legislature, though, when my colleagues switched their votes at the end. But, this was for real. No trick. We were winning! Finally, time ran out and a few stragglers voted in the well after the machines had been closed. The chairman then announced the vote, "On this amendment, the yeas are 131 and the nays are 244, and so the amendment is not agreed to."

Glory be! We had done it! After four straight years of voting to consolidate the Navy and Army helicopter pilot training, the U. S. House of Representatives had voted overwhelmingly against this onerous proposal that had upset so many people in the Milton and Northwest Florida area. The final vote of 131-244 are important numbers I will remember.

What a victory! It is easy to see why I have this date etched in memory. It was not an ordinary victory. It was so fantastic because it completely turned around a decision the House had made for four straight years, including 252-128 to consolidate a year ago.

The streamer across the top of page one in the Pensacola News-Journal the next day read, WHITING WINS HOUSE COPTER FIGHT. An inset box had my picture and a sub headline 'I FEEL BETTER!' EXCLAIMS HUTTO. Yes, I did feel better. I also was quoted as saying, "This is a big relief. I hope this has killed this issue for good!"

Congressman Jack Edwards (R-Alabama), a good friend but a fierce opponent in the consolidation fight, was the ranking minority member on the Defense Appropriations Subcommittee and he had spoken for Dickinson's amendment as he had year after year. Reporters wanted him to come out to the Speaker's Lobby to talk to them about the vote, but he declined because he was still involved in debate on the bill. But, according to the PNJ article, he sent out a terse message: "We got our fannies beat." Edwards also said, "I hope this ends the argument. Four years is enough!"

Dickinson was unavailable for comment. I was told that he was devastated. It apparently took him a long time to get over the defeat. But, to his credit, he bore no personal grudge against me and we worked together on the Armed Services Committee on many issues in later years.

Bill Dickinson was not the only one devastated by the defeat. Navy Secretary Graham Claytor took it hard...and Robert B. Pirie, Jr., Assistant Sec. Of Defense, said, "We may have been complacent. We certainly expected it to go through the House and Senate this year."

The Pensacola News-Journal ran an editorial titled, TIME TO BRING END TO 'COPTER DEBATE. The Milton Press-Gazette ran one titled HUTTO MAKES HIS MOVE OUT OF SIKES' SHADOW. One paragraph of that editorial read, *"It wasn't just that Hutto is a freshman legislator, and puny as all freshmen are, but Earl had the added burden of trying to fill the shoes left by Bob Sikes, the he-coon of Northwest Florida and its sugardaddy for 38 years in the House. It was just too much to expect of a mortal man, the sages explained. But he stopped it cold in the House, something Sikes had been unable to do the past four times the matter has come before Congress.*"

There were other complimentary articles and columns around the state, including Bruce Dudley's column in the Tampa Tribune of Sunday, September 29, 1979, titled CONGRESS LEARNS HUTTO CAN PROTECT HIS LAIR. The latter part of the article went like this: *How did Hutto do it?* "*He personally talked to over 300 congressmen himself,*" *said Hutto aide Tom Culligan,* "*He wrote personal letters to each congressman. Not form letters, but personal letters with personal notes. It's a hell of a victory and shows his style can work up here.*" *The word is out on Capitol Hill: the shoes of Robert L. F. Sikes have been filled.*

Just as stunned over the defeat as Dickinson were the two Alabama Senators, Howell Heflin and Don Stewart. The Alabama delegation conferred with DOD officials as to their next move. They decided to raise the issue on the Senate floor. About six weeks later, on November 9, they did that, offering an amendment for consolidating helicopter training from Whiting to Fort Rucker. Sensing that they had little support, they pulled the amendment before it came to a vote. By not voting, Senators Heflin and Stewart felt they could mount another drive for consolidation the next year.

Our Florida Senators, Lawton Chiles and Dick Stone, were disappointed there was no vote on the amendment. They knew they had the votes to kill it, but leaving it hanging probably meant that they would have to face this again in the future. Senator Chiles, in speaking of DOD's dilemma after the House defeat, said to the media, "They failed to figure into their calculations the Earl Hutto factor." I was grateful to both Senators for their support and laudatory comments. Senator Stone, later, in Milton, praised me for winning.

Senator William Proxmire (D-Wisconsin) and Alabama's Stewart accused the Carter administration of intentionally abandoning its fight to move the helicopter training from Florida to Alabama in order to help President Carter in a straw vote at the Florida Democratic state caucus. The White House denied it. I can deny it, too, because I remember the fire in the eyes of the Navy Secretary and other DOD officials as they lobbied to bring about the consolidation.

One thing you can say for the Alabama delegation, they have continually pressed DOD through the years to switch Navy helicopter training to Fort Rucker. Senator Stewart was defeated at the polls in 1980, but Senator Heflin, throughout his 18-year Senate career pressured DOD to consolidate. He, and Senator Richard Shelby, as late as 1995, were pushing for it in the base closure and realignment process. Senator Howard Metzenbaum (D-Ohio) was another ardent supporter of consolidation. But, the truth of the matter is, the overwhelming victory against consolidation on September 27, 1979, was the death knell for this movement.

Lori and Amy kept calling on my private line all afternoon wanting me to come home so they could open Lori's presents. Lori's birthday was even more special because of what happened that day!

I was awarded two beautiful plaques for winning the Whiting fight--one from the Pensacola Area Chamber of Commerce emboldened with a couple of spurs and proclaiming that I had "earned my spurs," and the other from the Santa Rosa Chamber which noted that I had earned my "Navy Wings of Gold."

Our prayers were answered. Right had prevailed. I was grateful to Tom Culligan and my staff, to the Association of Naval Aviation, and in particular to retired Rear Admiral Mark Hill, of the ANA, who provided me with a lot of good information and encouragement in this battle. I was likewise deeply appreciative of my colleagues for supporting me. I treasured the respect in which I was held by those with whom I served. It was a big, big issue, but now it was time to move on!

14

TIP O'NEILL COMES SOUTH

There are many congressional families in the Washington, D.C. area who are hurting. The children and the spouse have been plucked out of their home areas and thrust into an environment which many do not like while the congressional member is consumed by his or her responsibilities and other interests. They have lost their community involvement and have not made new friends. It is a lonely life--and sometimes leads to a breakup of the family. How sad.

When I came to the Congress and our family moved to Springfield, Virginia, Nancy and I resolved to maintain our family lifestyle as we had known it and not to get caught up in anything that would cause Lori and Amy not to have a loving home, or to feel neglected in any way by their parents. I made it a point to get home each evening so we could have family togetherness before the girls went to bed. We supported them in their school work and kept communications open with their teachers. One of the most important things we did was to establish ourselves with a church. This gave us a wonderful support group and made us feel like we belonged. The friends we gained at First Baptist Church in Springfield meant a lot to us. Much of our activities centered around the church and were especially beneficial to Lori and Amy as they grew up in that area.

Even though it was necessary for me to get back to my district often, I made sure, on the two or three weekends I did not go to Florida each month, we spent quality time together as a family. We had wonderful and memorable times during our girls' childhood.

It is understandable that it could be confusing and difficult for some to get used to living in two homes. We maintained our home in Panama City and I stayed there most nights when I was back in the district, unless I was scheduled for an early morning event at the other end of the district, in Pensacola or Milton. We wanted our girls to continue to be oriented to our part of the country. The family was back in Florida during the summer and during holiday periods. Lori found it more difficult to adjust than Amy. It was tough to leave your friends in one place and then, about the time you get used to new friends, you go back to the other place.

After losing Zack, Nancy and I thought it would be good to get the girls a new dog for Christmas, 1979. We found the cutest little snow-white poodle among a litter owned by a family in Panama City. On Christmas eve, after Lori and Amy were tucked in bed and we were sure they were fast asleep, Nancy's father and I went to get the little fellow. We put him in a box with a clicking clock, which we were told would make him feel like he was with his mother.

Can you imagine the joy the girls experienced when they found this adorable puppy under the Christmas tree the next morning? Though, like most American children, they had more than one present, they simply could not keep their hands off their new pet. Since he was not yet named, Amy suggested that maybe since he arrived at this time of year that perhaps we could name him St. Nicholas. This name was agreed to, but with the quick stipulation that he be called by his nickname, "Nicky". Thus, Nicky came into our lives and would remain with us for 13 years. He was the first indoor pet that we ever had and he was a fixture as "one of us." He grew quickly, but when he was grown he weighed no more than about eight or ten pounds. Back in Springfield, he was so white he blended with the snow when we put him outside. Each night, as I entered from the garage and made my way upstairs, there was Nicky, at the top of the stairs, waiting for me, standing on two feet with paws going up and down and barking with every breath until I picked him up and loved him. Nicky loved people and wanted the attention of everyone he saw. He had one big fault: he barked incessantly.

Both of our girls are very caring about pets. Amy wanted a gerbil and saved her money to get one. It was a good thing she also got the tubular house, in which it lived, because Nicky would not have wanted anything to compete with him for attention. We did not know if the new addition was male or female, so Amy named it Herman.

Herman gained a measure of fame. When the family went home to Florida that summer we left him at my office so that the staff could feed and water him (er..it). The news media learned of this and AP ran a story telling about Herman, the unique "intern" in Hutto's office. Another time when the family was in Florida and I was in Washington during the week, I had Herman at our Springfield home. But, I did a terrible thing. I forgot to feed it and Herman died.

Carol, my District Administrator in Pensacola, would often call at night. She would call collect and I would call her back on the

WATS line. Nancy suggested, during that time period, that Carol ask for Herman and we would know that it would be she who was calling. One night, after the family was back home, Carol called and Nancy answered the phone. The operator said, "I have a collect call for Herman Hutto from Carol Biven. Will you accept the charges?" In her devilish way, Nancy replied, "I'm sorry, Herman has expired." The operator, obviously saddened, sighed, "aww..I'm so sorry."

Members of Congress are busy people. I could never get caught up completely with what I wanted to do. Even after I got home at night and after the kids, and Nancy as well, were in bed, I was on the phone to people back in my Florida district. Oftentimes, I took the family into the capitol and did some work on Saturdays.

During the week I had a schedule card prepared by my staff that I kept in my pocket to tell me where and at what time I was supposed to be at this meeting or that. It was not unusual to have more than a half dozen receptions on my card toward the end of the day. Of course, there was no way I could attend all these receptions or dinners. Many of them I regretted, and others I would respond that I would attend if possible. I would have my secretary to put (ip) for those that I had advised "if possible." Usually, if I had constituents or people involved in the subject areas of my committees present, I would attend those receptions. Many times, if my family was back in Florida and I knew I would not get supper at our Springfield home, I attended the receptions I thought would have the best food.

I think it is a matter of vast importance that a Member of Congress not let his or her staff run their life by making out schedules which the member knows nothing about. These schedules are often loaded down with meetings, dinners and receptions which that member should not be attending. I fully believe I was blessed with the best staff in congress, but I made sure that I went through the invitations personally and okayed every event that I felt I should attend. Practically everyday I had a folder full of invitations to both Washington and Florida events placed on my desk.

I had no problem with my administrative assistant or secretary screening the invitations and making recommendations. But, I then wanted to read those invitations myself and decide what my schedule ahead was going to be. I also kept a featherweight date book in my pocket at all times so that I could better manage my time. I have seen some House members, and Senators, who are wound up like a clock. They just take that schedule card and go where it directs them, often spending time at unnecessary events.

In the busy workaday world of Congress, as in any occupation or routine of daily living, it is important to get exercise. I have always tried to stay physically fit. In my early years in Congress I utilized the House gym quite a bit, playing paddle ball with other members or shooting basketball if there were no paddle ball players around. I gradually quit using the gym. I mostly got my exercise by running around in our home, walking up the stairs of the office building, playing tennis infrequently with my daughters, and playing golf.

Once in a while when I was back home I would try to schedule a golf game with Homer Singletary, Al McLeod, and others in the Pensacola area. In Fort Walton Beach Fred Pryor would line up a foursome, and occasionally I played with church friends in Panama City. But, for the most part, I was on the go when I was in Northwest Florida speaking to churches, civic clubs, and special groups, as well as holding office hours, conducting town hall meetings, and attending other events.

In February of 1980 I was the recipient of the God and Government Award, sponsored by the Greater Cantonment Ministerial Association, at its fifth annual awards breakfast at the Sheraton Inn in Pensacola. Governor and Mrs. Fob James, of Alabama, were there and Mrs. Bobbie James was the featured speaker. I was most appreciative of the award, and in later years I have attended and served as the speaker at this award breakfast.

Congressional elections come all too frequently. One hardly has time to learn the ropes and get into the process before it is time to run again. Frankly, I have said for many years that the two-year House terms should be expanded to four years. In fact, I filed a bill for a constitutional amendment to accomplish this, and although I think most of my colleagues believe this should be done, it is a touchy matter and few want to be perceived as voting to extend their own terms. So, I got only a few members who signed on as co-sponsors. It is tough to get a two-thirds vote for a constitutional amendment, but I hope someday it can be passed.

I truly believe the time has come to have four-year House terms. Why? Because when the founders wrote the constitution they did not even have telephones, let alone the modern means of communications. Now, not only do we have telephones, we have radio, television, faxes, e-mail, and all kinds of instant communications. In those early days horseback was the best way to travel and it would take days or weeks to get back home. Now, with modern jet travel a congressman can be back in his district in no-time flat. The framers of the constitution rightly wanted the House to be close to the people. How close can you get? My bill provided staggered four-year terms with half of the House members up for election each two-year cycle. It would cut down by half the amount of money a House member would need to raise, providing at least a measure of campaign reform. It would allow congressmen more time for oversight of our government rather than spending so much time trying to raise money for their re-election.

Anyway, absent longer terms, I had to be ready every other year to get out there and campaign. Fortunately, I liked campaigning. I just didn't like to do it so often. And I hated raising money.

My supporters and I decided we should have fundraising dinners in our district's three largest cities--Panama City, Fort Walton Beach, and Pensacola in the first quarter of 1980. For these $50 per plate events we would try to have a speaker who would help us draw a crowd. But who could we get?

I saw Speaker Tip O'Neill, when he happened not to be in the speaker's chair, sitting in the chamber chatting with another member. That was early January. More or less out of courtesy, I decided to approach the speaker. I was quite sure he would not or could not come to my district for one of these dinners. But it would not hurt to ask. I said, "Mr. Speaker, I was wondering if you might do me the honor of speaking at a fundraiser in Panama City, Florida the night of February 8th?" "Ull (that's Bostonese for Earl), I will have to check my calendar and get back with you on that."

It was my thought that the speaker was nice to even consider speaking for a conservative Democrat in a district that had always been in the Democratic column. Later that afternoon, my secretary came into my office and said Speaker O'Neill wanted me on the phone. "Ull", he said, "that's a good date. I'll be happy to go down to Panama City and speak for you on the eighth of February."

I could not believe it! Tip O'Neill coming to Panama City? That ought to bring out some folks. We got busy planning the dinner for a Panama City Beach motel and everything shaped up real well. The day of the big event Tip flew into Panama City by private plane early enough for a round of golf. He loved the game. Wallace Kendrick, a member at Panama Country Club, set up a Friday afternoon game with Tip, Florida Lieutenant Governor Wayne Mixson, Tip's pilot Bill Rutherford, and me in the foursome. We had a ball and Wallace especially got a kick out of the high fives Tip gave him every time he made a good shot.

It was said that Tip O'Neill was the highest government official to visit Panama City. That night, as people gathered for the fundraising dinner, one gentleman, upon entering, was heard to ask, "Where is the bar?" He was quickly answered by someone nearby, "Are you kidding? A bar at an Earl Hutto event? You know, ol' Earl doesn't drink anything stronger than Coca-Cola." The inquiring person was told that he would need to go next door for his drink.

Tip O'Neill was a smashing success! A big crowd was there and Tip wowed them with his quick wit and vast repertoire of Irish jokes. Donnell Brookins, witty at the mike, was the emcee. My good friends with whom I served in the Florida legislature, Billy Joe Rish and Wayne Mixson, were there. Wayne, who was serving concurrently as Florida lieutenant governor with Thomas P. O'Neill, Jr, in the same job in Massachusetts, introduced Tip as the speaker. It was evident there was a lot of good will and excitement that night.

O'Neill, after keeping the crowd laughing for awhile, then spoke seriously and eloquently about the issues confronting our nation. I was relieved to hear him, in praising me, make it clear that he and I often differed on some of the votes taken in the House. I was, indeed, grateful for his good comments about me, and even more pleased that my constituents agreed with him wholeheartedly.

After dinner, people absolutely swarmed around Tip. They really loved the guy. The ladies all wanted to get their pictures taken with this affable Bostonian who had charmed them throughout the evening. In fact, the speaker's reception was so good that he would, a year or so later in the midst of a partisan struggle with the Republicans, mention in a Washington Post article how well he had been received in Panama City, Florida.

Speaker O'Neill wanted to get in another round of golf the morning following our Panama City fundraiser. He wanted me to play and I was sorry that I could not play with him again. But, on that Saturday, I had a full schedule of activities all across my district. However, we arranged for the speaker to play another course.

Lieutenant Governor Mixson was again in the foursome. After golf, Tip O'Neill flew back to Washington that afternoon, obviously pleased at the reception he had received in the conservative south.

I had first met Tip O'Neill after my first election when Andy Ireland, then a Democratic congressman from Winter Haven, who switched to the Republican party about six years later, took me to the speaker's office to introduce me to Tip. Winter Haven was the spring training site of the Boston Red Sox and both O'Neill and Ireland were rabid Red Sox fans. I think this common interest fueled their close friendship, which may have waned a bit when Andy switched parties later on. Anyway, I found the speaker to be warm and personable.

Back in Washington after the Tip visit, the Democratic Steering and Policy Committee voted unanimously on March 11, 1980 to put Earl Hutto on the House Armed Services Committee. This was super good news for me and my district. I had enjoyed serving on the Public Works and Transportation Committee, which I would now give up, and it was valuable that I had the opportunity to establish rapport with committee members and staff. But for my district, laden with military facilities, it was crucial that I have membership on the House Armed Services Committee (HASC).

Nomination by the Steering and Policy Committee is tantamount to election, and rarely is its recommendation overturned. So, the next day, March 12, the House of Representatives voted without dissent to put me on the committee. I expected, after failing to make the committee at the start of my first term, to get selected for this assignment in my second term. Now, I was ahead of schedule in achieving this goal, a pleasing turn of events.

The vacancy had been brought about when Daniel Flood (D-Pennsylvania) had resigned from Congress. Flood was a member of the Appropriations Committee and Vic Fazio (D-California), supported by the large California delegation, wanted to fill that slot on appropriations and was successful in getting it. That left the vacancy on armed services to which I was elected. My assignment met with favorable response from the media and my constituents back in Florida. A committee staffer was quoted as saying that my achievement in getting on the HASC now would give me the jump in seniority over those chosen for the committee in the next congress. This would inure to my benefit in getting a subcommittee chairmanship somewhere down the road.

Well, one of my campaign fundraisers was now taken care of, but we had two to go. Since I had asked the Speaker of the House, I thought perhaps I should also check with the Majority Leader about speaking at the other two dinners. So, I asked and, sure enough, Jim Wright consented to speak in Pensacola and Fort Walton Beach in successive appearances March 14 and 15, 1980.

Good going! To have the two top leaders of the House speaking on my behalf in my district was more than one could expect. I was pleased that Jim Wright, a southerner from Texas, would be with us. The Pensacola event was held at Grotto Hall, a meeting facility of the shriners. Six hundred people were on hand to hear the majority leader, who was one of the most dynamic public speakers in congress. Pat Lloyd, of the Pensacola News, ran teasers in her column over a period of several days about the dinners in Pensacola and Fort Walton Beach. Gerald Newman, Al McLeod, Dot Waldon, Pete Lord, and Henry Smith headed the ticket sales for Pensacola.

I blush when good things are said about me, so I am sure my face was red a good part of the time while Jim Wright was talking. He praised me, as he had when the two of us had held a news conference upon his arrival in town, for my election that week to the prestigious Armed Services Committee, a vital position for my district. The leader also spoke of my winning battle last September in keeping helicopter training at Whiting Field in Milton, Florida and not allowing it to be transferred elsewhere. He pointed out that my winning arguments were based on what is good for the United States of America. Bottom line--a good event! Two down and one to go.

The next night, March 15, our dinner was at the Ramada Inn in Fort Walton Beach. As in the other fundraisers we had a good turnout. Randy Knepper, my Administrative Assistant and a native of Fort Walton, did a lot of coordinating on this one. Some of those assisting were his parents, Harold and Myrtle Knepper, Frank Grubb, Jerry Hollingsworth, Fred Pryor, and Richard Duke. It went off well. Jim Wright made a good speech and gave me good marks for my first term achievements, pointing out my support of the military. He specifically mentioned my work on behalf of Eglin Air Force Base, Hurlburt Field, and Duke Field, all in Okaloosa County.

The last of my three planned fundraisers had been held and all were successful. I think we netted less than $30,000 on the three events, but with my low-budgeted campaigning this would go a long way in my re-election effort.

"So long, Tip. So long, Jim." Though Tip O'Neill and Jim Wright had both been well-received in northwest Florida, I could never again invite members of the Democratic leadership of the House to come to my district. The year following these events was when the Republican Party did a super job of portraying Tip O'Neill, in a media blitz, as a strong-armed liberal leader who twisted our arms to get us to vote his way. Of course, Tip was liberal, but he was no arm twister. I remember only one time in the eight years I served under him that the speaker personally asked me if I would vote his way on a certain bill, which I will explain later. Anyway, to have Tip or Jim Wright to come back into my conservative district after 1980 would have been flirting with political suicide.

There were only three other congressmen and one senator, however, that I brought into my district to speak for me during my next 14 years in Congress. All were conservatives. Bill Nichols (D-Alabama) spoke at a $50-per-plate dinner in Fort Walton Beach and did a fine job, although a couple of local doctors complained about the food. Can you believe that? How did they expect us to make any money for the campaign if we fed top-of-the-line steaks?

Sonny Montgomery (D-Mississippi) spoke at a luncheon for me in Pensacola one year, and in a later year Bill Chappell (D-Florida) spoke at a fundraising breakfast in Fort Walton Beach. Nichols and Montgomery were both cohorts of mine from Armed Serivices. Chappell chaired the Defense Appropriations Subcommittee.

Congressman Charlie Rangel (D-New York), a high ranking member of the Ways and Means Committee, whose wife, Alma, is from Panama City, came to visit his mother-in-law in the summer of 1981. He did not speak for me at a fundraiser, but we did stage a dinner at a beach restaurant so that some of the local community leaders could get to meet Charlie, a good friend, and a very personable and effective lawmaker of African-American descent.

Back to business, guess what happened at my very first meeting with the Armed Services Committee? Although I was given a warm welcome by the group, I quickly found myself in another battle with Bill Dickinson over helicopter consolidation. Oh no, I thought, this can't be. I was confident we had laid this matter to rest, but now it stared me in the face again. But, this was not as traumatic and I felt we would have no trouble winning this little set-to.

After we had overwhelmingly won the battle on the floor the previous year to save Navy helicopter training at Whiting Naval Air Station, I had worked to make sure Whiting had the resources it needed to do the job. Now, in my first official meeting as a member of HASC, we were marking up the defense authorization bill for FY81. There was funding in the bill in the amount of $33.6 million for T34c fixed wing training aircraft and for TH57 helicopters for Whiting. Now, here was Dickinson offering an amendment to delete this $33.6 million authorization. I think he felt that if he could deny funding he would starve the Navy program and force consolidation.

After Dickinson explained his amendment, Chairman Mel Price said, "Does the new member from Florida, Mr. Hutto, wish to be heard on this amendment?" A big chuckle went up from the committee. They all had remembered this issue for too long. When I responded, "Yes, Mr. Chairman, I sure do," another round of laughter was forthcoming. In my argument against the amendment, I basically pointed out that this issue should be moot in view of the House vote and it was necessary to provide our Navy the resources it needed to train its pilots. When the vote was taken, the committee soundly defeated Mr. Dickinson's amendment.

One of the most unpleasant tasks an employer has, in my opinion, is firing an employee. Dick Foreman had served me well as my administrative assistant in the Florida legislature. Dick had a beautiful family, including three very bright children. Unfortunately, he had problems with an alcoholic wife which greatly affected his work. Dick strived hard to keep his family together, which I appreciated. In view of this, although he had been slack in his performance, I continued to employ him by naming him my district administrator for the eastern part of the district when I was elected to congress. However, after some five months in this capacity, Dick's work continued to deteriorate. I had no choice but to let him go. Regrettably, Dick was divorced not long after that. But the good news is that he went into insurance and has done quite well.

At first I thought I might try to use volunteers to run the Panama City office, but after realizing it would be impossible to provide good service to constituents in five counties I knew I had to have a full-time replacement for Dick. Nancy had suggested that I should hire Earl Hadaway, with whom I had worked many years at Channel Seven, but I was hesitant to ask him because I knew he had more than 20 years service there and might be reluctant to leave because of retirement benefits. Surprisingly, I got a call from mutual friend, Donnell Brookins, suggesting that he thought Hadaway might be receptive. Indeed he was, so I hired Earl at that time and he remained with me throughout my congressional career.

Americans were deeply concerned and upset that 50 of our people had been held hostage in Iran for many months. In late April, 1980, a daring rescue attempt turned sour and was aborted after an on-ground collision and fire at a staging area in a desert in eastern Iran.The Pensacola News-Journal praised President Carter for ordering the rescue attempt and most everyone agreed that it was the right thing to do. But, despite the bravery of those involved, the failed mission pointed out the need for more emphasis on special operations. Our committee held a number of hearings on this tragic foul-up in Iran which, without a doubt, was the leading factor in getting the military, though sometimes grudgingly, to begin putting more emphasis on special operations.

The Iran debacle hit close to home. Five of the eight servicemen killed in the mishap were stationed at Hurlburt Field. The Air Force flew Senators Lawton Chiles and Dick Stone and me from Washington down to Hurlburt to attend a memorial service and to meet with the families in offering our support and sympathy. Nancy had sent along with me Gideon New Testaments for each of the families. These were true heroes who had given their lives for their country. And, in my view, it was not in vain because it kept our nation focused on the hostages and assisted Congress in getting the military to improve our capability to perform such missions.

I had expected to have opposition in my run for a second term, but no one surfaced until Warren Briggs announced on June 2, 1980 that he was going to run for Congress again. There had been some rumors that Warren might give it another try, but I could not quite understand why he would. I had a good first term that exceeded my expectations and, I am quite sure, the expectations of a lot of other people. We had reversed what could have been the eventual closing of Whiting NAS and now I had gained membership on the Armed Services Committee.

How did Warren think he could do any better than last time? I think the answer was that it appeared Ronald Reagan would be the Republican nominee for president. Running on the same ballot, with a well-financed hard-hitting campaign, I believe Warren thought, would give him the boost he needed. For whatever reason, Warren had what I thought was a good explanation in the paper. He said, "Last time was for practice. We had so much fun we thought we would try it again."

Another matter that I had to contend with was the influx of Cubans, many of them undesirable prisoners and mentally ill people which Fidel Castro turned loose on us through the Mariel boatlift. Eglin Air Force Base became one of the distribution centers with upwards of 10,000 of these folks crammed into "Tent City" or "Camp Libertad." I opposed using Eglin, particularly because we had done our part in handling Vietnamese refugees a few years earlier.

Cubans have become some of our best citizens. But the conditions were not good at Camp Libertad and residents in the area were against them being in their community. It was hot weather, there was a problem with sanitation, there had been a few escapees, and some of the refugees had been involved in a rock-throwing melee. My office and I worked with General Bobby Bond at Eglin, and John Macy of the Federal Emergency Management Agency in trying to expedite the settlement of the refugees. It took several weeks, but finally the camp was phased out.

Public officials have to take a lot of flack, some of it justified and much of it not. That's the nature of the game. I tried to have a thick skin and most of the time I could take this sort of thing in stride. In my first term in office I had voted for a windfall profits tax because, at the time, the oil companies were raking in the profits due to deregulation of oil prices. I thought it was the right thing to do, inasmuch as proceeds from the windfall bill would be used for research in developing alternate fuel sources and lessening our dependence on oil. In town hall meetings that I had held I received favorable comments and a good exchange of ideas. But, it was not exactly that way in Jay, Florida.

When I walked into city hall at Jay I was faced with a room full of folks who were not too happy with my vote. I was given a petition signed by 178 Jay residents who thought the windfall profits bill was a disgrace. Okay, I had to face the music. Oil had been discovered and production in progress in the Jay area of Santa Rosa county for the last few years. The small royalty holders would be hit by the new tax. I understood their being upset. In response to a question, I told them that the purpose was to look to the future of our country in the development of other fuel sources and a portion of the tax would reduce individual income taxes. The good folks in Jay were civil and understanding and I have been back there many times, always getting a royal welcome. I also received a high percentage vote in Jay through the years.

It was good to mix with the people at the various events in our part of Florida. I fondly remember one Independence Day in Westville at the town hall, formerly the old Westville school building. A number of federal, state, and local officials were on hand. A full row of celebrities were seated on stage and each was called on to say "a few words." Some went beyond a few words, but generally the comments were light and humorous. I will never forget the joke that a judge told about a visiting preacher who spent the night with a family of the local church. The preacher and the man of the house had a glass of milk before retiring for the evening. By pre-arrangement, unbeknownst to the preacher, the wife put her husband's nightly toddy in one of the glasses. It seems she got the glasses mixed up and the preacher got the one with the toddy. Asked how his milk was, he exulted that it was the best he had ever had and could he have a second glass?

I don't remember the exact punch line to the joke, but the funny thing that day in Westville related to one of the county officials who arrived after that story had been told. When it came this gentleman's time to speak he started out by saying, "I heard this story about a visiting preacher coming into town and staying in the home of a church member." Before he could finish the first sentence, the audience was roaring with laughter. As he kept telling it, the crowd became hysterical. I'm sure he must have thought that this was the funniest joke he ever told. Finally, Lieutenant Governor Wayne Mixson, seated nearby, tapped the official on the shoulder and told him that someone had already told that joke.

It always has given me a good warm feeling of satisfaction to help someone who is deserving. In the summer of 1980 I was able to get through the House and Senate and President Carter signed into law a bill to compensate David Cosson, a victim of a mistaken bombing during World War II. In August of 1944 the Army Air Corps at Eglin Air Base was doing night-time bombing practice when the release mechanism on one of the planes malfunctioned and dropped 16 fragmentation bombs on the Cosson home below. Four members of the family were killed and five were injured. David's father, uncle, and two cousins died. David, 12 years old, suffered a severed spinal cord and injuries which required the amputation of a leg. In 1945 a claim was paid by the Army for $259 and a sum of $6,000 was paid to the family for the father's estate. My bill provided David, 47 at time of enactment, an annual pension of about $18,000. I realized this, in and of itself, did not compensate David for a lifetime of paralysis and pain, but I felt it did indicate his country cared.

My election campaign of 1980 had a different twist to it. What happened, you ask? Well, believe it or not, I was run over by a Republican. You heard right. I was run over by a Republican in September, but vowed I would not be run over by one in November.

Here is how it happened: It was "batter up" in the annual congressional baseball (not softball) game between the Democrats and Republicans on September 24, 1980. This was the second of these games in which I had played and this one was later in the year than normal because of the busy congressional schedule. I was playing first base, as I had the year before. Big Pete McCloskey (R-California) was at the plate. Remember him? He's the liberal Republican who had run against Richard Nixon in a presidential primary. I do not know if Pete remembered the year before when I had put him out by catching a little pop fly near the first base bag. Maybe he did remember and was trying to avoid a repeat. This time he hit a little humpback liner down the line toward first base. I dashed in and leaned forward for the catch. I saw stars!

While I was attempting to catch the ball I saw stars as McCloskey's knee caught my chin. I was down on the field. Players from both sides gathered around. Baseball Commissioner Bowie Kuhn was in the stands and he came down to join the others in seeing how badly I was hurt. I was bleeding above my eye and that was what everyone was looking at. But I kept grunting, pointing to my chin, and mumbling "this is where it hurts." All agreed I should go to the emergency room with my injuries. Several offered to take me, but Nancy and the girls were there and she told them she would take me.

The family headed for Bethesda Naval Hospital, but we were sweating a low gas tank. We made it okay and the doctor cleaned my wound and took some stitches in my eyebrow. Nancy asked him about the hurting I had in my jaw. The doctor replied, "Ma'm, I don't know, I'm a pediatrician." We chuckled and went home for the night.

The next day I went to see an oral surgeon and found out the inevitable, I had a hairline fracture of the jaw. Dr. Russell said my jaw should be wired up but, realizing that I was about to start an election campaign, he was hesitant to do it. He suggested that we let it go for a few days and then take more x-rays to see if it were growing back properly. Since the Congress was about to adjourn and knowing that I would be back in my district within a few days, the doctor referred me to Dr. David Boggs at Eglin Air Force Base, Florida.

The jaw continued to hurt and I went by Eglin to see Dr. Boggs. After taking another round of x-rays, he determined that my jaws had to be wired shut and proceeded to do just that. Can you imagine a politician going through a campaign with one's jaws wired shut? Nancy had to mix up all my food in a blender and I sucked it with a straw through the corner of my mouth. I must have done that quite successfully as I did not lose any weight during the campaign.

The Associated Press and other media carried the collision story all over the nation. Here's what AP reported:

Washington (AP) - Congressmen of opposing teams usually clash in debates only, but Rep. Earl Hutto, D-Panama City, Fla., was nursing a fractured jaw Thursday after a smashing collision on the baseball field.

The Republican congressman who ran into Hutto--Rep. Pete McCloskey Jr. of California--was unscathed.

The collision took place Wednesday night during the annual charity baseball game in which the congressional Democrats play the Republicans.

McCloskey, trying to beat out a hit, collided with Hutto as both tried to occupy first base.

Hutto suffered a hairline fracture of the jaw and had to have several stitches in an eyebrow.

McCloskey not only was unhurt, he was safe.

But Hutto's side won the game, 21-7.

The morning after the clash, Pete McCloskey came by my office and brought a basket of flowers with a bottle of booze tucked inside. I could not use the booze, but it was thoughtful of McCloskey. He offered to come down and campaign for me, but I said, "No thanks, Pete, you're too liberal for me and my district."...and he was!

Don Priest, news director at WCOA, Pensacola, called me and told me Charles Osgood of CBS News wanted to feature me on his Osgood File broadcast. I guess he thought it would be unique and funny--a politician who could only mumble near-inaudible sounds through one side of his mouth. I agreed for Don to tape me by phone and Osgood made a production of it on his morning program on CBS.

Lo and behold, my opponent, challenger Warren Briggs offered through the media to debate me with *his jaws* wired shut. He was quoted as saying, "I'm up against a very perplexing situation. How do you run against a man who can't talk? I want to be fair and it occurred to me that maybe Earl would give me equal time if I wired my own jaws." I responded that I hoped Briggs would, indeed, follow my lead. "I understand he's been issuing daily medical reports on me all over the district. I do wish Doctor Briggs would have his mouth wired up."

The calamity I suffered on the baseball diamond caused a shuffle in family plans for that election season. I could not, with my broken jaw, handle the situation without Nancy being with me. So, our decision, which was the right one, was to take Lori and Amy out of school in Springfield and bring the whole family back to northwest Florida. Amy was enrolled in the fifth grade at their old school, Northside Elementary in Panama City where a good friend, June Grubb, was her teacher. Lori, though, because she was in the seventh grade, went to Mowat Junior High in nearby Lynn Haven, and had excellent teachers also. After the election, they returned to school in Springfield. We had wonderful cooperation with schools in both locations, but this was the last time we would change schools for our girls during a campaign.

The race was off and running, broken jaw and all. One of my volunteers, Pella Pompier, a resident of Pensacola who had worked on the Hill with Senator John Sparkman of Alabama, acted as my interpreter in debates and joint meetings with Briggs. I would whisper in my muffled tones to Pella what to say and she would relay it to the audience. The News-Journal ran a great picture of me speaking into Pella's ear and her looking smugly at Warren. He had a look on his face as if to say, "What in the world is going on here?"

As expected, Warren did tie himself to Ronald Reagan, and also to Bob Sikes again. When a gentleman from the audience asked if I were keeping a relationship with Congressman Sikes, I replied, "Yes, he is a constituent and whenever he comes by my office in Washington I see him like anybody else from our district." I noted that Sikes had once told me that if he were in congress he would have voted the same way I did in the 1979-80 session. That was a fact, but Briggs did not believe it and maintained that Sikes called him every few days with a lot of good advice. And one statement Briggs made astounded everyone. He said, about my winning of the helicopter fight for Whiting, "We must remember that most of that situation was solved by Bob Sikes."

Neither Briggs nor I had primary opposition, so it was just the two of us doing a repeat of two years before. I campaigned hard as I always did. But so did Warren. On the Friday before the election, as usual, the two congressional candidates met for a debate at the Tiger Bay luncheon in Pensacola. Nancy and I had a surprise up our sleeves. That morning we had gone by the doctor's office and had my jaws unwired. When we got to Pensacola for the debate, I did not let on and quietly had my usual milkshake for lunch. My friend John Hodges was there to introduce me, so he was the only one we shared this news with beforehand. We asked him to say something in his introduction like, "As you all know, Earl has a broken jaw and has had his mouth wired up. He has been unable to talk, but it is a pleasure for me to introduce at this time, his wife, Nancy."

I suspect that the audience thought Nancy was going to give some introductory remarks and then I would speak through an interpreter, as I had before, during the questioning period. Instead, she said, with some flare, "We have a Halloween surprise for you. Now, here's Earl!"

How happy I was! At long last I was liberated, and it felt good to be able to talk again. I went to the microphone and spoke plainly and forcefully. Wow! I was able to respond to some of the distortions and innuendoes of the last several months. I did it by saying something like this, on several different subjects: "You have heard statements that would indicate that I am a liberal. Do you know what's wrong with that? (Pause) It just isn't so."...and I explained that I was only one out of two in the House and one in the Senate who received a zero rating from the American Civil Liberties Union. How conservative can one get?

In my campaigning around the district I was thankful for old friends and new friends who stood by me. In Santa Rosa County, for example, Sam and Ethel Dixon, of Pace, who had been at Troy State part of the time I was there, were the only two people I really knew in the county when I first ran for congress. Sam had called me up when he first heard I was running to tell me he wanted to help. And help he did! I spent several nights in their home. Sam, and his brother-in-law, Earl Hawthorne, took me all over the county introducing me to a lot of people. Mr. Mason West, of the Jay area, was a big help in my early races before he passed away and Don and David West, with other members of the family, gave me good support. In later years, Mahlon McCall and Nora Jones chaired my campaign in Santa Rosa County.

Though I had less time to campaign in 1980 and was handicapped by my broken jaw, I worked just as hard as in any previous campaign. I never took anything for granted. That was the first time I had run for congress in a presidential election year. The presidential race, as well as the campaigns for county sheriffs, seems to always bring out a higher percentage of voters. That was the case on November 4. There was a heavy turnout at the polls as people exercised their American right to choose their leaders.

It was very difficult, each election night, for the Hutto family to find a way to celebrate with people all across the 100-plus miles expanse of the First Congressional District. However, each year, we did our best to have some kind of election-night party in each of the largest population centers. Initially, we started out with a Panama City celebration in early evening before the polls were closed, stopped by Fort Walton Beach at our headquarters, and then went on to Pensacola. When our children were with us, in those early years, this arrangement was tiring for all of us. So, in future campaigns we started out in Pensacola. After the first returns started coming in I would do interviews with the media and then we would head to Fort Walton and on to Panama City to wind up the evening at home.

It was most gratifying for us to receive the encouragement and best wishes from so many people during the campaign. And they expressed this when they went to vote in this second contest between Briggs and me. Ronald Reagan carried our district by a landslide. However, though I was bucking the tide of a very popular candidate of the other party, I also won a landslide victory. The final count showed Hutto with 119,829 votes and Briggs with 75,939. My total was the largest vote ever cast for a non-presidential candidate in our district. But, percentage-wise, Warren was two per cent better than in our first contest. Warren Briggs, as in our first election, conceded gracefully and called to congratulate me. He has continued as a community leader in Pensacola.

This had been a campaign to remember. I joked that I was run over by a Republican...on the field, but not at the polls... that I might have started a trend in national politics by going through a campaign with my jaws wired shut...I could not talk...but I won!

I was keenly aware my contract had to be renewed by the people every two years. I always felt, and said to my staff, that if we did our work as it should be done, the people would keep us in office.

As we approached the '82 election, the Senator who came down to speak for me was a famous one, Senator John Glenn (D-Ohio), the first American to orbit the earth. The event was held Saturday, May 15, at the Pensacola Interstate Fairgrounds. Mullet fish, when fried fresh, is delicious and it is sometimes, in our area, referred to as the "soul food of politicians" because it is served at a lot of rallies. Max Dickson, Chris Banakas, and other volunteers did a great job of frying and serving this delicacy. We charged only $10 for the John Glenn appearance and a good crowd showed up. Tickets were available around the area and also at the gate.

Who wouldn't want to see someone who had gone around the earth three times in five hours at 17,500 miles an hour and at maximum orbital altitude of 162 statute miles? Senator Glenn also was testing the waters for a presidential bid in 1984. So, this was the backdrop for the event and we were happy to have a lot of good supporters and potential supporters turn out, as well as many elected officials from the local to state level. Mayor Vince Whibbs presented Glenn with a key to the city. Lt. Governor Wayne Mixson emceed and among others present were Escambia County Commission Chairman John Frenkel Jr. and my predecessor, Bob Sikes.

"The Earl Hutto Fish Fry featuring Senator John Glenn" was a happy occasion. Bunny Bradley's Band played music for the late afternoon family event and everyone seemed to have a good time. During his speech, Senator Glenn mentioned his possible presidential candidacy in '84, but for me and my supporters his most important words were, "If it ain't broke, don't fix it. Earl is doing a good job for you in congress. Send him back."

Senator Glenn, and his wife, Annie, who Nancy really enjoyed getting to know better, were big hits with the people. Folks were clamoring to get autographs or have pictures made with our distinguished guests. We were very pleased, indeed, to have these outstanding people with us in northwest Florida.

In 1982, Terryl Bechtol, a former national Jaycees president who touted credentials of having worked for President Reagan, announced his candidacy against me with much ballyhoo. To demonstrate that he was going to run a mud-slinging contest, he threw out symbolic mud packets at his gatherings. It did not work. The vote count: Hutto 82,569, Bechtol 28,373. This was a solid 75 per cent victory, my highest. Bechtol since has taken on the nickname of "Bubba" and does motivational and humorous speaking.

After my first election to Congress, I did not have primary opposition for ten years. But I had a general election opponent every election except in 1984. That year no one announced against me, Democrat or Republican, so it was one of those "best kind of elections," a renewal for another two years on the job without my name even being on the ballot.

Before my election to Congress I had never been to a political convention. Subsequently, in 1980 my family and I attended the National Democratic Convention at Madison Square Garden in New York. This was the first time that Nancy and the girls had been to the big city. Besides watching the interesting convention sessions, we had an opportunity to see a lot of the Big Apple. Lori and Amy particularly enjoyed seeing a live network television program, David Letterman, who then had a daytime show on NBC.

In 1984, having no opposition, we decided to combine a trip to the National Democratic Convention in San Francisco with the only extended vacation we ever had. My smart wife lined up some low-cost transportation for the family. We drove by rental car from Panama City to New Orleans, where we took in the World's Fair, then flew to Phoenix, where we rented another car. The Grand Canyon was one of the first sights we saw out west, then we motored to San Diego so the girls could see the Koala Bears in the San Diego Zoo. After a couple of days there, we casually made our way up the coast to San Francisco by convention time. We arrived in time for the excitement of seeing the Olympic torch being run down the streets of San Francisco on the way to the '84 Olympics in Los Angeles.

This was the convention at which Geraldine Ferraro, with whom I had sat on the House Public Works Committee, was nominated as the first woman, in either of the major parties, to run for vice president. After the convention, we reverted to Nancy's super savers and flew back to New Orleans. There, we rented another vehicle and drove home to Panama City. It was 17 wonderful days together of which we have many photographic memories.

While we're on the campaign trail, let's run through my other elections to Congress. For the 1986 election I did not have to wonder who my opponent was going to be. A retired colonel announced a full year ahead of time his candidacy as a Republican, though he had previously been registered Democrat and Independent, back and forth a few times. In reality he conducted a vicious letter writing campaign a full two years before the election. Although the letters to the editor bore different names from time to time, it was obvious to most who the author was. I asked one of the elderly ladies we knew, whose name was listed on several letters, why she would write such erroneous letters. She admitted the colonel had written them. Thank God, the public could not be fooled. The election results: Earl Hutto 97,532, Greg Neubeck 55,459.

I had made a couple of very responsible votes which, nonetheless, I had to defend in that race. I not only voted for the Gramm-Rudman deficit reduction bill, I was in the chair presiding when the final conference report was passed in the House. Those who believed we should take tough steps to get the deficit under control voted for this. It provided automatic cuts through sequestrations if the deficit went beyond certain limits. It was not something we liked, but it was the only mechanism we had for trying to get the deficit under control. I had sought to get the conference committee to exempt military and civilian retiree cost of living adjustments from possible cuts, the same as Social Security. Failing this, even after Gramm-Rudman passage, I introduced legislation to exempt those making less than $12,000 from the cuts.

There was a great hue and cry about including these COLAs for possible sequestration. The argument was that every group should be treated the same. I agreed. There was a proposed budget that would do exactly that. It was known as the Leath amendment and I, and 55 other brave souls voted for it. Guess what? The same folks were highly critical of that vote, too.

There is a chapter of The Retired Officers Association which has a member, said to be a triple-dipper, who used the organization's newsletter he edited to launch an eight-year vendetta against me for my vote for Gramm-Rudman. He even passed out the newsletters at political gatherings. A federal case could have been lodged against him for using this non-profit organization's reduced mailing rate for political purposes. There was also no paid political advertising disclaimer, as required. However, I had no desire to hurt the man. A lot of his comrades, and particularly the national organization, were highly embarrassed by him.

I co-sponsored a balanced budget amendment throughout my congressional career and I feel strongly, that for our future generations, the deficit must be eliminated, so I was willing to take the political risks. I was pleased that a number of military and civilian retirees, some friends of my opponent, agreed with me that something had to be done about the deficit. In a district with more military retirees than any in the country, many obviously voted for me.

During some of our casual conversations in Congress, the subject would often turn to how our campaigns in '86 were shaping up back home. When I was asked what my opponent was saying about me, I would reply, "He says I'm a liberal." Everybody who heard that I had been referred to as a liberal laughed out loud. So, I got an idea for a campaign ad.

I had a TV camera set up and when several members came by, the question was asked, "Is Earl Hutto a liberal?" Each of them broke out laughing and we got that and their comments on tape. We edited it down to brief laughs and comments of three members-- Charles Stenholm (D-Texas), Sonny Montgomery (D-Mississippi), and Bill Whitehurst (R-Virginia). Whitehurst's comment was "If Earl Hutto's a liberal, Ronald Reagan's a liberal." We ran this 30-second spot on TV in my district and I haven't heard anyone else call me a liberal. Anyone who keeps up with these matters knows that my record is one of the most conservative in Congress.

I relied almost solely on volunteers in my campaigns. The few people I hired were generally part-time. In one election, Sarah Anne Gay was my coordinator and in another Chloe Hadaway served in that capacity, both in Panama City. Fran Boudolf and Edwina Hagler, on separate occasions, ran my Fort Walton Beach campaign office.

The 1988 Democratic Convention in Atlanta would be the last

one our family would attend. Michael Dukakis, of Massachusetts, was nominated for president. One of the speakers I had seen before at a Florida convention, but whom my family had not seen, was Arkansas Governor Bill Clinton. It was obvious this fellow was grooming himself to one day be president. But I thought he had absolutely doomed his chances forever with a boring speech that night at the Atlanta convention, which everyone thought would never end.

I had Democratic opposition in 1988 for the first time in ten years. Dr. Durell Peaden, a physician-lawyer from Crestview, threw his hat in the ring. I have had a whole host of steadfast supporters in Crestview over the years, including Al and Faye McLain, Pete and Tot Holloway, Inez Sikes, and Mattie Morgan. Peaden and I had a good clean campaign. I won that primary 72,508 to 28,883. Later, Dr. Peaden was elected to the Florida House of Representatives in 1994, where he now serves.

My general election opponent was Ed Armbruster, Republican of DeFuniak Springs. He had been appointed to a vacancy on the Walton County Commission by Governor Bob Martinez. I am not sure why Armbruster, a realtor, wanted to run against me because I had been helpful to him in a rather knotty problem regarding the FHA. Like in other areas, we have some loyal friends and supporters in Walton County, Armbruster's home. J. W. Adkison, Jack Huggins, Pete Hinote, Gwen Lyles, James McHenry, and Ron Pugh are just a few of the good folks who have worked on my behalf through the years. On November 8, 1988 I received 142,449 votes, the most any candidate ever received in the First Congressional District, eclipsing the vote of 119,829 I received in 1980 when the district had eight counties instead of the five in 1988. Armbruster got 70,534.

In 1990 I again had a primary opponent, Steve Hudson, a building inspector from Okaloosa County. We had a positive campaign and on September 4 I received 53,648 votes and Steve got 19,779. Terry Ketchel, a lawyer who had worked on the Hill with Congressman Guy Vander Jagt of Michigan and had come back to Fort Walton Beach where he had gone to high school, was my Republican opponent.

This was a tough year and people were getting more and more frustrated with the partisanship and bickering in congress. This was the year the leadership from the White House and leadership in congress had summit meetings at Andrews Air Force Base trying to work out a budget. Congress was in session seven days a week. We were frustrated as much as the people back home. The final adjournment came so late I had only a week to campaign. Also, give Terry credit for running a hard, though negative, campaign. When it was over, I got 52.2 per cent of the vote, my lowest ever. The final tally on November 6 was Hutto, 88,416, and Ketchel 80,851.

Though Okaloosa County became quite Republican and the registration surpassed Democrats, I still had a lot of loyal supporters. To mention a few who attended our volunteer meetings regularly, there were Fred and Mayrelizbeth Pryor, Gloria and Morris Battle, Basil and Sally Bethea and Jim Glenn. Gloria spent many hours running our headquarters. In earlier years, retired Colonel Frank Grubb provided great support.

The Hutto family had one of the best kept secrets imaginable. For three years, since 1989, we knew that 1992 was going to be my last election. It is a secret we continued to keep until 1994. I could have retired one term sooner and personally taken the $190,000 in my campaign fund. I did not think it was right, although lawful, to do this. Besides, that was not our timetable.

Our family, having been to New York for the '80 convention, opted not to go to that city for the '92 convention. It was unbelievable that Bill Clinton, with the ill-fated speech in Atlanta, the scandal about him and Gennifer Flowers, and his embracing of the gay community, could get the Democratic nomination, and even more surprising, be elected President of the United States, even though, with Ross Perot in the race, it was with a 43 per cent vote.

For the third straight election I had primary opposition in 1992, this time from two opponents--Ernie Padgett, county manager for Santa Rosa County and Harry Keller, a military retiree, from Mary Esther in Okaloosa County. We had a good hardfought campaign. However, I was able to win without a runoff with 60,346 votes to Padgett's 17,373, and Keller's 10,411.

Ketchel had sent a pretty clear signal after the '90 election he would be trying to oust me again. He was waiting in the wings for the '92 general election. So was a third candidate, Barbara Ann Rodgers Hendricks, a nice lady, who was running as a Green Party entrant. Terry's big line was that he came within "a handful of votes" of beating me in the last election. When I remarked, in one of our joint meetings, that 8,000 votes is more than a handful, he stopped using that line for a while.

There was one thing that rather irked me during this contest. A staffer from Vice President Dan Quayle's office called me at my office in Washington and told me the vice president wanted me to know that, on a certain date, the vice president was going into Pensacola, in my district. He wanted to advise me he was not coming for my opponent and that he would not even be on stage with him. Well, it turned out just the opposite. Ketchel not only was with the vice president, but this was an airport fundraiser for him. The bothersome thing was not that it happened like this, but just that I was specifically told otherwise. It is possible that only a staffer was involved and Dan knew nothing about it. I did let Dan know that this was not a principled thing to do.

The procedure through the years was to hold Hutto volunteer meetings Monday nights in Panama City, Tuesday nights in Fort Walton Beach, and in Pensacola Thursday nights. In at least a couple of campaigns, with the specific approval of the ethics committee, I used Carol Biven half on staff and half on the campaign. This allowed her to do some of the important campaign work during working hours, keeping accurate records of the time. In later campaigns, she led the volunteers only on a off-duty basis, such as running the Thursday night meetings and related activity. Ben Collins, for the last several campaigns, served in this capacity.

Our volunteer meetings were very positive and upbeat occasions for my family and me. It was a time of great fellowship and we felt close to those who cared enough to help us in our campaigns. In Pensacola, Homer Singletary, my longtime friend from TV days, without a doubt, lined up more people to be volunteers than anyone. I think he recruited a good portion of the congregation from his church, Warrington Presbyterian. Homer did anything that needed doing, not only during campaigns, but also, after his retirement, as an unpaid staffer for my office. His son, Lee, helped a lot.

I am grateful that Chappie and Alice Creighton were among the first to be recruited. They have been at our side every campaign. Chappie has a special ability to organize and he was helpful in numerous ways, including compiling lists of people, marking precinct maps, and especially preparing delicious foods, whether at the headquarters or at their home. Grace Hawke is someone Homer and

I worked with at Channel 3 and she and next door neighbor, Beth Little, have been super-active in every election.

Others who were stalwart workers included Sisters Pella Pompier and Eileen Huddleston, Rex and Lola Berry, Major and Eloise Jimmerson, Jack and 'Reen Stewart, Margaret Kavalaskia, Peggy Orgussar, Barney and Theresa Barnes, Jerry and Chris Glenn, Virgil and Florence Frey, Charlie Taite, Ira Handrop, Bobbie Adams, Bob and Pat McCrary, Jimmy Grady, Don and Dot Harmon, Bill and Earline O'Toole, Jim and Drew Pennewell, Don and Anna Tripp, Captain Don and Martha Krehely, Marge Restucher, Colonel Bob Morrison, Zo Wilkinson and, obviously, hundreds more. Lori Roswold provided us delicious chocolate chip cookies each election.

A. W. Long is not only an active citizen who often expresses his views in letters to the editor, he also can build anything, with a master's touch. So can his brother, Bill Long. You can understand how indispensable they, with support from spouses Viola and Mary, were to our campaigns, fixing up headquarters, making and repairing signs, and numerous other things. Bill was sign chairman and he mapped out all Escambia county and made sure signs were in the right places. Businessmen Jim Marks and Grover Robinson III provided good sign locations. Betty McGill supervised media scrapbooks.

You met Al McLeod and Gerald Newman, from Pensacola, in Chapter I. They were assisted by Dick Sherrill, Max Dickson, Ruth Fillingim, and others in collecting contributions. When it came to fundraising breakfasts, which were held the last few years at the Pensacola Grand Hotel, Fred Donovan was the spearhead and others who were big players were Vince Whibbs, John Hodges, Win Davis, and Travis Bradley. Dick Sherrill, especially, did a super job of selling tickets to these events.

As we approached what would be our last election, there were so many around the district, without knowing our secret, who continued their enthusiastic support. Among them were Billy and Shirley Booker, Ed Downs, George Dailey, and John Harrell in Panama City. In the new boundaries of the district, I only had a small portion of Bay County and most of these folks were helping me out of friendship because they were no longer in my district.

Although I lost nearly all of Bay County, Holmes County was back in the district for the first time in ten years. It was good to attend the political rallies and to renew acquaintances with a lot of people, including Clerk of the Court Cody Taylor.

It was impossible for me to attend all the rallies around the district because some were held simultaneously. Oftentimes, if I could not be present, I would send a speaker. On a few occasions, Lori and Amy would attend and one of them would speak for me. Can you believe those daughters, who were ten and eight when we went to Washington, were now out there on the stump for ol' dad? My chest swelled with pride when I heard reports of what a good job they did.

As usual in a presidential election year, there was a good turnout at the polls across northwest Florida on November 3, 1992. We had lost our home out of the district in the reapportionment, but good friend June Grubb was still in the district and she allowed us to use her apartment as a temporary address, and we were grateful because we wanted to vote in our own district, although the law allows someone not living in a district at the time to be elected. Although the new district was much less favorable to a Democrat, our spirits were high and we felt good about the situation. During a portion of the day we were joined by friends in waving to voters entering the fairgrounds to vote in the largest precinct in Escambia.

That election night was typical of so many others, but for Earl, Nancy, Lori, and Amy, it held special meaning. We knew this was the last one, and in a way it was a shame that we could not share our secret with even our closest friends. But I did not want to be in a lame-duck position for two years. We would have to keep it mum until the right time. As the returns began to be announced by the media, we became aware that the people were again ratifying the hard work we had done on their behalf. The final tally gave Hutto 118,941 votes, Ketchel 100,349, and Rodgers-Hendricks 9,341.

This was a very gratifying election. First, I had a much larger spread than two years before. Also, this election meant that I had won in three differently configured districts, the first one in '78 and '80 when District I had eight counties, the second in '82, '84, '86, '88, and '90 when it was comprised of four counties plus about 90 per cent of my home county of Bay, and the last one in '92, drawn by a panel of judges after the legislature deadlocked, decidedly more Republican, which has five counties plus a tiny sliver of the western end of our home county of Bay.

Tip O'Neill has the record for continuous service as Speaker of the House--ten years.
Earl Hutto served under Speaker O'Neill for eight of those years.

Nancy and Earl Hutto are shown with President George Bush at a Christmas Ball at
the White House.

15

PRESIDENT REAGAN ON THE LINE

A new administration was coming into power as I began my second term in Congress in January of 1981. Ronald Reagan had beaten President Jimmy Carter and it was interesting, in a manner of speaking, to watch the changing of the guard. How exciting to be present, in person, to see the change of power in the greatest nation on earth! How comforting to know that this takes place every four years, peacefully, and not at the point of guns. There were no tanks and troops surrounding the capitol.

Members of the Senate and House of Representatives assembled in their respective chambers and then marched to the ceremonial area on the west front of the capitol building. After we got to our seats, it was unbelievable to me that we were only a few feet from where all of this was going to take place. In every direction I looked, there was a mass of humanity, thousands and thousands of people physically present to see more history in the making. This was multiplied by millions watching by television throughout the nation and around the world. It was a pageant of color, and the air was filled with a feeling of expectancy. What a spectacle!

I looked down on the crowd to see if I could spot Nancy. Others around me were trying to locate their spouses. Most of us found them in that sea of folks. Yep, there she was. How pleased I was that my family could be there for this memorable event. Each congressman was given an allotment of tickets including a seat up front for spouse and other passes for family, friends, or staff, further back. Since this was a Republican administration coming into office, I had given several tickets to Republicans from northwest Florida who were otherwise not eligible to attend.

"I, Ronald Wilson Reagan, do solemnly swear to uphold the constitution....." The words reverberated over the loudspeakers as if the world stood still and listened. Not only was I present for the inauguration of America's 40th president, but I had a ringside seat. Was this a dream or something? Could a cotton pickin' little fella from the backwoods of rural Alabama be there in the midst of congressmen, senators, and the highest officials in the United States, watching the swearing-in of a President of the United States of America, the most important official in the world?

It was real all right. It was a long way from a humble beginning. How proud I was to be there representing a half million people of Northwest Florida....present in our nation's capitol participating in the governing of the world's greatest democracy. What a privilege! How blessed I was!

A political sidelight was the speculation on whether or not this change in administrations had anything to do with Iran's impending release of our hostages after 444 days of captivity. There were rumors about a so-called "October surprise" in which vice-presidential candidate George Bush had gone abroad to broker a release of the hostages that would take place only after the new president had been inaugurated. We found out during this ceremony that, indeed, our hostages were being set free. Americans everywhere rejoiced! But, I do not think anyone seriously thought there was such a thing as "a deal" like the aforementioned rumor.

When the hostages arrived in the United States and into our nation's capitol, a big parade honoring them and welcoming them home was held in Washington. Their fellow citizens turned out by the thousands to show their love and appreciation for those who had been imprisoned for so long, for no reason other than they were Americans. Fairfax County schools excused students for attending the parade, and we were glad Lori and Amy were able to experience this event. Our prayers were answered. It was good to know the former hostages were again able to breathe the fresh air of freedom in their native land.

Regardless of political affiliation, most Americans want to see our president do well and the nation progress. We had a new president who was Republican, and his party had won control of the Senate for the first time in years. The House remained Democratic.

President Reagan was conservative. But, conservatism was not exclusively the province of Republicans. There were quite a few of us Democrats who were just as conservative. If President Reagan was going to get his program passed, he would definitely need some votes from Democrats in the House. We knew we represented the balance of power for either side. If we voted with our party leaders, the Republicans could not win for the administration. If we voted with the president he could succeed if his own party stayed in line. It was that simple. We knew we were in the driver's seat.

It was this knowledge aforethought that prompted Charles Stenholm (D-Texas), a second-termer like me, who was a farmer from

Stamford, Texas, to call a meeting of conservative House Democrats, mostly from the south, but with a smattering from other regions, to get together to talk about organizing. We had a good initial turnout and, as we began to meet frequently, our numbers increased. We knew there was broad support for President Reagan and that a lot of our constituents felt that the liberal branch of our Democratic Party was not leading us in the right direction.

The Conservative Democratic Forum was the name we gave to what some would call a "renegade" group. Because most of us were from the deep south, and perhaps with remembrances of how southerners had played a big role in governing in years past, we were nicknamed by some as "Boll Weevils." It was not our intention to be a renegade organization, necessarily, but we did want to play a role in cutting spending, reducing the deficit, and bringing about a more efficient government. Our organization did not require a litmus test of its members. It was a forum, as the name implies, where we would get together and discuss the issues important to our constituents and the nation. Nobody's arm was twisted to vote a certain way, but we felt a sense of unity about our conservative philosophy, particularly as it related to the budget. We were also in tune with the folks back home.

Charlie Stenholm was our leader, and deservedly so, because he got it started. I don't believe we ever had a formal election of officers. It was unnecessary because it was an informal organization and Charlie was dedicated in leading us. Later, after several years, I knew Charlie was having to take a lot of flack and probably tiring of the job. At that time he named a nominating committee, with me as chairman, to come up with a new slate of officers. When the committee met, I expressed my feeling that we ought to keep Charlie. It was a sacrifice none of the rest of us wanted to make. Charlie and staff spent time keeping us informed and giving leadership recognized by House leaders and other members. My colleagues agreed and Stenholm has continued as leader of CDF through the years.

President Reagan's budget began a new era in America known as Reaganomics. Ronald Reagan, who had been a card-carrying union man and a Democrat in his younger days as a Hollywood actor, was now an arch conservative. His charisma and ability to perform on TV had made his face and name known throughout America, and in the political arena his service as Governor of California catapulted him to his party's presidential nomination and into the White House.

When the President put forward his first budget, it included a package of drastic cuts in spending and the largest tax cut in history. It also brought forth some first class partisan political battles. Liberal Democrats made it known, loud and clear, that now Vice President George Bush, in his run for president in earlier primaries had referred to Reagan's plan as "Voodoo Economics." Nonetheless, Ronald Reagan's administration, with Bush as a top player, knew how to win. They had to have discipline by Republicans in congress, and pick up enough Democrats to achieve a majority.

President Reagan was not at all averse to calling over to the White House groups of Democrats and Republicans in Congress, or getting on the telephone to them on an individual basis. He also utilized members of the cabinet in calling day or night.There reportedly was a lot of horse-trading and promises to members for voting with the administration. I can honestly say I never bargained my vote. I was not hesitant, however, if I voted their way on some measure, to remind members of the administration of that when I needed their assistance on matters relating to my district and Florida.

One memorable telephone call from President Reagan came to me at home on a weekend. It was not unexpected. The word was out from the media that President Reagan was busy trying to run down members of congress around the country in lining up support for his program. It was exciting when one of the girls answered the phone and the White House operator asked for Congressman Earl Hutto. I told Nancy, Lori, and Amy to get on the phone extensions. We had the whole family, except Nicky, on the line. When the president came on, I said, "Mr. President, I have my family on the line and would like very much to introduce them to you." He was very cordial and greeted each of them as I called their name. Wow! Talking to the President of the United States was something extraordinary! After they hung up, Mr. Reagan asked me about supporting his budget. I told him I was grateful for his call and was leaning his way on the forthcoming legislation.

The Conservative Democratic Forum met frequently with about 30 to 40 members, on call, mostly in the offices of Congressmen Dan Daniel (D-Virginia) or Sonny Montgomery (D-Mississippi). We discussed the budget and other issues of common interest. We knew we were in a good position and both parties had to listen to us. We were Democrats and we wanted to work within the party if possible, so from time to time some of our members, or at times the entire group, would meet with Speaker O'Neill or Majority Leader Wright.

The Washington Post, in April of 1981 carried a story headlined, AFTER TWO DECADES THE 'BOLL WEEVILS' ARE BACK, WHISTLING DIXIE. The article pointed out that "the old southern bloc, led by men like Sam Rayburn, Richard Russell of Georgia, and James O. Eastland of Mississippi, had a basic respect for party line and parliamentary hierarchy. They recognized congressional seniority as the source of authority. By winning term after term from safe Democratic districts, they used seniority to achieve power and prominence in both houses of Congress."

The Post write-up stated that "The new Boll Weevils, in contrast,have no clear leaders, and little individual power. And they exhibit a noticeably limited sense of allegiance to their party and its leaders." It went on to list 44 of us with a brief background of each. It was a factual article. Obviously, as individuals, we did not hold a lot of power, but collectively our group could carry the day. At our request, the leadership acquiesced in providing new seats on important committees, including three on Budget to CDF members. Still, we made no commitment to support the leadership budget.

In the CDF we talked about what we felt was the right way to go for our country. We felt strongly that we had to get a grip on spending and reduce the deficit. Proposals were worked on as possibilities to present as a substitute budget. Congressman Phil Gramm (D-Texas), a former economics professor at Texas A & M, was active in coming up with budgetary plans. The trouble with Phil was that he usually ran to the Republicans with those plans before we could get a response from our own side. He was one of those on the Budget Committee and he voted consistently with the Republicans which, of course, reflected our way of thinking.

When the budget resolution came to the floor of the House there was no question that my constituents were solidly back of the president. This was true throughout the south and other sections of the country. Gramm had been successful in getting the administration to include provisions the CDF wanted and the measure passed was known as the Gramm-Latta budget. The vote was 253 to 176 for this Reagan plan. Eight of eleven Florida Democratic House members voted for it, along with the four Republicans in the delegation.

Overall, 63 Democrats jumped the traces and went with the president.

The House leadership was stunned by the loss to the new president. This was the blueprint for government spending, but it would not be the last word. I would cast some of my toughest votes during this first year of the Reagan Administration. Speaker O'Neill and his leadership team worked hard to turn back the Reagan tide. A few weeks after this first budget vote, the leadership lost a close vote to preclude a vote on a reconciliation bill to by-pass or supersede control of various programs by committees and force them to reconcile their budgets to provisions of this bill. The White House had pulled out all the stops in its lobbying effort.

The Washington Post related a story about arm twisting and horse-trading by the administration with Democratic Members of Congress. Office of Management and Budget Director David Stockman said there were no deals, only "accommodations." "I went with the best deal," Representative John Breaux (D-Louisiana) was quoted as saying. Breaux was asked if his vote could be "sold," to which he responded, "No, it can be rented."

The vote was a squeaker. The conservative forces won again by a vote of 217-211. I was one of 29 Democrats voting for the bill, including five from Florida. Though it is no fun to go against one's own political party, I felt strongly that I voted the right way. We simply had to cut spending and this bill did it to the tune of nearly $40 billion. It was also what a vast majority of my constituents wanted.

There was acknowledgment from the Republican leadership in the House that the legislation had been put together somewhat hastily and haphazardly. After several hours of heated debate, there was a need for levity--and we got it. In putting the proposal together hurriedly, it contained a woman's name and phone number. This prompted Speaker O'Neill to ask if she were being written into law?

In a discussion with the bill's sponsor, Representative Del Latta (R-Ohio), O'Neill noted that the bill contained the words "Source, Rita Seymour, 225-(number). "Is that part of the permanent record?" O'Neill asked. "Maybe that's her golf score, Mr. Speaker," Latta stated, assuring O'Neill the name and number of the lady would be removed before passage.

The next part of the Reagan economic package called for a massive tax cut. I had some problems, not with cutting taxes, but with the size of the cut, and stated so publicly. But, the momentum was there from the public and I also felt that since this was part of the overall plan I had supported up to this point, that I should vote for it. There was a terrific onslaught of telephone calls. Southern Bell in Pensacola reported that there were 2,500 calls each for the two-day period, leading up to the vote, from the Pensacola-Panama City areas, practically all in support of the legislation.

This was the only time I recall, in the eight years I served under Speaker Tip O'Neill, that he personally asked me if I would vote a certain way. The night before the vote was to be taken, the speaker called and said, "Earl, we really need your vote against Reagan's tax cut tomorrow. Can you possibly go with us on it?" I said, "I'm sorry, Mr. Speaker, but my constituents don't see it that way. I plan to vote for it." Speaker O'Neill graciously replied, "I understand, Earl, you've got to go the way your folks want you to vote." Tip is the one who coined the phrase, "All politics is local." He understood that my constituents were different from his.

When it is likely there is going to be heavy lobbying by the leadership, as a member reaches the floor to vote, it is sometimes advisable, unless one wants to be lobbied, to ease into the chamber, vote quickly and get out. I had that feeling very few times, but the vote on the tax bill, known as Hance-Conable, unofficially named for CDF member Kent Hance (D-Texas) and Barber Conable (R-New York), was one of them. Others did the same thing. When the vote ended, there were 48 of us Democrats who joined all but two Republicans in passing the Reagan tax cut measure 238-195.

Though I voted against him numerous times, I maintained the deepest respect for Tip O'Neill. His word was good as gold. You could depend on him as a person of integrity. Tip was a warm, personable individual. A lovable person, he endeared himself to those who knew him. Though disagreeing often, members of our CDF held him in high regard, as did the Republicans. He seemingly never forgot a name. Tip was always gracious to Nancy and me and greeted us by name, even if we were in the midst of a large crowd.

As previously stated, I had some misgivings about the size of the tax cut. I believed that we should have a tax cut to spur the economy, but taking $750 billion dollars out of the treasury has to balloon the deficit. History reveals that is exactly what happened. It makes for good times here and now, but it leaves a legacy of a huge debt for our children and grandchildren. I liked the fact that President

Reagan stood firm for America with increased defense spending, which I wholeheartedly supported in committee and on the floor. But, I was disappointed that he did not have a deeper commitment to deficit reduction, after campaigning for it. In fact, he was even quoted as saying afterwards that deficits did not matter. The inordinate size of the tax cuts, hardly obvious to the average person, gave us more debt than in all history.

Tip O'Neill, unlike some other Democrats, did not threaten us conservatives who voted for the Reagan economic plan. It was certainly understandable, however, that Phil Gramm was in the doghouse due to his coziness with Republicans and sneering at the leadership during the budget debates. He would later resign and be re-elected as a Republican. Then, he was elected to the Senate and, as the world knows, Phil ran for president in the 1996 primaries.

I was asked by the media and others if I thought O'Neill would try to take away my Armed Services Committee assignment or take other action against those who voted against him. I replied that I did not think he would be vengeful, and indeed he was not. We felt the cold shoulder, however, from some of our more liberal colleagues. But it wasn't just in Washington. While my votes received overwhelming approval from most in the First District, there were several dyed-in-the-wool Democrats who denounced me for forsaking my party and were politically threatening.

Wes Ramsey, Editor of the Port St. Joe Star summarized my position and my feelings rather well when he ran an editorial titled, HUTTO REPRESENTS PEOPLE, NOT PARTY. Wes pointed out that he was a registered Democrat, but as he saw it, "Congressman Hutto was not sent to Washington to represent the Democratic Party, even though the large majority of his constituents are registered Democrats." To further paraphrase, the editorial said, "We feel that in really important things, Congressman Hutto has cast his vote like the majority of the people in his district want him to, whether his vote was cast in favor or against a Democratic program." Wes's additional comment that I was "one of the most honest men in Washington who would vote for what is best for the nation" was really appreciated.

As a Member of Congress I wanted to do all I could for the well being of the people of my district. From an economic standpoint that meant jobs and a decent living for families. I was pleased to work with the leaders of Escambia County and Pensacola, through the

Pensacola-Escambia Development Commission (PEDC) to acquire Ellyson Field, a former military helicopter base, as an industrial site. I interceded with the General Services Administration, with whom the PEDC negotiated to purchase the 600-acre Ellyson property for $3 million with only 10% down and the balance over a 20-year period. The House Governmental Operations Committee, though, questioned the GSA about these terms over the usual 20% down and 10 years to pay. But the committee did not disapprove and I announced the agreement April 12, 1981. The legislative delegation did its part covering costs through state grants. Ellyson is now filled with clean industries, providing jobs for thousands, ahead of all projections.

I wanted my offices to be pleasant work places, with happy people doing important work for our nation. Through the years I was blessed with having dedicated, loyal people on my staff. We had very little turnover, but over a 16-year period there are inevitable changes.

Tom Culligan had served me so well as Legislative Director, but after three years he accepted a job with McDonnell-Douglas, one of the nation's top builders of aircraft, and a major defense contractor. Tom advanced rapidly and in a few years was a vice president working directly with John McDonnell in the St. Louis headquarters. More recently, Tom took a job as a vice president of Allied Signal and watches over its European operations from Paris.

When I called Nancy to tell her about Tom's leaving, she said, "You know who to get to replace him, don't you?" "Tom Tamura?" I asked. "Exactly" was the reply. I had met Colonel Thomas T. Tamura, United States Air Force, in the first few weeks I was in Washington when I was invited to speak at the annual prayer breakfast at Bolling Air Force Base. I had sat next to the commanding officer of Bolling and his wife, Maile Tamura. After my speech, the colonel whispered to me, "You sound like a Baptist." I acknowledged that he was right, and Tom declared, "So am I."

It turned out the Tamuras were members of First Baptist in Springfield, where we now attended. In a few weeks we were in a Sunday School class taught by, guess who? Yep, Tom was mine and Nancy's teacher in a couples class. We became good friends and have been since.

Tamura, like the outgoing Culligan, is a bright guy with an engaging personality and a fine family of similar qualities. I recall that he had expressed to me an earlier interest in someday working on

Capitol Hill. So, when I called and offered him the job, Tom was excited. But, this would be a major decision. He was already a "bird colonel" and sure to be a future flag officer. He was getting ready to take a new and important assignment with the Rapid Deployment Force, headquartered in Tampa. Tom had a lot to consider and one can imagine that this telephone call was causing his mind to work overtime. He said, "Earl, can you give me a few days? Maile and I will have to do a lot of thinking and praying. But I am really intrigued about this." Nancy and I prayed, also, that Tom would take the job.

After excruciating deliberations, Tom joined my staff and worked with Culligan about three weeks before the changeover. He was a quick learner. Tom and Randy Knepper, my Administrative Assistant, got along famously and became good friends. Tom was about 15 years older than Randy and was a steadying force in his development. Colonel Tamura was called "Tom" by everybody, even our young staff people. This took some getting used to because he was accustomed to being called "Colonel Tamura" or "Sir." But after Tom got used to it he liked the camaraderie and informality of the office. He did great work for over six years as my military advisor, but also through a wide range of dealings with people in our district. However, he, too, was lured away by industry. Tom said the six years plus with me was the longest he had worked at one job, so apparently it was time for a change. Tom Tamura went with Douglas Aircraft in California and worked there until becoming Principal Deputy Assistant Secretary of Energy back in Washington in 1993.

Bob Flint, a good friend and a retired Army colonel, who had been hired by Congressman Solomon Ortiz (D-Texas) two or three years earlier, upon my recommendation, was a logical choice to replace Tom. Then, after Bob, my last military advisor was a young man, Brett Pfeffer, who had served as an enlisted man in the Air Force. Due to all the military in my district, this was an important position in which they served me and my district exceedingly well.

Some Members of Congress do their casework for constituents out of their Washington offices. My predecessor did that. I felt, however, that it would be better to do casework back in the home district so that those having problems with the federal government could go into their congressman's office and actually talk to a staffer, if necessary. Also, when I was back in northwest Florida, I often held office hours to meet with those who personally wanted to see me. So, I phased out the casework in Washington and shifted it to my Pensacola office. Mail we received in the way of casework was "orange bagged" to Pensacola. This arrangement allowed us to concentrate more on legislative work in the Washington office.

During President Reagan's first term, I got a call from then Deputy Secretary of Defense Frank Carlucci, not unusual since I was a member of the Armed Services Committee. But Carlucci, who several years later would become Secretary of Defense, was not calling about military matters. It was one of those times, I mentioned earlier, where the president staged an all-out press by lobbying, oftentimes through his cabinet officials, for his legislative proposals. It so happened that I already had decided to support the measure Carlucci was calling about and I so informed him. Then, I said, "Mr. Secretary, now there is something I need your help on." "What's that Mr. Congressman?" I went on to advise him that it was my understanding a study was going on in the Pentagon with the intention of contracting out the Naval Aviation Rework Facility in Pensacola that would cause about 4,100 people to lose their federal jobs. This meant it would be operated as a GOCO, government owned, contracted out facility. It was not at all wise, especially from a national security standpoint, and I told the secretary I would appreciate his stopping this study. He promised to look into it... and to make a long story short, the study was called off, pronto! Our senior Florida Senator, Lawton Chiles, supported me in this.

Military construction, in my view, was important in providing for our national defense. But, I readily admit that I wanted to get as much as possible for my congressional district. It was my job to see that our bases stayed strong. New construction not only provided a stabilizing effect, but it brought jobs to the building industry. As a member of the Military Installations and Facilities Subcommittee (Milcon), I was in the right place for acquiring megabucks for adding to our military bases in northwest Florida.

I did more than just support the projects the services recommended. I stayed in close touch with my military bases back home. I received briefings from the military and civilian leadership of each facility and oftentimes had my military legislative assistant to check on the needs of the bases. In this way, I could help expedite projects scheduled for the out years. One year, my staff and I looked at a list of five projects which were possible prospects for moving up for early construction. As I left my office to go to the subcommittee markup, Tom and Randy reminded me to try to get one or two of these projects included in the bill. They could not believe it when I got back to the office and advised them that we got all five projects added, for an extra $23 million for the Panhandle. It was a great pleasure for me to speak at the groundbreaking and dedication of a lot of these military projects during my time in Congress.

I have often expressed my disdain for partisan bickering in the political arena. It seemed to get worse year-by-year. One year, during an apparent impasse on the budget, I decided to write Speaker Tip O'Neill and President Ronald Reagan urging them to end the squabbling. In my letter I said, "Mr. President, the polarization that we see on your part and on the part of Speaker O'Neill is not in the best interest of the country. We hear you constantly lashing out at the Democrats in congress and Speaker O'Neill likewise ridiculing your administration. Are your efforts to elect a majority of Republicans in the House, and his to keep a majority of Democrats, more important than trying to do what is right for the nation? The people are suffering and they stand at your mercy." In the letter, which was identical to the one to O'Neill, with just a change of names, I pointed out that Budget Chairman Jim Jones (D-Oklahoma) and Ranking Minority Member Del Latta (R-Ohio) were capable and reasonable men who could work out the budget if only the political restraints were lifted. I released the letter to the press and said I expected an answer, but hoped it would not be the usual, "it's not me, it's him."

The budget is one thing that can be counted on to be a big issue. It was that way in the first Congress, each succeeding Congress, and will be for all those to come. An issue--yes--but it does not always have to be so contentious and such a partisan issue. There is no question that budget reform could help. I had what I thought, and still think, is at least a partial solution...a longer budget cycle. Early in my career I introduced a bill proposing biennial budgeting, including authorization and appropriations, and got three significant members from both parties as original co-sponsors-- Les Aspin, Democrat from Wisconsin; Trent Lott from Mississippi and Jim Courter, from New Jersey, both Republicans. The last few years my good friend, Sonny Callahan, and I introduced the biennial bill.

Obviously, it is very difficult to break the yoke in changing the annual appropriations process and, of course, we never came near getting the measure passed. But, hopefully we did get the ball rolling because it seemed every year that we got more and more co-sponsors. President Bush even called for biennial budgeting in one of his State of the Union speeches to Congress. To me, it makes a lot of sense. Agencies of government hurry to spend all they have so they can get more next year. A longer budget cycle would slow that spending down, give Congress more time to oversee spending by federal agencies, and more time to work on other important issues. Let us hope biennial budgeting gets enacted.

Social Security is a program that is helping many elderly people survive and I support it wholeheartedly. But it is a political football that is always being kicked around by the two major parties. In 1983, responding to recommendations of a bipartisan commission, we enacted legislation absolutely necessary to rescue Social Security from bankruptcy. Because of this legislation Social Security was made sound well into the next century. However, as there are fewer and fewer people proportionately paying into the system and more people reaching the age for benefits, there is need of planning for those who will reach retirement age after the first quarter of the 21st century.

One of the things that riles me up is organizations that rip off senior citizens by scaring them half to death with misleading information. They send out mass mailings telling seniors they are about to lose their Social Security and Medicare benefits and send $25, $15, $10, or any amount possible, so that they can persuade Congress to do something about it. Many members of Congress kowtow to these groups for fear of alienating their older constituents.

Some of us in Congress warned the American people about these ripoffs, especially James Roosevelt and his so-called Committee to Preserve Social Security and Medicare. There are others groups, too, including one that includes the name of columnist Jack Anderson. How cruel to prey on those who can least afford it! At one point we did an hour of special order speeches on the floor to blast these organizations for taking advantage of the needy and vulnerable..

The Subcommittee on Social Security of the House Ways and Means Committee, chaired by Rep. Andy Jacobs (D-Indiana), held hearings on several occasions to take testimony regarding these schemes aimed at senior citizens. I testified, along with several colleagues, against these ill-advised organizations. Practically every member of congress is a supporter of Social Security and it is foolish for elderly people to send money to these groups to lobby congress on something for which there is absolutely no need. In fact, they take the poor people's money and seldom contact members of Congress. I do not recall a single time anyone from these organizations came into my office to see me about anything.

I caught a lot of flack in my home district about the so-called "notch problem" in Social Security. Some very adamant senior citizens wanted me to co-sponsor a bill to change the formula. In reality, it again was the organizations raking in millions from senior citizens who created this mentality and led these folks astray. Again, many members of Congress, going with the seemingly prevailing sentiment, signed on as co-sponsors of the "notch" bill. In all good conscience, I could not support this and quite a few others, including the leadership of both parties, were of like mind.

There were, indeed, "notch years" involved in the Social Security formula, but it was more of a perceived problem than a real one. In summary, it came about when Congress passed an overly generous Social Security formula in 1972; and then in 1977, before I got there, passed legislation to correct the formula. In so doing, they made it prospective and phased it in so that those becoming eligible for benefits in the next few years, those born in the years 1917-21, would not receive such a drastically reduced amount. Those born before those years would be held harmless and would continue to get the higher benefit from the flawed formula. There had to be a stopping point. So, the formula was ratcheted down so those born in the notch years would actually fare better under the formula than all of us born after those years, as we would be on the revised formula. Some well-meaning people never understood this and felt because they were born during the notch years they were being cheated.

Apparently some of these organizations work overtime in coming up with ideas they can use to frighten people into sending more money. In order to add additional millions to the largess, they sent out more mass mailings, claiming that those born all the way up through 1926 were in the notch years. For the good of everyone on Social Security, and those expecting to be on it, be thankful this "notch bill" has never been passed in Congress and hopefully never will be. If it is ever passed it will devastate the Social Security Trust Fund. It would have saved me some grief if I had just gone along with the flow and signed on as co-sponsor of this bill, but most of those to whom I was able to explain it, understood I was doing the right thing.

The state of Florida is inhabited with a lot of veterans. Many are in our part of the state, but unfortunately they have, through the years, had to travel lengthy distances, such as downstate or to Montgomery, Alabama or Biloxi, Mississippi, to get treatment at VA facilities. I worked very hard, as did Senator Chiles, to get a VA Clinic in Northwest Florida. It wasn't easy. I exerted considerable effort to get the House Veterans Affairs Committee to approve the clinic. Then, the VA itself was dragging its feet. Senator Chiles and I wrote to newly appointed VA Administrator Harry Walters in 1983 telling him we were "appalled at the delaying tactics of this federal agency." This got the clinic off dead center and some three years later a fine VA Outpatient Clinic was dedicated in Pensacola. Joining Senator Chiles and me at the dedication in late July 1986 was General Thomas Turnage, the VA Administrator at that time. The facility has provided outstanding medical treatment to thousands of veterans.

Still, our veterans deserved a full-fledged VA hospital and for years we worked to get one. At one point, I lined up a congressional hearing, the first ever in Okaloosa County, to hear testimony on the need for a hospital. Congressman Dan Mica, chairman of the medical subcommittee of the House Committee on Veterans Affairs, brought his committee for a hearing to Okaloosa-Walton Community College, where many veterans from throughout the Panhandle testified on the need for a hospital. Subsequently, we were able to get on the list for a facility. Florida was the only state where new VA hospitals were being built. We moved up to as high as second on that list, but budgetary constraints and privatization efforts have stopped construction of more new VA hospitals.

The Cold War continued to rage. It was in 1983 that the Soviets shot down a Korean Airline plane that killed 268 people including our colleague, Congressman Larry McDonald, an arch conservative Democrat from Georgia. It was in the fall of that year that 230 U. S. Marines were killed in Lebanon from a terrorist bomb..

The American public was upset about our Marines being killed and questioned the security of our forces in Beirut. Some expressed doubts about the advisability of our troops being there. We were there following the taking of several American hostages and as part of a multi-national force to keep peace after Israel invaded Lebanon.

I was in a delegation, headed by Representative Sonny

Montgomery (D-Mississippi), that went to Beirut a few days after our Marines were bombed. On the way, we landed at our base in Frankfort, Germany and visited those wounded and transferred to the military hospital in Wiesbaden, Germany. I tried to cheer them up with chocolate chip cookies Nancy had baked for them. Several of the Marines were from my district and I was pleased to bring back reports of our visits to their loved ones in the states. One of the saddest things was our visit to the morgue at Rhein Mein Air Base where the bodies were being identified. This was a grim reminder to be grateful for those who have made the supreme sacrifice for our great nation.

After visiting the the bombing site in Beirut, it was obvious to us that our troops were in harm's way. We reported back to our committee and Representative Bill Nichols, Chairman of the Investigations Subcommittee, held hearings on the safety of our Marines. This forced some changes to be made prior to our troops being pulled out of Lebanon.

Members of the congressional delegation on that trip were dressed in military camouflage uniforms before going into Beirut. We were only on the ground a couple of hours to view the damage of the bombing and get briefings. Authorities felt that we should not change clothing before departing. When we landed in Athens, Greece, on the way back, and were bussed to the Athens Hilton Hotel downtown, we were still wearing our Marine uniforms. Then, a rather humorous incident happened. Several American tourists were in front of the hotel and as we began to unload they realized that we were Americans and asked, "Where are you coming from?" When we said, "Beirut", they began cheering and slapping us on our backs. They thought we were real Marines who had survived the bombing in Beirut.

It was in 1983 that Armed Services Committee Chairman Mel Price appointed me to chair the Technology Transfer Panel, a special committee to look into the slippage of our technology to the Soviet Union. Those named to serve on the panel were Representatives Jim Courter (R-New Jersey), Beverly Byron (D-Maryland), Marilyn Lloyd (D-Tennessee), Frank McCloskey (D-Indiana), Ken Kramer (R-Colorado), and Duncan Hunter (R-California).

It was common knowledge that the Soviet Union was using every method possible to get their hands on western technology. We felt very strongly that we needed to stop this flow of technology to our opponent in the cold war. There needed to be better safeguards.

Our panel did not have legislative authority, but after our hearings we came to the conclusion that, administratively, we could work with the Defense Department in tightening up security and also offer amendments to the Export Administration Act, under the jurisdiction of the Foreign Affairs Committee, when it came to the floor. However, there was then, and still is, a tug of war between the Defense and Commerce departments regarding transfer of technology. Commerce was much more lenient in allowing technology in the market place than was the Department of Defense.

The Coordinating Committee--comprised of several countries, including the U.S., and headquartered in Paris--was responsible for determining what products to allow to be sold to the Soviet Union and eastern bloc nations. But Co-Com, as it was called, had little staff and was highly ineffective. Our efforts were to try to strengthen Co-Com as well as to require proper screening before products with sensitive technology were allowed to be shipped out of our country. These efforts were fought by many big businesses with overseas markets. The common response was "If we do not sell it to them our allies will get the business." It was a tough fight and our efforts were only minimally successful.

The Secretary of the Navy for President Reagan was a hard charging young man by the name of John Lehman. At times he was controversial. But I liked the guy. Secretary Lehman believed in a strong defense and, especially, a strong Navy. This was reason enough to like him, but I also liked John from a personal standpoint because he was easy to talk with. He was diligent about returning my phone calls and he worked with me on issues relating to the Navy.

A major command, the Naval Education and Training Command, in charge of Navy training worldwide, has been headquartered in Pensacola for many years. A three-star admiral is the Chief of Naval Education and Training (CNET). I had what seemed like a constant battle keeping this command, or at least portions of it, from being transferred to Millington, Tennessee. Senator James Sasser (D-Tennessee) and Representative Jamie Whitten, from just over the border in Mississippi, successfully got legislation passed, to protect Millington from cuts, making it in essence, unlawful for Millington to go below its level of operations of each prior year. Secretary Lehman's orders to streamline commands caused pressure to be brought to bear in moving functions from

Pensacola to Millington. Also, some in the naval aviation "lobby" favored separating the Chief of Naval Air Training (CNATRA), based in Corpus Christi, from CNET.

Vice Admiral James Sagerholm, one of a long line of outstanding commanding officers of CNET, was under the gun to streamline. He consulted with me all the way on this and one weekend flew over to Panama City to brief me on what he had put together. He did a fine job in trimming military and civilian staff personnel and his plan, approved by John Lehman, kept Pensacola's three-star billet, and CNATRA still under CNET. Another bullet dodged!

Secretary Lehman established a goal of a 600-ship U. S. Navy. He also put forth a plan for strategic homeporting. I strongly supported this from a national defense standpoint as well as a parochial position. Envisioned in the plan was disbursement of ships to many ports, rather than having all of them congregated in San Diego, Norfolk, and a few other homeport locations. A part of Lehman's plan, which made sense militarily as well as politically, was to establish a Surface Action Group (SAG) in the Gulf of Mexico, to include the battleship USS Wisconsin and supporting destroyers and frigates. In a smart move, which probably was calculated to gain congressional support, the Secretary set up competition among potential ports in Florida, Mississippi, Louisiana, and Texas, and asked for communities to present their proposals.

Pensacolians, especially from the military and business community, were excited about the possibility of Pensacola becoming the homeport of the Gulf Coast fleet. A Homeporting Commission was organized with a distinguished group of members chaired by Ted Nickinson with retired Navy Captain Brad Butcher as Executive Director, and an all-out effort was made to obtain the ships and the influx of dollars that would help the community economically. The proposal they came up with, I believe, was excellent, but it did not provide the level of funding which the state and local governments of Texas and Mississippi offered. Nonetheless, we felt the existing Navy facilities in the Pensacola area and the history of strong Navy support from Escambia and Santa Rosa counties made the proposal attractive.

The envelope, please! Who is going to win the fleet of the Gulf Coast? Everybody was a little nervous. Still we felt pretty good about the chances for Pensacola. In July, 1985, Secretary of Defense Casper Weinberger made the big announcement on homeporting.

Wow! What a shocker! Weinberger announced plans for placing 29 ships in the Gulf and not just the half dozen or so ships in the Surface Action Group. Corpus Christi was pronounced the winner of the USS Wisconsin and attendant ships, but Pensacola was awarded a big-deck operational carrier. All the locations in the competition were to receive ships such as cruisers, destroyers, frigates, and oilers.

The USS Kitty Hawk was a big plum for Pensacola. It is understandable, in some respects, that we were all a little disappointed at not getting the SAG since that was the goal on which we focused. But getting the large carrier was the best deal. It fit. As the home of Naval Aviation, it would continue our long and close ties with the Naval aviation community that would move us into the next century.

Two other ports were added in the announced homeporting plan--Everett, Washington, and Staten Island, New York. Now, the ball shifted to our court--the U. S. Congress. We had to fund these grandiose plans. I was in the middle of that fight, but fortunately was in a key position on the milcon subcommittee which had jurisdiction. There was opposition to homeporting in congress from members who were never good supporters of defense, and also from a lot of inlanders who felt this proposition was just too expensive.

I generally carried the ball on our subcommittee, with good help from Mississippi's Sonny Montgomery and Texas's Solomon Ortiz. Bill Dickinson, of Alabama, although Mobile was to be a recipient of ships, was, to say the least, lukewarm toward homeporting. Bill favored Mobile as a homeport, but Everett and Staten Island were the first for which funding was requested because there apparently was a lot more work to be done in those ports. The funding requests for the other homeports would come the next year.

I felt very strongly that we had to keep the homeporting package together or we would lose the whole thing. One day, when the subcommittee broke for lunch, I called Secretary Lehman and the congressman from Mobile, Jack Edwards, and told them that they needed to talk to Bill Dickinson because we needed Bill's vote to pass homeporting out of the subcommittee. When the subcommittee resumed that afternoon, Dickinson laughed and said to me, "You must have called everybody in congress and in the Pentagon about me." I joined him in a good-natured chuckle. We did vote to keep homeporting alive and Dickinson voted with us. During the subcommittee debate, pushy Congressman Norm Dicks (D-

Washington) was constantly calling us about approving his homeport. Maybe that helped sway some of the members.

We continued to prepare for homeporting the next few years by authorizing and appropriating funds, including money for the NAS pier to accommodate the USS Kitty Hawk in Pensacola.. While this renovation was going on the Pensacola folks cooperated in a plan that brought the USS Lexington to a pier in downtown Pensacola.

But, alas, something happened on the way to "floating these boats" in the Gulf fleet and in the proposed homeports in the states of Washington and New York. The homeporting plans of a 600-ship Navy began to unravel for two reasons--budgetary constraints and a thaw in the Cold War. For years I worked to get a replacement for the Lady Lex, our aging training carrier in Pensacola. The homeporting scheme to bring an operational carrier to Pensacola would shift the Lexington to Corpus Christi. When the homeporting plan came apart, we lost the promise of getting the USS Kitty Hawk, but were able to keep the Lexington in Pensacola, pending a replacement. The Navy subsequently announced that an operational/training carrier, the USS Forrestal, would replace the Lexington. I made sure the Lexington did not depart until the new vessel arrived in Pensacola.

Finally, in February of 1992, the big day came when the Forrestal, fresh from service in the Persian Gulf, arrived in Pensacola. Nancy and I joined Navy and community leaders in flying, by helicopter, out into the gulf where we landed aboard the big vessel and rode it in for its big welcome. It was raining as we arrived and the carrier was moored to the expanded pier at Pensacola Naval Air Station. We waited until the rain slackened before going ashore for the ceremony welcoming the USS Forrestal to its new home. The rain did not dampen the spirits of Pensacolians who were, as usual, very supportive of this new addition to the area.

The downsizing of the Navy saw the decommissioning of the USS Lexington, which was taken to Corpus Christi to become a museum. It was sad to see the Lex leave after so many years. In fact, the military downsizing brought to our nation a lot of sorrow with the deactivation of many bases and units in all the services.

We knew the Forrestal would be in Pensacola only a short time before going into dry dock for an extensive overhaul. In September it departed for Philadelphia. A few months after the distinguished ship arrived there, Admiral Kelso, the Chief of Naval

Operations, announced that, due to cutbacks in the Navy, renovations of the USS Forrestal would be halted, the ship would be decommissioned and dismantled. This was sad news. Unfortunately, that was the end of a long era of the Navy having a dedicated training carrier. The decision was made to henceforth use fleet carriers for training pilots to land on aircraft carriers.

Aside from defense, one of my greatest concerns has been the deterioration of the family unit in America. In 1983, Renn Vara, my legislative assistant from Bonifay, Florida, called to my attention that Senator Arlen Spector, (R-Pennsylvania) had introduced a strong bill to fight child pornography. Renn, after reading a Ladies Home Journal article on the subject and conferring with the Senator's staff, felt it would be good for me to introduce a companion bill in the House. I agreed and introduced the Sexual Exploitation of Children Act. These measures got the attention of the judiciary committees in both bodies. I testified before the Subcommittee on Crime which marked up a bill that included most of the provisions of my bill. It would raise fines from $10,000 for first offenses and $15,000 for subsequent offenses to $100,000 and $200,000, respectively; expand the law to cover both commercial and non-commercial pornography; and eliminate the requirement that obscenity be proven. It also redefined "minor" as any individual under 18, instead of 16.

It took a year, but in mid-1984, I was one of those invited to the White House to witness President Reagan signing the Child Protection Act of 1984. Since then, the strengthened law has been effective in getting more convictions for exploitation of children. This kind of conduct remains an intolerable blight on our society.

My staff and I wanted to do everything we could to help people. Sometimes this meant helping constituents cut through the red tape and bureaucracy of the federal government. In other situations, it might require legislation. In this context, let me relate the story of Teddy Salanga. As a six-year-old boy, in his native Philippine Islands during World War II, little Teddy smuggled food, medicine, and other needs to American prisoners interned in a Japanese prison camp. He was small enough to slip through the camp fences, according to his sister, Josephine Britt, who assisted him, along with other members of the family. Years later, Salanga married a Vietnamese woman and spent seven years working for the U. S. in Vietnam as an engineer. After the war, the parents of Salanga's wife were executed as a direct result of their son-in-law's work for the Americans.

What does this have to do with Earl Hutto? Well, in 1983, it seems that just about everybody in Niceville, Florida, in my district, was rallying to the cause of Teddy Salanga, who at that time was biding his time by helping his sister, Josephine, in her restaurant. He was in the U. S. on a temporary visa trying to obtain legal residence. Teddy wanted to become a U.S.citizen and bring his wife and their three children, whom he had not seen in five years, to this country.

When Josephine Salanga Britt received a letter from the American Embassy in the Philippines in 1981 denying her brother's special immigrant application, she was angry, but did not give up. After the denial, she collected affidavits from seven former POWs attesting to Salanga's bravery and urging he be accepted.

I introduced a bill in February of 1983 to provide legal residence to Salanga. Attorney Hill Moore helped Josephine mount a campaign and sent letters and copies of the affidavits to President Reagan, Senator Barry Goldwater, and Actor Jimmy Stewart, urging them to support Salanga and my bill. I am not quite sure why Jimmy Stewart was included on the list. Anyway, I worked to get the measure passed. Although my colleagues felt that someone who had done as much for American citizens as Teddy Salanga should be granted residence in our country, it took me over a year to get this legislation into law. Finally, in late 1984, the bill passed the House September 18, and Senate three days later. President Reagan signed the bill granting legal residence to Teddy Salanga and I announced to the family and the people of Niceville the president's approval, and said, "It's a great day, a beautiful day for the Salangas."

Let me make myself clear, I was pleased that I could do this for Teddy Salanga, and I was able to get other worthy immigration legislation passed during my time in congress. I appreciate the fact that our country is a melting pot, a nation of people with diverse backgrounds, who have been productive citizens, making America what it is today. But, I support efforts to get control of our borders. Thousands of illegal immigrants are coming to the United States every year. We cannot indiscriminately open our borders to all who want to come to this land of freedom and opportunity.

As I continued to grapple with national and local problems, I always felt the closeness of my wonderful, loving family--Nancy, Lori, and Amy, and of course, our dog of dogs, Nicky. Family togetherness was priority number one in our busy lifestyle.

We watched with joy the growth of Lori and Amy as they moved through the public school system of Fairfax County, Virginia. After they finished the fifth and third grades, respectively, at West Springfield Elementary School, they transferred to Hunt Valley Elementary, nearer to where we had bought our house. Lori was there only for the sixth grade before she went to Washington Irving Intermediate School for the seventh and eighth grades. When she moved on to Irving it was the first time our girls had gone to different schools. That scenario continued when Amy advanced to Washington Irving because, that same year, Lori started at West Springfield High.

When Amy graduated from Washington Irving she wanted to go to West Springfield High where her big sister was enrolled, but unfortunately there was school redistricting that year and Amy was assigned to Robert E. Lee High School. She did not like this a little bit. Believe me, she let it be known. She took it upon herself to write the school superintendent, school board members, and even the governor telling them that this was unfair and please change the boundaries so that she could attend West Springfield. Her appeal was not successful, but we were proud of her for taking a stand. When it came time to start school in the fall, however, she went to Lee High and never complained about it one time the four years she was there.

In 1986, at the West Springfield football stadium, we were proud to see Lori walk across the stage and receive her diploma. She had already been writing to colleges and we had gone with her to scout out several. We wanted our girls to go to a college somewhere in the southeast and I even tried to interest them in my alma mater, Troy State. Lori seemed to like Troy, but she also liked other schools and narrowed her choice to Samford University in Birmingham and Auburn University. Her decision was to attend Auburn, where she did exceedingly well in her studies and extracurricular activities, such as being a member of Tigerettes, Mortar Board, and ODK. She also ran for student senate and when I called the night of the election, she said, "Well, Daddy, you are only a Representative...I want you to know I am a Senator." Touche'! I got the message. She had won!

Amy graduated from Lee High School in 1988 where she did well, even though Lee had not been her first choice. Her graduation, held on the football field at Lee, provided us with a rather interesting night. Of course, all of us parents experienced the pride of seeing our student march across the stage and get that diploma. But, the added attraction was the spectacle of the beach balls which rose from the graduates seated in front of the stage. They began slowly with a single balloon floating up and being quickly taken in tow by teachers nearby. Soon, there was another, and then another until several balls were batted around, bringing amusement to the crowd. A graduation to remember for Amy and for us!

Like her sister, Amy had scouted around for the college she wanted to attend. Before her decision she got a letter from Lori, suggesting Auburn. Lori said, "You know, Amy, we haven't been in the same school since we both attended Hunt Valley Elementary." This was real touching to Nancy and me. That sisterly love has always been strong. Lori's letter, without a doubt, was the catalyst. Amy joined Lori at Auburn University and they were in the same school, again, until Lori graduated two years later, in 1990.

Now, allow me to mention a few more of my staffers. In my early Washington office, Vickie Baird, who later worked with a couple of California congressmen, including Vic Fazio of the House leadership, was a whiz at speed typing. Nancy Spruill, who was with me about two years, was one of my first receptionists. Mary Sharp, who came to us from Senator Dan Quayle, was at the front desk from 1983-89 and her bubbly personality made everyone who came to see us, or called my office by telephone, feel welcome.

A valuable legislative assistant, Mark Kronenberg, worked well with Tom Culligan and later, Tom Tamura, as well as with Randy and me. Leisa Harris Dove, a native of Pensacola, was a legislative assistant from 1985-89 whose good writing I joked about being books. Robyn Roberts, of Panama City, and later Wade Warren, Dan Stech, Jennifer Rich, and Elliot Kaye were all outstanding members of the Hutto team. Whether analyzing bills, responding to letters, writing news releases or whatever I asked, they did a super job!

Our staff had a lot of fun together. Oftentimes, we got together in the office to celebrate someone's birthday or for any reason. Sometimes there was no reason, except to have a good time and enjoy each other's company. At times, particularly during holidays, we invited all of them to our house. One occasion we will always remember was when Randy volunteered to make banana ice cream for dessert. He concocted his specialty and operated the freezer on our patio.

Our mouths were salivating in great anticipation of this delicacy; that is, until Randy started dipping it up. The bananas he used were green and unripened and the ice cream would not turn loose of the dipper. Randy's face was getting more red every minute as he tried to get the ice cream into the dishes. He turned the scoop upside down and it would still stick like glue. Needless to say, we did not have banana ice cream that night. Randy took a lot of razzing and will never live this down. How funny! But he was a good sport about it, although he never again seriously offered to make banana ice cream for the group. If he had, I am sure the idea would have been vetoed out of hand!

President Ronald Reagan is shown meeting in the Oval Office with four members of the House Armed Services Committee. Left to right--President Reagan; Dan Daniel, Virginia (back to camera);Charles Bennett, Florida; Vice President George Bush; Earl Hutto, Florida; and Sonny Montgomery, Mississippi.

Congressman Hutto, right, who sponsored the House bill promoting "Just Say No to Drugs", watches with co-sponsors as President Reagan signs the measure into law. Left to right--Rep. Ben Gillman, New York; Sen. Bob Graham, Florida, sponsor of the Senate bill; Rep. Charlie Rangel, New York; Vice Pres. George Bush; and Rep. Connie Morella, Maryland.

16

MISTER CHAIRMAN

The nineteen-eighties, particularly the first half of the decade, were interesting years in America's dealing with the rest of the world. The Cold War raged. President Reagan referred to the Soviet Union as the "Evil Empire." There was continued turbulence in the Middle East with our involvement in Lebanon, the bombing of Libya after provocations by Moammar Khadafy, the encroachment of communism in Central America marked by controversy in our support of the Contras in Nicaragua, and the invasion by our forces to liberate the little island of Granada.

The saying goes, "We cannot be the policeman of the world," and I subscribe to that philosophy. But, there is no question, as the leader of the free world, we have a high stake in maintaining and supporting strong armed forces in defense of freedom. I firmly believe that, as a peace-loving nation, we were building up our military in the eighties, not for war, but for peace. There are those who feel like we are wasting money and there is no need to have a strong defense in peace time. That mindset has been refuted time and time again.

No matter what goes on in this world, the elective process must continue. Since I had no opposition in '84, I was more relaxed at election time. In the Presidential election, the Reagan-Bush team scored an overwhelming victory over the Mondale-Ferraro ticket.

When inauguration time came around in January of 1985, the weather was not at all cooperative. Washington was covered with snow and for several days the temperature was sub-freezing. On Sunday prior to the inauguration, I was asked by WUSA-TV to appear on their morning program to talk about my proposed legislation to prohibit alcohol advertising on radio and TV. It was easy to drive to the parking garage at the Capitol, but I did not know the city well enough to try negotiating those streets in that kind of weather. So, I brought my family with me to the garage and we took a taxi and made it on time for the program at the TV station.

The on-the-air debate was with a lobbyist representing alcohol interests. Of course, he contended that advertising alcohol on radio and TV did not cause anyone to drink, it only helped them to choose one brand over another. I believe everyone knows better. In fact, all surveys showed that the American people believed there should not be advertising of alcohol in the broadcast media. After all, cigarette advertising on radio and TV was prohibited by Congress years ago.

As I have indicated previously, I do not condemn anyone for drinking. However, I am living proof that one does not have to drink alcoholic beverages to feel good, be happy, and be productive. I was brought up by parents who did not drink. I never have had the desire to drink. Of course, there has been pressure. The peer pressure for young people, particularly, to drink is enormous. This is especially true of those going into the military where, for years, drinking has been, at least tacitly, encouraged. In the past, it seems the one who could handle the most booze was held up to be the real "he-man." Now, this is being changed by doing away with happy hours and bargain prices on alcoholic beverages at our military installations.

Both in and out of the military, one who chooses to abstain is often made to feel like a prude. The alcoholic beverage industry capitalizes on this by spending millions of dollars on glamorous ads that portray youths having a great time. Star athletes are shown in beer ads that make drinking appear to be the thing to do. Certainly, this barrage of beer commercials causes young people to start drinking. Three million persons under 18 have serious drinking problems. Yet, a study showed the typical adolescent is exposed to nearly 1,000 alcoholic beverage ads per year. Public service spots warning of the dangers of alcohol abuse, in contrast, are low-budget productions, rarely aired in prime time.

Billions of dollars are lost each year, just in productivity to American industry, because of the alcohol problem. Billions more are spent by governments at every level on law enforcement and rehabilitative programs. Families break up, children go hungry, innocent people are killed--yet there is constant promotion of alcohol. Just recently, the deaths of a carload of drinking teenagers, and another accident where a drinking teenager caused the deaths of innocent people was deeply saddening. Alcohol has been deemed by the surgeon general and the Commission on Alcohol and Drugs as the nation's number one drug. We need to do more about this problem and banning ads of alcohol on radio and TV would be a step forward.

I am not advocating going back to prohibition, but it makes all the sense in the world to realize the terrible impact of alcohol on our society and do something about it. Mothers Against Drunk Driving and Students Against Drunk Driving perform a good service. There are many good rehabilitation programs. But, we need to do something up front, before drinking starts. Young people need to know that, though everyone else at the party may be imbibing, they do not have to drink, and in the long run will be respected. I am glad to see movement in this direction, such as alcohol-free events like First Night Pensacola, a terrific program for all ages, on New Year's Eve.

After I had appeared on WUSA-TV, Channel 9, Washington, I also was asked to be on C-SPAN's call-in program to discuss the possibility of my introducing legislation to ban alcohol advertising on radio and TV. The calls on C-SPAN, from all over the country, were overwhelmingly in favor of such legislation, just as are all surveys on this subject. One young lady caller said the advertisements did make drinking attractive to her, but maintained that she herself did not drink. But she did know older friends who drank. The caller was 10; her "older friends," the drinkers, were 12.

I really energized the alcohol and broadcast lobbies with my discussion and they were quick to contact Members of Congress. It became obvious to me that unless the people really demand this of their elected representatives legislation cannot be passed. So, at that time, realizing it would not pass, I decided not to introduce the bill. The will of the people, although in favor, must be expressed or an advertising ban, such as the one on tobacco, will not be passed. I hope the people will counter the alcohol and broadcast lobbies and demand this be done. It would be in the best interest of our nation and would result in saved lives and lessening of crime.

The bitter cold and snow forced the second inauguration of President Ronald Reagan to be moved indoors to the Capitol Rotunda. That meant that thousands of people who had made the trek to Washington would be unable to see President Reagan take the oath of office for his second term. I felt sorry for them, including those who had come from our district. Due to the limitation of space in the rotunda, only a privileged few were able to witness the ceremony. As a Member of Congress, I was among those privileged few. There were no chairs and everyone stood. The crowd was made up mainly of members of the House and Senate, cabinet members, and the president's family and friends. I was standing six feet from actor Jimmy Stewart, an old Hollywood friend of the president.

As I began my fourth term in Congress in January of 1985, a major change was made in the House Armed Services Committee.

Longtime Chairman Mel Price (D-Ill) was ousted by Les Aspin (D-Wisc) in the Democratic Caucus organization for the 99th Congress.

I had mixed feelings about this situation. Mr. Price was at an advanced age and quite feeble. He should have retired a few years earlier, but like others, he preferred to hang on, some said at the insistence of his wife. Anyway, it was obvious that staff was making most of the decisions for Mel and some members believed strongly that it was time for him to bow out in favor of a new chairman.

Les Aspin had been meeting with a number of mostly moderate and liberal members, apparently over the course of a year, drumming up support for plans to stage the coup d'etat at the organizational caucus. The rules provide an up-or-down vote on each chairman. If the chairman is voted down the Steering and Policy Committee provides another nomination, usually the next ranking committee member. Then, nominations are in order from the floor.

So, the first vote was to oust or retain the chairman. Aspin's strategy was to vote down Chairman Mel Price and then he would be nominated from the floor. I supported Mel, despite his frailties, and voted to keep him because I believe in the seniority system and, also, I was not particularly fond of Aspin. It was a nip-and-tuck vote, but Mel was voted down by one or two votes. It was heartbreaking for the old gentleman, but he had brought it on himself by not voluntarily giving up his chairmanship or retiring sooner.

That vote meant that the HASC was going to have a new chairman for the first time in a number of years. The Democratic Steering and Policy Committee presented, as expected, the name of the next ranking Democrat, Representative Charles Bennett, my colleague from Florida to be the chairman. Then, Aspin was nominated from the floor and it became a two-man race. All of this voting was by secret ballot as members went to the speaker's desk, marked their ballot, and put it in a box. There was no question for me about who to vote for in this contest. I was for Charlie Bennett. But, when the votes were counted, it was evident Aspin had done his work and would be chairman of the House Armed Services Committee.

It was a bad day for Charlie Bennett. Charlie, who had been in Congress some 37 years at that time, had waited such a long time to be the chairman of the committee. He wanted it more than anything. But Charlie was bucking the support that Aspin had built up. Too, although there was high regard for Charlie's integrity, there were some members who did not like him because of his dogmatic demeanor. The outcome left Charlie in tears and he felt terribly let down. I, and others, sought to console him by telling him that he still had a very important role to play as Chairman of the Seapower and Strategic and Critical Materials Subcommittee.

I did not personally dislike Les Aspin. At times he displayed a warm and jovial personality. I just did not like some of the positions he took and the detached manner in which he operated. Les loved the spotlight. Yet, I sensed there was a lot of loneliness in his life. For years, he probably issued more news releases than any member of congress. When he led a delegation to the Soviet Union in 1989, newspeople were included on the trip, and true to his nature, he spent most of his time with the media instead of his members.

Everyone acknowledged that Aspin was a bright guy, an intellectual with a lot of savvy about defense matters. He had been a young Army lieutenant in the Pentagon and served under Secretary of Defense Robert S. McNamara. At the time of his ascendency to the committee chairmanship, Les had been in Congress for sixteen years. Yet, the conservatives and pro-defense members of the committee did not care for Aspin because they did not believe he supported a strong defense, and he rarely attended committee meetings. Be that as it may, Les Aspin was our new chairman.

My biggest beef with Aspin was that I felt that there were others more senior who should have had a shot at the chairmanship. Aspin was number seven in seniority on the majority side. In committee, as I looked up at the top row from my second row seat, I saw people like Bill Nichols (Alabama), Dan Daniel (Virginia), Sam Stratton (NewYork), and Sonny Montgomery (Mississippi), and others with more seniority who had no chance to be chairman.

I was in agreement with the fact that members should have the opportunity to change a chairman if they chose to do so. But, my feeling was that the rules should be changed so that if a chairman is voted down the next in line should be voted on and, if he is turned down, the next in line should be voted on, and so on down the list in order of seniority until a chairman is elected. This would still allow someone like Aspin to be chosen provided he got his forces to vote down each member ahead of him in seniority.

I promulgated an amendment to the rules to provide that each member, unless they yielded, would be voted on in order of seniority until a chairman was elected. I believe it might have passed, but I agreed not to offer it on the floor with the understanding that the Committee on Organization and Rules of the caucus would consider this procedure for the next congress. They did, at a later date, ask me to testify on the matter, but the change was turned down by the committee, which had several ambitious young members who apparently felt that it would hamper their desire to move up.

Let me hasten to add that Aspin did do some good work with the committee. He was not anti-defense, as some charged, but in order to keep his chairmanship he had to kowtow to the liberal wing of the party. In fact, there were times when he took strong defense stands which alienated liberals. Because of his support for the MX Missile, Aspin himself was voted down as chairman by a coalition of liberals and by conservatives who felt he was weak on defense, at the beginning of the next Congress in January,1987. He was saved, however, when he was nominated from the floor and was re-elected in a race with Charlie Bennett, Marvin Leath (D-Texas), and Nick Mavroules (D-Massachusetts). This was another heartbreaker for Charlie, who was rejected a second time for chairman.

Most of the HASC supported the Contras against the communist Sandanista regime that had taken over Nicaraugua. However, we had little authority on the issue because this was a foreign policy matter carried out by the executive branch, the Reagan administration. In Congress, the issue was more in the domain of the Foreign Affairs Committee. After a weekend trip to El Salvador, which had a strong insurgency threat of its own, and to Nicaraugua with my colleagues Bill Nelson (D-Florida), George Wortley (R-New York), and Norm Shumway (R-California), I was convinced we needed to support the Contras. Incidentally, with Florida's proximity to Latin America, our state delegation was pretty much unified on matters relating to that part of the hemisphere.

One of the big scandals that drew headlines for a long time was the Iran-Contra affair involving the Reagan administration. There was a period of time when funding was not provided by the Congress for the Contras in Central America. One morning America woke up to the news that arms provided by the United States to Israel were being sold to Iran at inflated prices and millions of dollars from these arms sales were then diverted to the Contras. National Security Advisor John Poindexter resigned and his aide, Marine Lieutenant

Colonel Ollie North, was relieved of his duties as a result of the revelations. The President claimed no knowledge that this had been going on. A joint Senate-House Iran-Contra Committee held hearings and the nation was captivated by the testimony of Colonel North, who was later indicted and convicted for his role in the scandal.

Representative Jack Brinkley (D-Georgia) was my chairman on the Installations and Facilities Subcommittee, but he retired after my first term on the committee. That was frightening news to a lot of us because Representative Ronald Dellums (D-California) was next in line to be chairman. In the image of most Americans, Ron is a wild liberal from Berkeley. There was no question he was against building up our nation's defense. So, it was little wonder that we did not look forward to having this man as our chairman of the subcommittee.

There is a saying that, "You can't always tell a book by its cover." This would certainly apply to Ron Dellums. We were scared to death when he was elected chairman of the subcommittee which we referred to as the "Milcon Subcommittee." Our fear was unfounded. What a surprise when we found out that Mr. Dellums would lean over backwards to be fair and make sure everyone was heard in his subcommittee. He gained the respect of even the Republicans, who still sing his praises for being fair. He sometimes voted against his own bill, but everyone knew he would not try to do anything without due process. We disagreed with Dellums, but respected his fairness.

After my first term on the Armed Services Committee I chose Readiness as one of my subcommittees and dropped the R & D Subcommittee. Readiness Chairman Dan Daniel (D-Virginia) became somewhat of a mentor to me. In 1984 Dan appointed me to be the Chairman of the Special Operations Forces Panel. He was deeply disturbed, along with me and others, that the services were giving short shrift to special operations. These forces, perhaps not as glamorous to the leaders of the services, were low priority. One could expect that if cuts were made they would come out of special operations. The SOF Panel's mission was to conduct extensive inquiries into all facets of the readiness of our special forces and report to the House Armed Services Committee. Dan felt so strongly about special forces he publicly called for a sixth service to handle this job. I think Dan did this to get the Pentagon to listen.

We definitely got the attention of each of the services. But even after our panel held hearings and determined that we should prevail on Pentagon leaders to revitalize and put more emphasis on special operations, they were slow in doing it. We had a staffer, Ted Lunger, who was an expert on SOF and low intensity warfare. Lunger, with a vast knowledge in this area, was not always popular with other staffers who had less understanding of the issue. Representative John Kasich (R-Ohio) was a leader with Dan and me, and in the other body Senators Sam Nunn (D-Georgia) and Bill Cohen (R-Maine) were active on the subject of special operations on their side of the Capitol. It made sense in today's world, with seemingly a constant threat of terrorism or low-intensity conflict, that our SOF Forces ought to be better prepared for these situations.

We could no longer wait around for something to be done by the military services. The case had been made clear after the debacle in the Iranian desert, the foul-ups and perhaps unnecessary loss of life in Granada, despite its success, and a long list of situations that pointed out the need for building up and training special operations forces. A glaring example: the infamous telephone booth credit card call from Granada in connection with that invasion.

The Defense Department and the military services would not do it, so....Congress acted! We added an amendment to the Defense Authorization Bill for FY 1986 creating the U. S. Special Operations Command. The legislation provided for an Assistant Secretary of Defense for Special Operations and Low-intensity Conflict (SOLIC), Major Force Program Eleven (MFP-11) for budgetary authority, and many other features, including the provision for a four-star flag officer as the Commander-in-Chief of Special Operations Command (CINSOC), a new unified command. We meant business! The SOF problem was going to be fixed!

Our amendment became a part of the Goldwater-Nichols Act, named for Senator Barry Goldwater (R-Arizona) and Representative Bill Nichols (D-Alabama), which was the most far-reaching reform legislation for the military in half a century. Goldwater-Nichols provided for more jointness in the military services and, among other things, a greater role in decision-making for the CINCs, the commanders-in-chief in the field, who had been burdened down and restricted by having to go through Washington for every move.

Even after the passage of this landmark SOF legislation, we had to push hard to get the Pentagon to fully implement it. We felt, and this was specified in the legislation, that the headquarters of The

United States Special Operations Command (USSOCOM) should not be in Washington. So, accordingly, it was established at MacDill Air Force Base, in Tampa. Army General Jim Lindsay was appointed as the first CINCSOC. General Lindsay had a big task of getting the command organized and functioning, and he did a superb job.

After much foot dragging, Jim Locher, a former Senate staffer and a knowledgeable strong supporter of SOF, was appointed by the President and confirmed by the Senate to be Assistant Secretary for SOLIC, as provided in law. It was our intent that SOF be endowed with proper funding and assets to accomplish the job. Locher, General Lindsay, and others had to battle the Pentagon for it to happen..

Since the command's formation, our special forces have improved immensely. They are generally the first to go in any conflict. These forces are tough, well-trained, brave, and courageous, and a great credit to our nation. After a slow start, the USSOCOM has continued to move in the direction we in congress intended. We who worked on this legislation for SOF, are real proud. After General Lindsay's tenure, he was followed by General Carl Stiner, and by General Wayne Downing, during my time in Congress. All have served with distinction. The value of the new unified command has been demonstrated many times during the last ten years.

Tyndall Air Force Base, at Panama City, has been at the forefront of air defense for years. It has been the home base for many outstanding units, including the Air Defense Weapons Center. I vividly remember taking a flight at Tyndall in a F-l06 jet fighter, a beautifully proportioned aircraft and, a few years after that, going up in the fantastic F-15 jet. I have fond memories of working with General Creech, the commanding officer of the Tactical Air Command, in speeding up the addition of the F-15s to Tyndall. These planes continue to brighten the skies over Bay County.

It was in 1985 that I had the pleasure of announcing that a new hovercraft fleet would be established at the Naval Coastal Systems Center, also in Panama City. Assault Craft Unit 5 employed personnel from the Navy and Marine Corps. NCSC, which has had outstanding people doing vital research, especially in mines and mine countermeasures, was at that time named the military's main site for research and development of amphibious warfare equipment. The Landing Craft Air Cushion (LCAC) vehicles have been seen a lot in testing in St. Andrew Bay at Panama City for many years.

In Washington, one of the most prestigious titles that is revered probably more than Congressman or Senator is that of "Mister Chairman." I had previously been honored by being appointed to chair the Technology Transfer Panel and the Special Operation Forces Panel, but at the start of the 100th Congress in 1987, I had gained enough seniority to get a full subcommitte chairmanship. I was elected by the Merchant Marine and Fisheries Committee to be the Chairman of the Coast Guard and Navigations Subcommittee.

As chairman, I was able to hire my own staff and set my agenda for this subcommittee. It is so important to have good staff, so I was pleased to hire Gene Hamel, a former staffer for Senator Lawton Chiles, as the staff director of the Coast Guard and Navigations Subcommittee. Before going with Senator Chiles, Hamel had been with the General Accounting Office. As his assistant, I took Jeanne Timmins from my personal staff. It was a good move for Jeanne who had been on the Hill before I came to Congress and had served me well in several capacities. It was a new challenge for Jeanne and, working with Gene Hamel, the two did a good job for me. In the two-year period as chairman, we provided a lot for the Coast Guard, including improvement of boating safety for the public. In 1988 I was honored to receive the Legislative Award presented by the National Association of State Boating Law Administrators.

A big problem with the Coast Guard is that it is in the Department of Transportation. There are good arguments for putting it in the Defense Department, but those sentiments have not prevailed. However, the Coast Guard is assigned to Defense during time of war. Anyway, the subcommittee always had to fight hard with the appropriations subcommittee on transportation to get proper funding. Coast Guard Commandant Paul Yost testified before our subcommittee often and worked closely with us trying to keep funding at a level for the Coast Guard to do such jobs as search and rescue, navigation aids, boating safety, and coastal defense.

I realized that the appropriations people had tough decisions to make on surface, air, and water transportation and it was not an easy job. But Coast Guard should not be a secondary consideration for funding. Since they were not willing to appropriate sufficient amounts for the Coast Guard, I went to another appropriations subcommittee. Florida's own Bill Chappell was Chairman of the Defense Appropriations Subcommittee at that time and, more than once, I worked it out with Bill to provide some needed funds for the Coast Guard out of defense appropriations. This was generally for specific missions, such as drug interdiction.

In managing the Coast Guard authorization bill on the floor, I had to try to ward off amendments that would hurt the Coast Guard. Although members were generally supportive of the Coast Guard, it was difficult to vote against amendments to cut two or three per cent. Those kinds of amendments on our bill could really do damage.

The Coast Guard then, as now, has a major responsibility for fighting the war on drugs.This was a difficult task to accomplish with the limited amount of funding it received. In 1988 I introduced a bill to give the Coast Guard an additional $346 million to fight drug smuggling. The Coast Guard had been forced to reduce its routine patrols for drug smugglers by 55 per cent because of a $60 million budget shortfall. The money in my bill would buy, relocate and equip vessels, aircraft, radar and equipment for drug interdiction, and fund 500 more jobs to train pilots and other personnel.

My bill was folded into an omnibus drug bill which was passed by the Congress. I was pleased that the Coast Guard could receive these funds and get back to doing its business of interdicting drugs. The use of drugs, in whatever form, is a scourge on our nation.

In addition to my work with the Coast Guard on the drug problem, I sponsored and got passed in the House, a couple of times, a "Just Say No To Drugs" bill. It is my belief that filling the love and acceptance void in young hearts and getting a strong anti-drug message to them is the best way to fight this problem. If the demand is not there, the drug problem will end. First Lady Nancy Reagan was involved in the "Just Say No To Drugs" movement and I was invited to the White House to witness the President signing these bills.

One weekend in March,1987, I was in my home district when Carol Biven Davis, my district administrator for Escambia and Santa Rosa Counties, shocked me by informing me that she wanted to retire from the job. Carol had recently married Win Davis and she wanted to have more time to travel with Win and to start a small business. I was really sorry to see Carol leave because she had done outstanding work for the people of the First District and would be hard to replace.

As I departed for the airport to return to Washington, Carol gave me a folder of papers, as she often did, to look over on my return flight. After boarding, I opened the folder and among the papers was a resume' from Ben Collins. Mr. Collins, whom I did not know, had recently retired from Monsanto. His letter stated he had plenty of time and wanted to be of service to me as a volunteer. I was impressed with his resume, which included information about his background as a personnel manager and his supervision of people.

Volunteer? I got an idea. This guy could be more than a volunteer. He might be just who I was looking for to replace Carol. As soon as I got to Washington I tried to call Ben, who lives in Milton. Ben and his wife, Vergie, were out of town for a while and son, Steve, checked their messages and got in touch with his dad. To make a long story short, I was able to set up an appointment with Ben the next weekend in Pensacola. We met at Burger King for lunch and I explained the job and asked if he would be interested. He was.

After checking references, I called Ben a few days later and offered him the job, which he accepted. Ben was not looking for money, just something productive to do, and the salary did not matter. I, nonetheless, hired him at what I thought was a fair salary. Ben started working with Carol to learn the job and, when she left the office, Ben took over without missing a lick. He endeared himself to the office staff and to the people, just as Carol had done, and continued in the position of district administrator for the rest of my congressional career. Ben's family thanked me several times for hiring him because they said he was miserable without the regular routine of a job, after having worked so many years.

Carol and Ben had great staff support. In addition to those mentioned, Joy Reiter, Pam Price, Linda Mitchell, Ruby Boyd, Traci Weidlich, Dolores Drennan, and Summer Jimmerson did good work.

Elected officials are called on for a lot of things. My good friend and supporter John Deese invited me to a hunting camp to award trophies for the Dog Hunters Association. "Sure, John, I'll be glad to do it," I said. "Okay, Earl, be at the lodge about three a.m. Saturday morning," John replied, "and we will have breakfast before giving out the awards." Three a.m.?

I was the house guest of Homer and Laura Singletary the night before the awards were to be made and Homer volunteered to get up and go with me to the lodge, somewhere in the woods of northern Escambia County. It was hardly worth going to bed. We had to get up at one a.m. in order to be there on time. We made it!

The lodge was a beehive of activity. The hunters were

drifting in and the ladies were busy cooking breakfast. Mmm...what a delightful aroma! Pretty soon we were served a delicious breakfast of eggs, bacon, grits, and biscuits. Homer was probably a bigger eater than I, which is saying a lot, so we both ate with gusto. The thing that I most remember about this occasion was our host, John Deese, getting upset when he put his filled plate to the side, to do some chore, and another hunter's dog got into his breakfast. It was not funny to John, but it was to Homer and me, although we refrained from laughing as much as we could.

In January of 1988, my good friend, Congressman Dan Daniel, died unexpectedly from a heart attack. Nancy and I joined a congressional delegation for the funeral at a Baptist church in Danville. It seemed the whole town turned out to say goodbye to this much loved great American patriot. It was a personal loss for me.

I was asked by President Reagan to be in a delegation to represent the United States at the funeral of Republic of China's President Chiang Chang-kuo. So, as soon as we got back to Washington from Dan's funeral, I boarded a military aircraft at Andrews Air Force Base and headed for Taiwan. Leading the delegation to Taipei was Reagan's former Attorney General, William French Smith. Others in the group were former Nevada Senator Paul Laxalt, Senator Frank Murkowski (R-Alaska), Senator Malcolm Wallop (R-Wyoming), and Representatives Bob Livingston (R-Louisiana) and Bill Thomas (R-California). It was, indeed, an honor for me to be chosen by the president as the only Democrat in the group. This could have been because I had spoken to the World Anti-Communist League the previous August in Taipei and was probably one of the last congressmen to speak with the late President Chiang.

The funeral ceremony, very moving and impressive, was much like a protestant American funeral. We extended the condolences of President Reagan and the American people to the family and to the leading officials in Taiwan.

The day after the ceremony we had a good session with Taiwan's new President Lih, who was educated in the United States, and with other government leaders. Although in 1979 the United States recognized the People's Republic of China and withdrew recognition of Taiwan, we continued relations through non-government offices authorized by Congress. We got in a "few licks" about our trade deficit with Taiwan and were encouraged by the response. Taiwan had recently reduced tariffs on 3,000 import products and officials indicated they would consider reducing tariffs on 1,700 other items. I appreciate Taiwan for its strong anti-communist stand and feel we should maintain close ties.

In early 1989 former Vice President George Bush was taking over the top office to lead America for the next four years. At that time I had a choice to make, but it was easy. I had gained enough seniority on the Armed Services Committee to become a chairman of one of its subcommittees. The rules allow a member to chair only one subcommittee, so I had to drop my chairmanship of the Coast Guard and Navigation Subcommittee. I really enjoyed that subcommittee, but I chose to take the Readiness Subcommittee on Armed Services because it had about a $90 billion dollar annual budget, whereas Coast Guard was about $3 billion. Besides, with the military in my district, this is what I was waiting for.

Unlike the Coast Guard Subcommittee, I was not allowed to hire my own subcommittee staff on Readiness, except for one person. I had to use the professional nonpartisan staff of the committee which, in accordance with my conservative philosophy, was just fine. Will Cofer, formerly with GAO, was staff director. Will served Readiness Chairman Dan Daniel, as well as Nick Mavroules, chairman for the year following Dan's passing. Cofer, Steve Rossetti, Pete Steffes, Kathy Lipovac and Peggy Cosseboom were mainstays of the staff. Will retired in '93 and Steve became staff director.

When I was elected chairman of the Readiness Subcommittee, no one challenged me. Generally, I worked well with Chairman Aspin. The biggest problem I had was getting an audience with him. Sometimes when I needed to talk with him I found the best way was to catch him on the floor during a vote, and even then he always seemed to be on the run. He was bad about not returning my phone calls. Les was somewhat detached from his members.

Although the rules allowed me to hire one person on the Readiness staff, I had a terrible time getting Aspin to approve it. I fought for a year to make it happen. As usual, I had trouble getting in to see him. I even got our mutual friend, Ike Skelton (D-Missouri), to talk to Aspin, but to no avail. I worked through Aspin's staff and finally was able to get an arrangement where I would have half of a staffer's salary paid by the committee and the staffer would have access to the committee and staff. This was some help to me.

Since the Special Operations Forces panel, which I had headed for three or four years, was under the Readiness Subcommittee which I now chaired, I decided I could pursue my interest in SOF without continuing the panel and would save the taxpayers a little money. There was another important panel under the jurisdiction of the Readiness Subcommittee and that was the one on Morale, Welfare, and Recreation. Marvin Leath (D-Texas) had been chairman of the MWR Panel and wanted to continue. I allowed him to do so.

When Leath retired two years after that, I had intentions of appointing Solomon Ortiz (D-Texas) who was in line for chairmanship of the MWR Panel. But, hold on. Aspin, apparently in a further move to consolidate power and control, decided to make the MWR Panel a full committee panel instead of leaving it under the jurisdiction of Readiness. I heard that this was in the works, but Aspin did not come to me and advise me of it, as he should have done.

Knowing that I was upset about the matter, the chairman sent some of his top aides to talk to me. Aspin appointed Martin Lancaster (D-North Carolina), a close ally but with less seniority than Ortiz, as the new chairman of the panel. Lancaster did a nice job, but to me it was purely a political move by Aspin, and the panel, which had functioned well, should remain as a panel under Readiness. The only concession was that the Readiness Subcommittee Chairman, which was me, would sit as ex-officio member of the panel.

Randy Knepper left my staff in May of 1989, after ten years as administrative assistant, to become President and CEO of American Bank and Trust in Pensacola. It was at this point that I prevailed on another military officer to retire and come to work with me. Gary Pulliam, who was in Air Force Legislative Liaison and who, with his family, attended our church, seemed an ideal choice. I knew Gary was about to complete his twenty years with the Air Force and, as a lieutenant colonel, was trying to make a decision as to whether he should continue his military career and go for full colonel or retire and seek other employment. He and his wife, Darlene, came to our home to talk with Nancy and me about his taking the AA job that Randy was leaving. Among his questions to me was, "How much longer do you think you will stay in Congress?" I leveled with him, but asked him not to relay this information to anyone else. I replied, "about five years." Indeed, as I mentioned earlier, Nancy and I established 1994 as our time frame for leaving Congress.

It was May, and Gary Pulliam could not get out of the Air Force until November. So, the question was: Could I make it without an AA until November? If I could, then he would accept the job. I decided that, although it would be difficult, we could hold off on filling the job until that time.

Though our staff was probably as stable as any in Congress, it is normal to have some changes from time to time. Back when I took the Coast Guard Subcommittee chairmanship and moved Jeanne Timmins over to the subcommittee staff, I gave Betts Spracher, a longtime holdover employee from Mr. Sikes's staff, the responsibility of being my secretary. Betts, who was a good typist, served me in that capacity for a year or so before her retirement.

One day I was working at my desk when I broke out laughing so loud the whole staff heard me. Since I had an open door policy, they came dashing in to see what was so funny. Sometimes, instead of dictating answers to personal letters, I would just make a note to Betts telling her briefly how to answer. At this particular time, I had received a letter from a lady in our district with some pictures she wanted me to have. So, I scribbled a note on the letter that accompanied the photos that said, "Betts, thank her for the pics." Betts composed and typed the letter and put it in my "in box" where my letters to sign were placed. When I picked it up to sign, I read, "Dear Jane: Thank you for the pies. They were simply delicious!" That's when I roared with laughter. Betts had read my note to say "pies" instead of "pics."

Another good friend and colleague on the Armed Services Committee, Representative Bill Nichols (D-Alabama) died suddenly of a heart attack in his office after coming to work early one morning in December, 1988. The night before, Nancy had let our daughter, Lori, take her place in attending the White House Christmas party with me. Lori and I had seen Bill Nichols and wife, Carolyn, in a joyful mood, just before we departed from the White House that night. I was on board an aircraft at Washington National Airport the next morning, ready to depart for Florida, when an attendant brought a note informing me of the death of Mr. Nichols. This was a real shock! The Nicholses were good friends and we had a special attachment due to the fact that Bill was an alumnus and on the Board of Trustees of Auburn University where Lori was attending and where Amy later would enroll.

Mr. Nichols had an excellent staffer that we wanted to bring to our staff and I gave Randy the green light in trying to get her to work with us. Cathie McCarley, who had worked with Congressman Nichols for fifteen years, liked our office and people and, after talking with Randy and me, she accepted the job as executive secretary. In the past I had given my secretary other responsibilities, but Cathie was hired to be full-time secretary for Randy and me and with her experience she, in reality, served as somewhat of an office manager.

So, a few months later, when I would decide to hire Gary Pulliam and wait five months for him to report to work, I was confident in knowing that Cathie, now working in the office next to mine, within hearing range, would be a big help in getting us through the time before Gary came on board.

In April of that year, we added as replacement for the retiring receptionist Mary Sharp, at the front desk, a lady by the name of Helen Berry. Helen was someone who was well known to me, Nancy, Randy, and to Gary Pulliam, our forthcoming administrative assistant, because she also attended our church in Springfield. Additionally, Nancy and I had known Helen and her husband, John, when we patronized a paint and wallpaper store they owned.

Helen and John decided to close their store after more than 20 years in business because the landlord of the shopping center increased their rent too much. This was timely for me because Helen was just what we needed at our front desk. She was a joy for all of us to work with and, like Mary before her, made everyone who came into the office or called feel welcome. Helen had come to Washington from Russellville, Alabama out of high school and worked with the FBI until she and John married. Now she was back at work with the federal government. Helen and Cathie developed a very close relationship and both did splendid work, especially during the interim when we did not have an administrative assistant.

Finally, November arrived. Gary, after a nice retirement ceremony, was back in civilian life after 20 years. Some of the issues he had dealt with the last several years, while in legislative liaison for the Air Force, would be issues he would continue to work in his employment with me. In addition to being the AA, Gary, with his military experience, would be a key player with me and the First Congressional District of Florida in staying abreast of military matters, especially the defense drawdown which became even more severe after the Gulf War. Since Aspin allowed me a half-staffer, Gary was the one I put on as a part-time employee of the Readiness Subcommittee. This was good for Gary and me due to the fact that, in addition to serving as my AA, he was generally treated as a full committee staffer and was able to attend important staff meetings.

Serving as chairman of the Readiness Subcommittee was a great responsibility which I did not take lightly. Readiness is the key to success for our armed forces. Our subcommittee had jurisdiction for authorizing funding for operation and maintenance of our forces worldwide. We had specific jurisdiction over special operations, exercises and training, civilian personnel, commissaries, exchanges, and morale, welfare, and recreation of our troops.

The Readiness Subcommittee had responsibility for more of the defense budget than any subcommittee, in the neighborhood of $90 billion annually, which was enacted under the operations and maintenance title of the defense authorization bill. Our subcommittee drafted this title and reported it to the full committee to incorporate with titles by other subcommittees such as Procurement, Research and Development, Personnel, and Military Construction.

Each year the full committee, after consideration of many amendments and much debate, passed the bill and sent it to the rules committee which promulgated a rule under which the bill was debated on the floor of the House. Of course, this same procedure was followed in the Senate. When each of the two bodies passed its defense bills, a conference committee was appointed to iron out the differences. Then the conference report went to both bodies for approval before sending it on to the president.

Conferees are appointed by the speaker, on recommendation of the committee chairs, from subcommittee chairmen and senior members. I was on the conference committee a couple of years before I became a subcommittee chairman. I never will forget, one year, going into the conference and looking across the table and seeing at least five former presidential candidates. Wow! What a lineup! There was Strom Thurmond (R-South Carolina), who ran as a Dixiecrat in 1948; Barry Goldwater (R-Arizona), who was the Republican candidate in 1964; as well as Ted Kennedy (D-Massachusetts), Gary Hart (D-Colorado), and John Glenn (D-Ohio), all of whom had run in primaries. Also present were two others who later ran: Phil Gramm(R-Texas) and Pete Wilson (R-California).

The procedure for the conferences would first find all of the conferees of the House and Senate meeting jointly in a secure room. Then the conferees were divided into groups, according to subject matter. The subcommittees of the House did not match up precisely with the subcommittees of the Senate, so it was sometimes difficult to figure out who the negotiators from the Senate were. But the full committee chairmen would determine who was to be on each group. The smaller groups scheduled separate meetings to try to come to agreement on the literally hundreds of issues in the defense bill. The chairmanship of the conference committee rotated from year to year between the House and Senate. The same was true of the sub-groups.

In 1986, my first year on the conference committee, Senator Goldwater was chairman of the Armed Services Committee in the Senate and Mel Price was chairman of our committee. It was the Senate's time to chair, so Senator Goldwater was chairman. He depended a great deal on Senator Sam Nunn (D-Georgia), the ranking minority member. I remember, on more than one contentious issue, Senator Goldwater would say, "Sam, what do you think about this?" Senator Nunn would say something like, "Mr. Chairman, I believe we ought to do this (or that)." Whereupon, Senator Goldwater would reply, "Okay, let's do it."

The staff, in consultation with the chairmen and members, would do a lot of the work in ironing out the differences in the two versions of the bill. On some of the more controversial provisions, the groups would meet more often. Many times it would take more than two weeks to come to full agreement in the conference, but generally it was done in two or three weeks.

The Republicans lost control of the Senate after six years and beginning in 1987 Democrats were in the majority through the rest of my time in congress. Senator Nunn was the Senate Armed Services Committee (SASC) chairman. On the House side Les Aspin, following his overthrow of Mel Price, continued as our chairman until he was appointed Secretary of Defense by President Bill Clinton in 1993. Aspin was then succeeded by Ron Dellums (D-California).

As subcommittee chairman, every other year I was chairman of our negotiating group. The chairman from the Senate I faced most was Senator Alan Dixon (D-Illinois) and, after his defeat in 1992, I went up against Senator John Glenn (D-Ohio). Both were enjoyable to work with. Senator Dixon had a rather exuberant personality and it was fun to hear him plead for his viewpoint, in somewhat whining tones, from time to time. Of course, Senator Glenn was strong in holding his positions, but was reasonable.

I remember one year when Senator Dixon put in $2 million in the Senate bill for a Navy project in connection with the Museum of Science and Industry in Chicago. I felt very strongly that if the senator was going to authorize appropriations to that institution I was going to do likewise for the National Naval Aviation Museum in Pensacola, which is an outstanding museum that needed funds for its continued growth. I put the money in and both projects were funded. I am proud to serve on the Board of Trustees of the Naval Aviation Museum, which now has a six-story tall IMAX theater and is attracting visitors from throughout the world.

Already mentioned were some of our involvements in the first half of the decade of the eighties. In the second half, we still had to contend with hostile leaders of the world, such as Moammar Khadafy in Libya, Manuel Noriega in Panama, and Saddam Hussein in Iraq.

One morning at two a.m. Nancy and I were sleeping soundly in our home in Springfield when the telephone rang. It was Dave Gribben, Assistant Secretary of Defense, on the line. "Mr. Hutto, I am calling for Secretary Cheney who wanted me to let you know we have just begun 'Operation Just Cause' and our forces are beginning to invade Panama," he stated. That was all he had to report on the invasion, so I said, "Thanks, Dave, I appreciate your letting me know." I knew that we had to get Noriega out of there and I was confident our forces would do a good job. With that assurance in mind, I turned over and went back to sleep.

We had barely gotten back home to Florida in late October 1990, with only a week or so to campaign, when President Bush called the armed services committees and the appropriations committees of the House and Senate back to Washington to consult with us about Iraq's invasion of Kuwait and to advise us of the administration's decision to deploy military forces to the Persian Gulf.

President Bush did an outstanding job, through the UN, of rallying other nations to the cause and getting them to supply troops as well as financial support. There was a great debate in Congress as the president sought congressional support for sending troops to the desert to stop the advances of Saddam and to drive the Iraqi forces out of Kuwait. In my view we had to act. If we had not, it is likely

Saddam would have continued into Saudi Arabia and who knows where else? Closing the debate in the House, with a dynamic speech for giving the president the authority he asked for, was a liberal Democrat from New York, Steve Solarz. I supported the president, and thankfully a bipartisan majority in Congress voted approval.

Operation Desert Shield saw the relatively quick and orderly movement of a half million of our troops to Saudi Arabia. It was obvious to most of us that we could not allow Saddam Hussein to invade Kuwait and get away with it. A high percentage of the world's oil flows through the Persian Gulf, so it was of great national interest to us as well as other nations. Though it was in our interest and we would lead the way, it was also the responsibility of a lot of other nations, none the least of which were Kuwait and Saudi Arabia. Incidentally, it was our only war where the expenses were paid for by other nations, namely these two.

U. S. and allied forces were ready. Nancy was back in our home district with me. We were walking out of Wednesday night prayer meeting in Panama City, headed for Pensacola, when we met a couple of young girls who said, "We were just listening to the radio and heard that our planes are bombing Iraq!" We knew the war was on. Operation Desert Storm had started! As we drove on Highway 98 we heard reports. Upon arrival in Pensacola, WEAR-TV had a news crew waiting to interview me.

Though there were complaints from the news media about restrictions, there is no question the Persian Gulf War, with the U. S. and allied forces under the command of General Norman Schwarzkopf, of the U. S. Army, was the most covered war in history. There were uneasy moments as Saddam fired his Scud Missiles, but it was good to hear reports that our Patriot Missiles were intercepting and blasting from the sky the incoming Scuds.

The air war, directed by General Chuck Horner, whom I had known and played golf with when he was at Tyndall, was highly successful as we pounded strategic targets in Baghdad and elsewhere. But, realizing that Saddam Hussein was not going to surrender, the world waited anxiously for the ground war to begin. We were confident our forces could win, but at what cost? Thankfully, when it started, it was no contest and the war was over quickly. Although our casualties were relatively low, I am grateful, and I believe all Americans feel the same way, for the sacrifices made by those who did not return. They were heroes. Included were 13 men aboard an AC-130 gunship, from Hurlburt Field in my district, which was shot down just off the Kuwaiti coast. I attended memorial services for these brave warriors and met with their families to express my condolences and gratitude for the sacrifices made by their loved ones.

When Iraq surrendered, the objective of driving Saddam's forces out of Kuwait had succeeded. Frankly, I and many Americans felt the world, and without a doubt the suffering people of Iraq, would have been better off if we had a further objective of capturing Saddam and bringing him to justice, like with Noriega of Panama. Saddam continues to be a tyrant who defies the civilized world.

There were many heroes in Desert Storm, but most noted was the commander of the allied forces, Stormin' Norman Schwarzkopf. Senator Trent Lott (R-Mississippi) sponsored in the Senate and asked me to sponsor in the House, legislation to award the Congressional Gold Medal to General Schwarzkopf. I agreed and our bill passed.

General Schwarzkopf was invited to address a joint session of congress. It was a pleasure to present, with Senator Lott and Representative Sonny Montgomery (D-Mississippi), a framed copy of the Joint Resolution passed by Congress authorizing the Congressional Gold Medal to General Schwarzkopf in a ceremony in the speaker's office prior to his speech. It was good to meet the Schwarzkopf family who accompanied him to Washington. The actual medal was presented at the White House by President Bush.

Due to the fact that Secretary of Defense Dick Cheney and Chairman of the Joint Chiefs of Staff Colin Powell played such leadership roles in the Desert Storm victory, we decided that they, too, should be recognized with Congressional Gold Medals. So, authorization legislation was passed and I was privileged to be invited to the White House to witness the president making these awards.

The gunship that went down off Kuwait, along with other units and personnel from Hurlburt who were in the Gulf War, was another example of this base's involvement when duty calls. In just about every conflict in which America has interests, the first to go are troops from Hurlburt, Eglin Air Force Base, and Duke Field, the reserve Air Force base near Crestview. The 33rd Fighter Wing from Eglin, with their F-15s, played a major role in Desert Storm and knocked down more Iraqi planes than any other unit.

In 1990, the 23rd Air Force, which had come to Hurlburt from

Scott Air Force Base, Illinois, was upgraded to become the U. S. Air Force Special Operations Command, a major Air Force command reporting directly to the Air Force chief of staff. I had a close working relationship with the special forces community and it was with great pleasure that I made the announcement about the upgrade at Hurlburt, which added 100 military personnel, and further increased the stature of Hurlburt Field.

In Northwest Florida we love the military--all branches. In keeping our bases strong I was supported by chambers of commerce and other groups and people who went to great lengths to show our military services they are welcome and respected in the Panhandle.

My office and I welcomed the input of the local communities. In the Fort Walton Beach area which has the Air Force facilities at Eglin, Hurlburt, and Duke, I sometimes had difficulty, however, in knowing which group spoke for the community. We got different signals. There were constant rumors about the Air Force planning to make big cuts, or actually making plans to close Eglin. The rumors were usually just that, but we spent an awful lot of time trying to track them down. After he returned from the Gulf War, Larry Williamson worked for me in Okaloosa County and helped a lot in working with the different factions.

I would be remiss, though, in not stating that there were a lot of outstanding people with a great deal of knowledge about military matters in that area. It was evident that many did not realize the work that I had done on their behalf. With the military drawdown, it is impossible to protect every unit and every job. But, even against those odds, we managed to keep Okaloosa's military on the plus side.

One of the biggest battles I had was with Air Force Secretary Don Rice over changes connected with the disestablishment of the Munitions System Division (MSD) at Eglin, a move that potentially could cost the area about 2,500 jobs. The proposed changes were in the Defense Management Review (DMR) to restructure the armed services' troubled procurement system. After doing a bit of research, I found a provision in the law that would prohibit this kind of realignment without approval of Congress. I made the case with General Bernard Randolph, commander of the Air Force Systems Command, and persuaded him to leave the MSD at Eglin, at least temporarily. General Randolph was in the process of retiring at about that time, but his successor, General Ron Yates, agreed with my interpretation of the law.

The ball game was not over. There apparently was a difference of opinion by the legal experts in the Pentagon and the matter rocked on for several months. Air Force Secretary Rice had the disestablishment of MSD as part of major changes he planned for streamlining the service. I asked Secretary Rice to come over to my office and huddle with our Florida Senators Bob Graham and Connie Mack. Still, no resolution. Meanwhile, the doomsayers, each with a different story, kept calling from the Eglin area with more rumors.

I had great respect for Secretary Rice as being an honorable man and I believe he respected me in the same way. In fact, he even picked me to be in his foursome in the Air Force Secretary's golf tournament. That did not appease me, and I don't think he expected that it would. It was a tough, drawn-out battle, but one that I believe was fought with integrity. I was glad to have Gary Pulliam, who formerly worked in Air Force legislative liaison, on my staff. Gary knew how they worked in the Pentagon and knew a lot of those involved in helping Secretary Rice with his decisions.

The fear was the possibility of losing a lot of Eglin's development personnel to the Aeronautical Systems Division (ASD) at Wright-Patterson Air Force Base in Dayton, Ohio. I was adamant about not losing these jobs. Gary communicated with people in the Pentagon about what was going on and from time-to-time, through staffers, Secretary Rice would float a proposal to me. Each of them we found unacceptable. Once, Gary listened on the phone as a letter to me from Rice was read to him which still proposed the disestablishment of MSD with a considerable loss of jobs. I told Gary to tell the Pentagon folks to advise Secretary Rice not to send the letter. It was completely unacceptable. The letter was not sent.

Finally, after months of negotiating, the Secretary called me with a proposal. He was agreeable to keeping the jobs at Eglin in what amounted to an ASD-South and he proposed to replace the Munitions Systems Division with a Tactical Test Center. I wanted Eglin to continue with development and testing of weapon systems, so I suggested that, instead of Tactical Test Center, that it be called the Air Force Development and Test Center (AFDTC). Rice accepted that and finally, after some six months, the squabble was over! He was true to his word and there was no loss of jobs at Eglin. In fact there was a net gain.

Okaloosa County wanted to renew its lease with Eglin for the use of its Okaloosa airport and terminal building. Eglin refused, saying that increased commercial air service would be incompatible with increased military flights after the year 2,000. The county commissioners came to me for help. I asked Secretary of Defense Casper Weinberger to have DOD do an airspace study. It found Eglin would have no problem accommodating the commercial service for years into the future. The airport lease was extended to the year2,012.

There were numerous other things we did for the county, including passage of legislation providing for a swap of land between the federal and state governments for a new Okaloosa Walton Community College--University of West Florida Education Center that has been built. I also got legislation passed to relieve tower height restrictions, and worked to get easements for the new Mid-Bay Bridge connecting Destin with the Niceville area.

When I first started my congressional career, I had frequent meetings and telephone conferences with the Bay County Chamber of Commerce in Panama City, but for a period of several years afterward I was getting little or no support from my hometown leaders. So, I decided to have lunch with three or four of the business people to see if I could establish a better rapport.

When I met with these folks, I told them that in both Pensacola and Fort Walton Beach the chambers had been working closely with me and expressed to them my disappointment that I was not getting better support from the chamber in Panama City. Apparently the membership of the chamber was unaware of this disconnection and John Robbins, one of those in the group, began working to change the situation. It was about that time that my good friend, Hugh Roche, with whom I had worked at Channel 7, moved back to Panama City to manage Channel 13. After Hugh and I talked about the lack of support I was getting in the business community, he started the ball rolling. Hugh and John did a fine job and pretty soon an annual visit to Washington was coordinated with my office.

During the visits to Washington by these groups, the major emphasis was on the military with regard to Tyndall AFB and the Naval Coastal Systems Center by the folks from Panama City; Eglin AFB, Hurlburt Field, and Duke Field by those from the Fort Walton Beach area; and Pensacola Naval Air Station, Whiting Naval Air Station, and all of the naval units in the area by the Pensacola-Milton delegation. Of course, these were separate trips by the three groups.

I was able to line up meetings with key people in the Pentagon--military and civilian--with jurisdiction over the matters in which they were interested. Often, the Navy Secretary and Air Force Secretary, as well as the Chief of Staff of the Air Force and the Chief of Naval Operations were included in our visits. After my years on the HASC and through my Readiness Subcommittee dealings with these leaders, I was on a first name basis with them. This definitely facilitated our confabs and we left nearly every meeting feeling good about the military facilities back home.

The annual visits of the Pensacola folks had been started while Mr. Sikes was in office, a few years before I got to Congress. The first year I was there, only a few people from the Chamber of Commerce and the Naval Air Station made up the delegation which referred to themselves as a committee. After that, we organized a three-day program each year that began with the arrival of the visitors in Washington on a Sunday. That evening they would host Nancy, me, and our staff at dinner.

Meetings were scheduled, mostly at the Pentagon, for Monday. This was followed by a meeting in my office on Tuesday morning, then at noon by a luncheon on Capitol Hill that we referred to as the Pensacola Day Luncheon. This event grew so much we had to schedule larger rooms, such as the Cannon Caucus Room, to accommodate all the Navy and Marine Corps folks who were invited. I remember Sam Lovelace, who worked as the civilian facilities manager at Pensacola Naval Air Station for over 50 years, was in charge of coordinating the event for a long time before his retirement.

I have rarely seen so much Navy brass in one place as when this luncheon convened. Everybody, who might have anything to do with the U. S. Navy and Marine Corps down our way, was invited and nearly all of them attended. It became an annual ritual and the Washington invitees loved it. Many who had been stationed in Pensacola were there. The attendance numbered as many as 150 people. There was no question that it was a wonderful good will happening for the Escambia-Santa Rosa County area.

It was my job to emcee the Pensacola Day Luncheon. Many of my colleagues, mostly Armed Services and Appropriations Committee members who were invited, dropped by and I would call on them to say a few words. Our Florida Senators were invited.

Secretary of Defense Casper Weinberger had lunch with us a time or two. I was honored that he accepted my invitation and more pleased at the nice things he said about me and Pensacola. The Navy Secretary made several of the luncheons, and we always had a bunch of assistant secretaries, congressional and military staffers.

In the Tuesday sessions in my office, the Pensacola group, led by Sam Lovelace, would enlighten me on the status of military construction projects for the present and future, and any other subjects relating to the Navy's presence in Pensacola. Sam is a fine gentleman with whom I enjoyed working. We got along famously and I agreed with Sam on just about everything--except one.

The Naval Air Station badly needed a new brig, but I disagreed with my friend, Sam, on the location which he had planned for it. It was close to the Barrancas National Cemetery and I knew that, in the future, that land would be needed for burial sites. Sam finally agreed and found another location. After that, we always kidded about the "brig."

The delegation from Pensacola that made the annual trek to Washington was comprised of only Escambia people for the longest time. But in the last two or three years of my time in Congress, Santa Rosa Countians were added to the group. This was good because the leaders of the two counties have not seen eye-to-eye on a lot of things, and still don't. But progress has been made and including the Santa Rosa folks on the Washington trip was definitely a step in the right direction.

There was one person whom we greatly missed on those last few Pensacola visits, and that was Sam Lovelace. Sam was almost a landmark. I doubt if anyone has ever worked at the Naval Air Station as long as he did. But, finally, he retired and then his health began to fail. So, Sam was not included on the Pensacola visits to Washington.

Sam saw the need of a new bridge crossing from Pensacola to the Naval Air Station. He was right in his advocacy, not only because of the employees, but also the increasing thousands of people visiting the National Naval Aviation Museum. When I obtained the $6 million funding for the multi-laned bridge in the mid-eighties, it was only fitting that it be named the Sam Lovelace Bridge as a memorial to a man who did so much for his community and his country.

Admiral Paul Yost, Commandant of the United States Coast Guard, greets
Congressman Earl Hutto, Chairman of the Coast Guard and Navigation
Subcommittee, before testifying at a hearing in Washington.

Earl Hutto, Chairman of the Readiness Subcommittee of the House Armed
Services Committee for six years, interacts with a hearing witness.

Congressman Earl Hutto and Senator Trent Lott present copy of legislation awarding the Congressional Gold Medal to General Stormin' Norman Schwarzkopf, hero of the Gulf War, and Mrs. Schwarzkopf.

Congressman Earl Hutto, second from left, confers with Congressmen Newt Gingrich (R-Ga)), Sonny Montgomery (D-Mississippi), and Minority Leader Bob Michel (R-Ill.) on an amendment being considered on the floor.

17

AVOIDING POTOMAC FEVER

A lot of people who serve in Congress, in the military, in government jobs, or any other jobs in the Washington area cannot, somehow, break loose and leave the Capitol area when they retire or give up those vocations that took them there. This is called "Potomac Fever," and many folks seem to catch it. I guess they feel that Washington is where the action is and that is where they need to be.

It is true that Washington is an exciting place. It is not only the seat of government for the greatest nation on earth, it is, in essence, the capitol of the world. Indeed, as the leader of the free world, and especially since the demise of the Soviet Union, we are the one super power left. Many decisions made in Washington have worldwide ramifications. I can understand how people get caught up in believing that they are an awesome part of all this power.

I have no problem with those who succumb to "Potomac Fever" and have a lot of friends who have chosen to stay in our nation's capitol. I enjoyed Washington. I enjoyed serving in Congress. But, frankly, I like a better feeling of community. In reality, I had rather be a big fish in a little pond than the reverse. I love the part of the country where I was born and raised. I like to be able to get in my old car and know I can get to most any place in town in 15 or 20 minutes, unless my conveyance conks out. I enjoy seeing and being with family and friends. Washington is too big--it's too busy.

So, as I have indicated, Nancy and I wanted our children to be oriented to the southeast. We steered them that way and it took. Yes, it is all right with me if others want to stay in Washington, but as for me and my house, give us "Home, Sweet Home."

During our sixteen years in the Washington area, we stayed in touch with relatives and with people generally. This was not just for political reasons, though this was certainly necessary, but it was also because we love people.

We might have lived a thousand miles away from our real home during our Washington sojourn, but our hearts did not stray from our upbringing. Our lifestyle changed little and we are still the same folks we were when duty called and the good people of Northwest Florida hired us to head north and represent them in the Congress of the United States.

Family--and I am not speaking just of our immediate family, but our extended family of loved ones and relatives--means so much to us. Even while in Congress, I made it a point to be home the fourth Sunday of every July to attend the Kelly-Mathis Reunion, which is held in an old refurbished one-room schoolhouse now used as a community center at a crossroads near Dothan, called Grimes.

The reunion has not always been held there. As a small child, I remember attending the event with my parents and brother and sister when it was held at the home of Uncle Meredith Kelly, a great uncle, out in the country in Barbour County, Alabama. Our mother was a Mathis and her mother was a Kelly. After Uncle Meredith's death, the reunion was moved to the shade trees at Salem Baptist Church, not far away. Then, for a period of time it was held at the state park in Blue Springs, still in that general area. It was a delightful place to have a gathering, but one of our cousins objected to the presence of all those scantily-clad girls in their bathing suits. A bigger reason to move it, though, was that it was hot as blazes outside at that time of year. Ah, how wonderful it is that we now have air conditioning inside for the reunion, although I doubt there was air conditioning in that building at Grimes when it was used as a school.

Now, I'll admit that I do not know everybody who attends this reunion. I vividly recall that Mama would often say, "Son, do you see that lady over there in the red dress? She's your cousin." Nowadays, that's sometimes the comment I make to Lori and Amy. It used to be the older folks I did not know, but now it is the younger ones. We miss those great uncles and my mother and her four brothers and now my own brother, all of whom have passed on. But, it is still good to attend the reunion and visit with relatives who are my peers, to see their children and grandchildren, and remember those not with us.

You have met our two daughters and may recall that Lori graduated from Auburn in 1990 with a degree in history. She received a graduate teaching assistantship, and although she had not planned to work on a graduate degree, she said, "Daddy, if they are going to pay me, I think I will accept it." But, in the midst of her second quarter, she felt the calling to become a staff member of Campus Crusade for Christ, as had her best friend, Cary Crawford. She was assigned to the University of Alabama where Cary was already working. Can you imagine Auburn girls having to work at Alabama? Cary adapted pretty well to Crimson Tide sports, but Lori is too much of a loyalist. After she had been in Tuscaloosa awhile, I was talking with her on the phone and she said, "Daddy, there is one thing I just cannot bring myself to do." I inquired, "Lori, what in the world is that?" She replied, "I just cannot bring myself to say, 'Roll Tide!' "

Lori, after two years at Alabama, spent a year at Georgia Tech, and now is in her third year as Associate Campus Director at FSU in Tallahassee. She has had several summer overseas trips to Eastern Europe, working with students. Lori is making a difference in the lives of young people and we are proud of her.

Amy graduated from Auburn in 1992 with a major in speech communications. Afterwards, she had a wonderful 3-month internship in Atlanta with Coca-Cola. They sent her on assignments to the Wisconsin State Fair in Milwaukee, to New York City for the 10th anniversary of Diet Coke, and to Tampa for a sendoff of Olympians to Barcelona. After the Coca-Cola stint, she enjoyed a six-months internship with Baptist Hospital, Pensacola before landing a job as Program Coordinator for American Lung Association of NW Florida.

Amy married Marty Stubblefield in a lovely ceremony at First Baptist Church in Pensacola on November 5, 1994. We welcomed Marty into our family with open arms. I am not hesitant to brag on this young man, who at age 31, was named City President of AmSouth Bank in Tallahassee in the Spring of 1996. We love Marty as we do our wonderful daughters.

In July of 1995, I lost my only brother, Rex, who passed away at age 57. Rex was a perfect specimen of health, with athletic ability, except for one thing--an arterio-vascular malformation (AVM), a matting of the veins in the back of his head. He was unaware of this until he began having severe headaches when he was about 30. He endured much pain, but continued to work at Southtrust Bank of Ozark, where he was assistant vice-president and loan officer. I don't see how he did this year after year. The AVM erupted on May 21, 1995, but we still had hope as Rex was conscious for about two weeks before suffering further hemorrhaging that eventually took his life. Rex is survived by his wife, Sara, and by a son and daughter, Alan and Kristi. He was much loved, as was shown by the overflow crowds at the visitation and the touching funeral service.

My sister, Merle, and her husband, Bill, live in Ozark most of the time, but have a trailer near Milton, Florida and we visit with each other quite often. Earlier, I had mentioned the birth of her daughter,

Wanda. Wanda and Frank live in Ozark. Wanda's two sons, Bobby and Doug are in Good Hope, Alabama, and daughter, Amy, who lives in British Columbia is engaged to be married. Bobby is married to Ralena and they have an infant daughter, Whitney.

On Nancy's side, her father, Aubrey Myers, age 92, and mother, Vera, 85, live in Oviedo, Florida and are doing well. Her dad still hunts. Nancy's brother, Albert Myers, lives in Orlando where he has an insurance business. Albert has a daughter, Shannon, in college at Montgomery, Alabama. Nancy has two aunts on her father's side, Hazel Porter, age 94, in Rome, Georgia, and Helen Cordell, 85, in Albany, Georgia. We don't see Aunt Hazel and her family very much, but get together with Helen, Aubrey, Vera, and Albert quite often. In the last few years we've gathered in Pensacola for Christmas.

Nancy has a few cousins, mostly in Georgia, and I have a whole slew of them, mostly in Alabama. It is good to communicate with them although, for some of them, it is only occasionally. As you can tell, I deeply love my family.

Back in 1989 when Nancy and I had decided, with concurrence of Lori and Amy, that 1994 would be my last year in congress, we started planning. First, we anticipated that in 1992, following the decennial census in 1990, the Florida Legislature would more than likely reapportion Bay County, or at least most of it, out of District One due to Florida's growth. We wanted to run again in the new district in 1992 for two reasons--to try to hold our area military intact in the face of the drawdown and to prove to myself that I could win in the new district, which would be the third district configuration I had served since my first election in 1978.

Our reasoning was that we would probably need to move westward to stay in District One and at the same time we were thinking about our home for retirement. It was then that we bought a lot on River Gardens Circle in Pensacola. We put our house in Springfield up for sale, but after a year or so, when the contract with the realtor ran out, we had not sold and decided to take it off the market for a while. We figured we had plenty of time and the longer we waited to sell, the more equity we would have. In early 1993, we put our house at 7404 Gambrill Road, Springfield, up for sale again by nailing a sign to a tree. We sold this Washington area home where we lived for about 14 years and rented a small two-bedroom condo until we finished our service in Congress.

Our furniture from the Springfield home was crammed into the little condo. One of the two bedrooms was used only for storage. It was quite an ordeal living with one bedroom and not even having enough room for a table to eat on. It was really cramped living, to say the least, and almost gave us claustrophobia. But we decided, since Nancy would be in Pensacola most of the time watching over the building of our new home, we could handle it. Since the 1992 reapportionment had turned out as we expected, we had moved from our Panama City residence to a patio home in Pensacola. Then, we were able to sell our Panama City home. The equity from the sale of our two homes helped us to build our dreamhouse.

During my time in congress some amazing things took place on the world stage. Who would have believed the Berlin Wall would come down and West and East Germany unified again. Even more remarkable, who could have forecast the Soviet Union falling apart?

When our armed services committee delegation was in the Soviet Union in August of 1989 for about 10 days we could see signs of tensions easing and attitudes changing. Gorbachev's "glasnost" was changing things. We flew around, in an Aeroflat Soviet airliner, with members of the Soviet Defense and Security Committee of the Supreme Soviet, to military installations throughout the republics of the Soviet Union. Our hosts were quite open in showing us military hardware and staging firing demonstrations by their soldiers.

It was obvious, also, that the people were anxious for change. For example, when a couple of my colleagues and I ventured out into a park one night in Kiev, there were groups of people gathered in clusters. Although, due to the language barrier, we could not understand them, we were told that some of the fiery speeches that were being made were calling for independence for Ukraine.

Take heart, o' younger generation! There is still hope for peace in your lifetime. On an uplifting day in a place called Sarny our delegation saw a Soviet team--watched by the U. S. On-Site Inspection Team--render useless launchers for SS-20 missiles that could have mutilated any point in Western Europe. The launchers were cut apart by acetylene torches in accordance with the Intermediate Nuclear Force (INF) Treaty which provided that all SS-20 missiles and our ground-launched cruise missiles and Pershing II missiles be eliminated.

This was a great step for mankind. It was unbelievable to see the Soviet Union completely crumble less than two years after our visit. Certainly, it is good to know that the old adversary is no longer a super power. However, the time has not come when all hostile nations can beat their swords into plow shares. We know there are continuing threats, and our nation and the freedom-loving nations of the world must be strong and ready to defend against tyranny.

The last few years in Congress were such that Nancy and I had no doubt that we had made the right decision in our timetable. We would be ready to come back home and get out of the rat race. It was definitely not as pleasant as when we first went to Washington. The constant partisan bickering was not much fun. Then, too, I felt, and still do, that the defense drawdown was too much, too quick.

I certainly agreed that with these astounding world happenings and apparent end of the cold war, there had to be a drawdown. However, we have drawn down too much after every conflict in our history and should take lessons from the past. Be that as it may, the reality of it is that, with this lessening of the major threat and burgeoning national debt, somebody's bases are going to be closed.

Even before the Soviet breakup, and commensurate with Gorbachev's "glasnost" and the signing of the INF Treaty, Representative Dick Armey (R-Texas) proposed a base closing bill in 1988. In keeping with my previous statement, I voted against it, but it passed. It was signed into law and the procedure got underway.

We had worked hard to make our bases in Northwest Florida healthy. They were blessed with excellent military and civilian leadership and I felt pretty good about our bases not getting on the list. But, one never knows. So, we sweated. Retired Congressman Jack Edwards (D-Alabama), my friend and colleague from Mobile who had been an adversary in our Whiting battles, was co-chairman of the Base Closure and Realignment Commission (BRACC). This caused some concern and I razzed Jack a bit by saying, "Jack, don't do this to me!" He just smiled. Jack is a man of integrity and since the Navy did not offer up Whiting, he would not try to add it.

When the big day came and decisions were made, it was good news for Northwest Florida! We came away unscathed and breathed a sigh of relief. However, as the favorable turn of events continued internationally and with severe budgetary constraints, Defense Secretary Dick Cheney suggested further base closings. We passed legislation providing for future closures in 1991, 1993, and 1995. In

1991 we almost escaped again, but were hit with a downgrade of the Naval Coastal Systems Center in Panama City to the Naval Coastal Systems Station, with some reductions of personnel through attrition over a five-year period.

Then, in the 1993 round of closures and realignments, the Naval Coastal Systems Station in Panama City got well again when it received more positions than would have been lost under the '91 announcements. But, in the '93 round, the Pensacola area was hit when the Naval Aviation Depot was listed, with other NADEPS, for closure. This hurt because the some 3,800 skilled people who worked there had good jobs which meant a lot to the community. However, in NADEP's place, the Naval Aviation Technical Training Center (NATTC) was transferred from Millington, Tennessee, to Pensacola. The community and I, through a well-organized effort, fought hard to keep NADEP, which had employed generations of Pensacolians.

The coming of the NATTC would actually provide more people than we had before the NADEP closure began, but we still bemoaned the loss of those skilled jobs. The new tenants at NAS, however, would require a lot of new construction and this would be a boost for the economy. Nearly $300 million was put in the base closure fund by our committee for the new construction in Pensacola. Additionally, the permanent staff and students at NATTC will help maintain needed jobs for the area. There were times when it appeared that this move might, in some ways, become unraveled because of efforts made by the Tennessee delegation, who claimed that the construction funds for Pensacola were unnecessary and a drain on the budget. The Navy contacted me and asked me to protect the funding authorization and appropriations for Pensacola construction so the plan could proceed. The funding stayed intact.

A congressman's constituents have a right to know what their congressman is doing. I sought to keep the folks back home informed. Holding town hall meetings back in the district is one way to inform, but it is an even better way to listen to their suggestions, criticisms, and comments. Sometimes, when they were unhappy about something, I heard more than I wanted to hear. Other ways to inform are to send out news releases, and audio and video tapes.

At the beginning of my congressional career, I did not hire a full-time press secretary (or more appropriately, media director). Because of my media background experience, I felt that I could handle the contacts with the media and hold down the number of staffers. I soon realized I needed some help. First, I assigned part-time media duties to Mary Anne Williams. Mary Anne retired after five or so years to be near her children back in Florida and Jeanne Timmins filled in at this job, as did others. As I recall, Brian Keeter was my first full-time media director and he conscientiously handled the media for me for close to five years, to be followed by Elizabeth (E.R.) Gregory for the remainder of my tenure.

"Congressional Report" was said to be the longest running congressional TV program on the air, dating back to the early seventies. Congressman Jack Edwards, who is from Mobile, had made arrangements with that city's WKRG-TV to run the half-hour program once a week. Since Channel Five's signal reaches all three congressional districts, it featured Congressman Bob Sikes, Congressman Trent Lott, and Edwards, not necessarily in that order. In fact, Edwards was the host at the outset and then host duties were rotated from week-to-week. When I was elected, I was contacted almost immediately about taking Sikes's place on the show. Naturally I agreed because that's right down my alley.

The TV program was taped on Thursdays at the House Recording Studio in Washington and sent to Channel Five in Mobile, where it went on the air at 11:00 a.m. on Sundays. That is the church hour and we sometimes joked about having an audience of sinners. We had an informal discussion of what was going on in congress. Edwards and Lott, of course, were Republicans and I a Democrat. Was it difficult to work with these folks? Not at all. At times we disagreed, but generally, since I am just as conservative as those two, we were on the same wave-length. I enjoyed the show and, off camera, we had a good time chiding each other about naming the show "The Jack Edwards Show" or "Trent Lott Show" because of one or the other hogging the air time.

Jack Edwards retired at the end of 1984 and was succeeded by Sonny Callahan, of Mobile. Sonny fit right in with the TV program. In fact, he was like a senator doing a filibuster and it was hard for Trent or me to get in a word edgewise (Just kidding, Sonny). But, Trent and I refused to let it be the Sonny Callahan Show and we had a good time trying to butt in. When Trent was elected to the senate in 1988, he was succeeded by Larkin Smith, a former sheriff in south Mississippi. It was a pleasure to work with Larkin on

"Congressional Report," but we were shocked and saddened when he was killed in a plane crash in August of 1989.

Gene Taylor, of Pascagoula, was elected to replace Larkin. Gene is a Democrat, so for the first time the shoe was on the other foot, so to speak. For the first time, there were two Democrats and only one Republican on the program. We still had good discussions and, as always, the show seemed to be well received by the public. But, apparently because of scheduling, we only did the program spasmodically. For one thing, NBA Basketball telecasts sometimes caused the station to either put us on at another time or cancel the show. Trent, even after going over to the senate, would sometimes come back and be on the program.

"I love a Parade" could be the theme of just about every congressman. At least, I am assuming that most of them are invited to a lot of parades, like I was. In the early days when Washington County was in our district, Nancy, and the girls and I enjoyed the Watermelon Festival in Chipley and especially riding in the parade on the watermelons in the back of Mr. Farrell Nelson's pickup. In the Bonifay Rodeo Parade, I rode a horse (a gentle one). But, most times I walked, like in Lynn Haven's Fourth of July Parade, Wausau's Possum Day Parade, Milton's Scratch Ankle Festival Parade, and the Chautauqua Festival Parade in DeFuniak Springs. Also, I walked in the Panama City, Fort Walton Beach, Pensacola, Crestview, Niceville, and Destin Christmas Parades.

I am very thankful that I did not have to spend large amounts of money to get elected. It is unbelievable that many candidates are now spending a million dollars or more, both in primary and general elections. That is why our nation cries out for meaningful campaign reform. There has been a lot of talk, a few proposals, and a noticeable lack of action by both major parties in accomplishing reform. Most of my campaigns were run on less than $100,000. I accepted PAC money, but had my self-imposed limits and would not accept funds from sources which might expect me to take positions counter to my conscience. There were several times that I returned checks to contributors.

My feelings on campaign reform? First of all, I believe we need a constitutional amendment to limit the amount of overall spending in congressional campaigns. Although I believe PACs are better than allowing corporate contributions, I support the amount that a PAC can give to a candidate be limited to $1,000 instead of the present $5,000 per election. A plan for free or reduced broadcast times should be devised. I have generally been against public financing, but the time may have arrived when some program, similar to presidential funding, should be implemented.

People who know me, especially those who worked for me, will tell you that I am more stingy with the taxpayers money than I am my own. I do not believe in wasteful spending. I ran my offices in a business-like way. Each congressional office operates with two accounts. One is called "clerk hire" and from this account all salaries are paid. The other account is "official expenses" and all other expenses such as office equipment, supplies, travel, and so on are paid from this account. The amount in the clerk hire account is the same for all offices, but the official expenses allotted varies from office to office, depending on the distance from Washington to the home district. The funds in these accounts are not in the hands of a congressman or his staff, but the expenses are vouchered through the House Finance Office.

Each congressional office is allowed 18 full-time employees, including those in the home district, and four part-time employees. I never used my allotted number of employees. Generally, I had 16 staffers, but for a while during an extremely busy time, had 17. I used only a portion of my expense accounts and, through the years, I have turned back many thousands of dollars unused.

There are numerous organizations that rate a congressman on his voting record. Some of these ratings hold little credence with me because they are taken from a selected number of issues out of literally hundreds of votes cast. The ultimate rating is the one that comes from the people who vote for you. Nonetheless, these ratings are often used, pro and con, in political races. Thankfully, I had good ratings with the legitimate organizations, but I think it is wrong to vote a certain way just to get high marks with a rating service.

One of the gratifying things about being a congressman is being able to nominate young men and women to the military service academies. Due to the fact that our district has a lot of military, I suspect that my office received as many applications, or perhaps more, than any district in America. I held an annual Academy Day in the middle of my district each year at either Fort Walton Beach, Choctawhatchee, Niceville, or Crestview High Schools for students to come and hear representatives from each academy speak, and to visit the exhibit desks for information about the academies. We had a lot of high schoolers in attendance on a Saturday morning.

It was not an easy task to pick nominees for the academies. From the many excellent applications received I, with assistance from a member of my staff, would spend many hours studying them and painstakingly narrowing the list to the best possible selections for the Naval Academy, Air Force Academy, Military Academy, and the Merchant Marine Academy. The Coast Guard Academy does not choose its students through congress, but they still had representatives at our Academy Days. It is always heartwarming to hear from military officers, whom I appointed to the academies, who have made good and write to thank me for giving them a start in their military careers.

Did I expect to stay in Congress long enough to serve under four presidents? No, but in my 16 years there, I served under two Democratic and two Republican presidents. In number of years, I served 12 under Republicans and only four under Democrats.

The president in the White House when I arrived in Washington was President Jimmy Carter (D-Georgia). President Carter was a good man, but unfortunately, in my opinion, he was hampered by the people around him. His staffers, generally, did not serve him well, although there were some good ones in the bunch. His relationship with Congress was not the best. Remember Speaker Tip O'Neill referring to Chief of Staff Hamilton Jordan as Hannabal Jerkin'? To his credit, President Carter was considered a person of high integrity. Perhaps more than any ex-president, Mr. Carter is still serving people well through his diplomatic missions, as well as his work in building homes with Habitat for Humanity.

President Ronald Reagan won the White House in 1980. He was an inspirational, uplifting leader who brought about a feeling of patriotism and helped Americans feel good about themselves. President Carter initially campaigned for defense cuts, but after a couple of years he saw that this was wrong and asked for increases in defense spending. Then, in comes President Reagan and it was he who provided leadership in building up our military might that brought about an end to the cold war. It is obvious to me we can only deal from a position of strength. Give President Reagan credit. I fully believe our defense buildup, and particularly the introduction of the so-called star wars, plus the disastrous Soviet economy, led to the demise of the "Evil Empire." Unfortunately, President Reagan also left the legacy of more debt than all other presidents combined. Another thing I wish he had not done was to allow China access to our nuclear technology. Now, China is exporting missiles to irresponsible nations such as Iran.

President George Bush was my favorite of the four presidents. I know that he lost favor with even a lot of Republicans, but I believe he was a good president. He generally had good people in places of responsibility. Through his leadership, we were able to line up a coalition of nations to help us in driving Saddam Hussein out of Kuwait during the Persian Gulf War. George Bush was a very decent, likeable person with a warm personality.

I especially remember a time in 1992 when Mr. Bush had the Florida delegation over to the White House to discuss a matter of importance. As he entered the cabinet room where we were gathered, he said to me, "Earl, when we finish I would like to see you for a minute." When the meeting was over, the President asked me to come into the Oval Office with him. He said to me, "I really enjoyed being in Pensacola last week and I am sorry my staff was not in touch with you in time to invite you to be with us." No apology was necessary. The staff had notified me, although it was a little late, but I was unable to get down there anyway. I thought it was a nice gesture by the president, and still treasure a picture of President Bush and me seated in the Oval Office that day.

My last two years in Congress were during the first two years of President Bill Clinton's administration. I have already expressed my surprise at Mr. Clinton's election. In many ways he is brilliant and has done some good things, but he has veered greatly from his Southern Baptist upbringing on the issue of abortion and other moral issues, which has about destroyed the Democratic Party in the south.

Speakers of the House under which I served were less numerous than presidents. I served under three--Tip O'Neill, Jim Wright, and Tom Foley. I have already expressed my admiration for Speaker O'Neill and he was my favorite, although we were miles apart on a lot of the issues before Congress. Jim Wright certainly was one of the more dynamic speechmakers that I have seen. Although fully capable, he ran into trouble, and chiefly through the prodding of Newt Gingrich, resigned from Congress. Tom Foley was a likeable fellow and smooth in his demeanor. All of them were beholden, apparently, to the liberal wing of the party and gave us conservatives little consideration in their agendas, although O'Neill made us feel a little more a part of the party. I also served with two fine Republican leaders--John Rhodes of Arizona and Bob Michel of Illinois.

On Saturday, April 4, 1994, a memorable event took place. Our good friends and supporters, Chappie and Alice Creighton, hosted the Hutto family and our supporters at a fish fry in their back yard in Pensacola, as they had done many times before. This one would be different. The big secret our family had harbored for nearly five years was about to be let out of the bag. I had chosen this time and place to announce my retirement. In so doing, I had to commit a few other people to secrecy. I told my staff about it the day before and prepared a news release that E. R. would fax to the media from Washington about the time the fish fry was to begin. Nancy and I also felt that I should tell friend Homer Singletary and the Creightons before the program got underway.

As the crowd began gathering around four o'clock that afternoon, the cookers were starting to fry the mullet fish and a savory aroma filled the air. Charles Creighton, David Creighton, Bill Long, David McCluskey, Bob Schrader, Snooky Ward, and Ken Grady were doing the cooking that day and these fellows know how to do it. The helpers inside were Dot Ward, Edna Rivers, Annie Tripp, Dot McCluskey, Garnet Grady, Grace Hawke, and Beth Little.

We greeted folks that were truly our friends who had spent many hours working on our behalf in many campaigns dating back to 1978. There were close to 200 people on hand for a good time of fellowship, eating fish, and hearing Hutto lay out his plans for the forthcoming campaign. They did not know it yet, but they would not hear plans for campaigning this time. Nancy, Lori, and Amy, and my sister and her husband, Merle and Bill, were present; so were my Pensacola office staffers and Earl Hadaway from Panama City, as well as two former staffers, Carol Davis and Randy Knepper.

It was a good time together...folks eating fish, talking, laughing and enjoying themselves. Then, it was time for Chappie to introduce me. Homer had rigged up a microphone and as I stood up to speak and looked into the faces of these good friends, I held my composure real well, better than I thought I would. After the preliminary remarks of expressing pleasure to be together again, I talked for probably about 10 minutes about what was going on in

Washington....and then, it was time to break the news.

I do not remember the exact words I uttered, but I reminisced about the campaigns of past years and conveyed to them our love and appreciation for all they had done for us through the years. "These have been 16 great years and we are grateful to all of you and the good people of Florida's First Congressional District for the honor you have given us to serve. Nancy, Lori, Amy, and I decided about five years ago that this would be the time we would leave congress. I know you understand this was a secret we had to keep until this time." I went on to tell them I had another nine months to serve and would continue to live and work in their midst. When I finished speaking our assembled friends, as always, supported our decision.

The media got word of my retirement announcement and began tracking me down for further comment. WEAR-TV asked me to come out and be live on the 10 o'clock news that night. John Richardson, the anchor, did the interview and I reiterated that I felt 22 years in public office, including six in the Florida Legislature, was enough and that I was imposing my own term limits. I listed a number of things I would probably be doing--spending more time with my family, doing some speaking, some writing, perhaps sit on a few boards, do a little teaching, maybe a little consulting, some traveling, and playing a lot more golf.

Although, as usual, there had been some speculation, as in 1992, that I might retire, my announcement seemed to catch everybody by surprise. The media, both print and broadcasting, did wonderful stories. The Pensacola News-Journal carried a big front page picture and story that was very well written and complimentary and the Northwest Florida Daily News, Panama City News-Herald, Santa Rosa Press Gazette, DeFuniak Springs Herald-Breeze, and the two Bonifay papers also did nice stories.

The papers carried a lot of quotes from my constituents warmingly praising me, saying that they hated to see me retire, and that I would be greatly missed. I joked that "now, everybody loves me." It did seem that way, but I was grateful for all the good comments. Of course, I got calls from people wanting me to reconsider. Following the Okaloosa Chamber of Commerce's annual Military Affairs black-tie dinner at Indian Bayou Country Club in Destin a few weeks after my retirement announcement, Basil Bethea, a good friend and supporter, got me in a room full of community leaders who tried to get me to change my mind. I appreciated their friendship and support, but my plans had been made a long time ago.

When I returned to Washington, following my weekend announcement in Florida, many of my colleagues likewise expressed surprise. They had kind remarks to make, but understood why I made my decision and wished me well.

We still had a way to go before I left the big city. In fact, we still had our defense authorization bill as well as all the appropriations bills to pass before Congress could adjourn in October to let members get back to their districts to campaign for re-election. I still had the things to do that had been my routine for all these years. I must say, however, that although I am a calm person, not noted for a lot of worry, I did feel more relaxed in carrying out my responsibilities.

One of the most important things for me to do, in the phase-down, was to assist my staff in every way possible in getting new jobs. I told them I would appreciate it if they could work it out to stay as long as possible before leaving, but if they were able to obtain the right kind of employment anytime before we closed the office, I would be supportive. None of them wanted to be left hanging. For example, Cathie McCarley is a single parent and, with her daughter, Kellee, about to enter college, she jumped at the opportunity to go with another member who needed her. Helen Berry was able to get a job with the inspector general of the Department of Defense so that she could get in the number of years she needed for retirement without having the risk of elections every two years. In September Gary Pulliam seized the opportunity to go with Aerospace Corporation. I was pleased that most of my staff had lined up jobs before closing of the office at the end of the year.

Gary's departure meant that I had to have an administrative assistant. I turned to my legislative director, Delisa Harmon, and promoted her so the work that Gary had started in getting the office phased down could continue in an orderly way without disrupting the remaining work that we had to do. I am happy to say that, with the right kind of planning in which we looked ahead and anticipated all the things needed to be done, we had a smooth drawdown.

Believe me, there was much to be done in making sure that all the furniture, equipment, supplies, and everything in the office was inventoried, and all the files were properly dispensed. I had been asked by two or three institutions about receiving my papers and I chose the University of West Florida in Pensacola. Several months later, I read in the Pensacola News Journal an article in which Curator Dean Debolt was quoted as saying they had received about 6,000 pounds of my papers.

When I made my announcement on April 4, we had been in our new house about a month and we loved it. However, we still did not have all of our furniture from Springfield. Later in the year, in September, I rented a truck and got Homer to fly up from Pensacola and help me with the move. In addition to the home furniture, a lot of things from my office, including desk and chair, which are the only pieces of furniture I was allowed to buy, were loaded on to the 20-foot truck. We had quite a load when we started our two-day trip south. Homer and I joked about being the Ace Moving Company. He had assisted me in similar moves from Panama City to Pensacola and had helped me move Lori from Atlanta to Tallahassee. We were getting good at it, but never seriously considered going into that kind of business. In fact, just the opposite was true. Boy...what a big task! Nancy and I are not considering any further moves.

I am not fond of goodbyes, but when I am confronted with the need to bid farewell I usually try to be casual about it, with the notion that this is not forever and, whoever it is, we'll be seeing again. Without this kind of approach, I could get emotional. The truth of the matter is that, in this case, there probably were a number of folks that I will never see again. I made a lot of friends on Capitol Hill, both in congress and out. As for the staff, we do stay in touch.

After the adjournment of Congress in October of 1994, Nancy and I went home to Florida for several weeks. As the holiday season approached, we returned to D.C for the last time to wrap things up in our office, to spend some time with our staff and friends, and to attend our final White House Christmas Party. At the White house, we mingled with congressional friends of both parties. Some of our Democratic friends were asking "Where did you get that crystal ball? How did you know this was the time to leave?" I explained to them that I had read that crystal ball five years ago.

My office at 2435 Rayburn House Office Building was rather barren, but re-elected members who had enough seniority to get into the Rayburn Building were coming by to scout it out. I must say that our office, through the years, had been the envy of a lot of members. I give credit to Nancy for making it one of the best-looking offices on the Hill. Newly-wed Representative Bill Paxon (R-New York) came by and told me that he had chosen my office. His wife, Representative Susan Molinari (R-New York) selected the office right across the hall. Then, they did a switch and Susan, who in 1996 would be the keynote speaker for the Republican National Convention, took my office.

As Nancy and I left my office the night of the staff Christmas party, we pulled the door shut and heard the lock click. We looked at each other and knew that it was final. We would not enter that door again. We headed for the "C" Street House, within walking distance, for our very last event, the annual Christmas party with our beloved staff. Nancy and I treasured that last time together with these special folks. They were like family. We tried to have a happy time and carry this out like we always had done before. We did talk and laugh and enjoyed being together. But, despite that feeling of togetherness and love toward one another, perhaps even because of it, there was an underlying feeling of sadness that the old gang was breaking up.

At the end of the evening, everyone posed for a final group picture and tears flowed as we said goodbyes before leaving "C" Street house. As I walked down the sidewalk I looked back and saw Nancy, and those with her, huddled in the middle of the street hugging each other. More tears were shed. Those were not the last ones. As we departed the Capitol area and ascended the ramp onto Shirley Highway, Nancy looked back a last time and wept. Departing was such sweet sorrow.

I have a 1979 Olds Cutlass Supreme I purchased in November of 1978. I drove it throughout my years in Congress and continue to drive it to this day. For about the last 10 years, my staff joked about it and gave it clever names. My wife, a few weeks before time to leave Washington, said, "You can't drive that thing to Pensacola. It will never make it. Sell it or give it away." How cruel...to talk about my fine automobile like that. No way. I would not sell it!

Nancy was apprehensive. But the day after our Christmas Party, I got behind the wheel of this wonderful vehicle, Nancy followed in a rental car, and we headed to Pensacola. Guess what? My jalopy made it! It purred as smoothly as a kitten and had no problem at all negotiating those 1,000 miles from Washington, D. C. to Florida's beautiful Gulf Coast.

We were back home to stay! And we experienced no symptoms, whatsoever, of Potomac Fever!

Earl and President Jimmy Carter during Hutto's freshman term in Congress.

President Ronald Reagan greets Congressman Earl Hutto in the Oval Office.

President George Bush invited Earl to the Oval Office to express to him and the people of Pensacola his appreciation for a good trip to Pensacola in 1992.

Bill Clinton was the last of four Presidents Earl served under and here he talked with President Clinton when he came to a dinner on Capitol Hill.

Baseball great Mickey Mantle, shown here at the Capitol with Earl, gave his support to March of Dimes Walk America in Washington.

Arnold Palmer, one of the all-time great golfers, was another supporter of the March of Dimes effort. He is with Congressmen Hutto and Antonio Won Pat of Guam.

President Anwar Sadat of Egypt with Congressman Hutto during visit at Aswan Dam on the Nile River a year or so before his assassination.

Hutto and other members of Congress met with Egyptian President Hosni Mabarak in Washington shortly after he became leader following Sadat's assassination.

Mother Teresa addresses the National Prayer Breakfast at the Washington Hilton Hotel in 1994. Earl Hutto, Vice President Al Gore, and Tipper Gore are shown applauding.

Earl Hutto and King Hussein of Jordan are shown during the King's visit to Washington in 1994. King Hussein had met with Hutto and his Readiness Subcomittee the previous year when the Americans saw a demonstration by Jordanian special forces.

Here Earl greets Israeli Prime Minister Menachem Begin as Speaker Tip
O'Neill looks on. At right is House Minority Leader John Rhodes (R-Ariz).

Congressman Hutto is shown here with President Arpad Goncz of Hungary at a prayer
luncheon in the U. S. Capitol January 31, 1991.

Earl Hutto with Soviet dissident Anatoly Scharansky during his visit to
Washington in May 1986 following his release from prison.

Congressman Hutto talks with President Duarte of El Salvador in
Washington. At right center is Congressman Matt McHugh (D-Ny).

Grown-up Hutto daughters, Lori
& Amy, home from college, with
parents at Capitol

Earl & Nancy in London at
British Parliament

Congressional delegation on 50th
Anniversary of D-Day in France

Nancy joins husband Earl at Capitol

Congressman Hutto speaks to crowd on arrival of USS Forrestal in Pensacola.

Earl and General Al Gray, Commandant of Marine Corps, in Washington in 1987.

Earl and Defense Appropriations Chairman Bill Chappell (D-Fla.), center,
discuss Naval matters with Chief of Naval Operations, Admiral Carl Trost.

Congressmen Trent Lott (R-Mississippi), Sonny Callahan (R-Alabama) and Earl Hutto (D-Florida) chat on the Capitol steps prior to taping their weekly television program, "Congressional Report."

Amy, Earl, Nancy, and Lori applaud returns of the 1992 election. They were excited that this was Earl's last run for Congress, a secret they had to keep until 1994.

Famed Oceanographer Jacques Cousteau talks with Earl Hutto, Coast Guard Sub-Committee Chairman, at Capitol.

Congressman Hutto visits with Secretary of State George Schultz, one of President Reagan's top cabinet members.

Earl Hutto with former Senator Paula Hawkins, a conservative, and '84 VP candidate Geraldine Ferraro, a liberal

Earl and Claude Pepper during a golf game on Pepper's 86th birthday

Earl and Nancy, on their last day in Washington, pause on the grounds of
the U. S. Capitol and reflect on sixteen years in Congress.

18

"Life is like a roller coaster." I have heard that expression many times. There surely is an element of truth to it. Everyone has ups and downs along life's way. But, in reflecting on my life, I would have to say it has been like a flight "on the wings of an eagle," or maybe, like a Navy expression, "fair winds and following seas."

Life is a good smooth ride for me. Oh yes, there are a few bumps in the road. But God has truly blessed me in countless ways. Indeed, I cannot begin to enumerate them, but I will try to share from my heart some of the things I have always found difficult to express. In so doing, forgive me for vacating my humble nature at times.

I have pretty much been a happy person all my life. Oh, I can remember some times when things were not going as well as I would have liked. But when the going has been tough, there has still been a feeling of peace deep inside me and a faith that sustained me with the assurance that things would get better. They always have.

I had a good upbringing. One could question how I could say that, remembering that life was such a struggle for my parents and us children in the meager circumstances in which we grew up in rural Alabama. Looking back, I did not know, during those early years, that one day I would benefit greatly from those experiences and be proud of my heritage.

God has forgiven me for actually being ashamed, in the growing years, of being seen with my parents because we were poor and "lived on the other side of the tracks." We barely had the necessities of life. It hurts me now to remember that Mama had to take in washings and ironings to make ends meet and Daddy, when he could get work, had to labor so hard with the double hernia he had in order to get enough money so that their children could have clothing for school. It does not hurt because they were humble enough to do this for their children, but because it makes me realize what tremendous struggles they experienced. One can understand that when I realized our poverty, plus my small size, at times I felt inferior.

Yet, I now rejoice and am very proud of this legacy. We managed to get by. These were times that were hard for a lot of people. Our parents gave us a lot more than material things, such as love and personal responsibility. Our home was one that was filled with love all the time, and happiness most of the time. Nowadays, as I see and hear about children being brought up in homes under such terrible circumstances, I realize how fortunate I am to have had such a humble beginning, in a stable home, that instilled in me and my brother and sister values that have endured.

Out of this setting, who would have thought that admirals and generals and high government officials would one day be opening doors for me? I had to chuckle to myself when, indeed, I was treated so royally by such distinguished people. My mind always harked back to my days in Navy boot camp when I was scared to death to be in the presence of any officer, no matter what their rank.

However, as the saying goes, "fame is fleeting." I had that rude awakening in mid-1994, after I had announced my retirement from Congress. As a member of the House Armed Services Committee, I visited a lot of military bases, especially in my home district. Always, when I arrived, usually with my local staff person, there would be a parking place designated for "Congressman Hutto." The admiral or general, as the case might be, would be waiting to open the door, greet me and usher me in. Well, on this particular occasion, as we drove up, there was no sign for the congressman. Not only that, but the flag officer was not waiting for me, although the visit had been arranged with his staff. In fact, I was even asked by the receptionist who I was there to see? After advising her of my appointment, she told me I could go upstairs and his office would be at the end of the hall. When I got to the high official's outer office, he was not waiting for me. We were told to have a seat and he would be informed I was there. He appeared several minutes later.

Friends, this is not proper protocol! I am not one to want any special favors, but I was not prepared for that kind of treatment. When I arrived home and told Nancy about this, she laughed and said, "Welcome to the real world, Hutto. Just remember, you will soon be a former congressman!" Okay, I get it.....and yes, I can get by without protocol, and without those perks!

Paperboy....Army PXClerk.....Navy seaman.....teacher.....radio announcer...TV sportscaster...FM station owner...state legislator...ad agency owner...congressman. Gee whiz..that sounds like I have really been around, doesn't it? I will have to say that, vocationally, I may not have been the greatest role model. I have kind of drifted into each of these jobs. It seems one just naturally led to the other and I enjoyed them all immensely. Each job was meaningful to me and was a learning experience. In everything I have done, I worked hard to be the best that I could be.

Can you remember turning points in your life? There have been some definite turning points in my life. One of the earliest might have been the fact that I was kept in the first grade for two years, at a time when more maturity was so vital in my young life. Certainly, there were teachers along the way who made a difference. One was my elementary school teacher, Miss Napier, who encouraged me to memorize a reading and instilled in me the confidence to tell it to the class.   Others included my high school diversified occupations instructor, Mr. Bittner, who became a real friend as well as a teacher. Still another was college professor, Miss Stout, whose instruction in speech led to my broadcasting career.

My service in the Navy and utilization of the GI Bill to attend college definitely were turning points, because I otherwise would not have gone to college.   Yes, even Mr. Swicegood's wise counsel advising me that I had an acceptable voice and not an exceptional voice, gave me an added touch of humility that has stayed with me.

There are silver linings behind storm clouds. I know, because I have experienced them more than once.   Out of adversities have come good things. An example was the struggle I had with WPEX-FM that eventually led to our selling the station. This was another turning point because had the station been successful I probably would have still been with it. Remember how disappointed Nancy and I were at not getting the job as Auburn's football play-by-play radio announcer? That was another case of a disappointment being a launching pad for something better. Had I been selected for that job, I most likely would be working in broadcasting in Birmingham, and would never have run for Congress.

I'll bet you can guess the very biggest turning point in my life. Outside of my acceptance of Christ when a child growing up in a wonderful family, my marriage to Nancy has been the single greatest turning point for me. She brought a dimension to my life. Without her I could never have achieved what I have. Our love for each other and the births of our precious daughters have blessed me with fulfillment and great happiness.

I have always enjoyed singing around the house, in the car, at the office, wherever I am, provided there is not an alien audience around. I think happy people should sing, hum, or whistle, to express themselves, and I do. It is a hand-me-down from my mother and father, who enjoyed singing the old hymns. The problem is that I don't know a thing about music. But I like to sing hymns and popular songs. I know only about a verse of some of them, and just a few words of others.

There were times, as Nancy and I were in the elevator going up to my office in the Rayburn Building at the U. S. Capitol, when something she said would remind me of a song and I started bellowing it out. If the elevator opened, she would shush me up. The staff probably did not worry about my coming in and catching them not working because, more often than not, they would hear me singing or whistling down the hallway. I like singing hymns such as, "How Great Thou Art," "Because He Lives," "Amazing Grace," or popular or show tunes like, "The Song from Moulin Rouge," and "The Sound of Music." Of course, I have a ball singing Christmas carols. My crooning, however, is generally confined to the shower or around the house. Too bad the public is not tuned in to hear the virtuoso that Nancy has on her hands (ha, ha).

Frankly, I don't think my singing is all that bad. As a matter of fact, on at least two occasions ladies in front of me in church have turned around, after the service, and said, "You ought to be in the choir." I thought these were compliments. But Nancy told me afterwards, when I bragged about the comments, "Don't kid yourself. They thought if you were in the choir you could not be heard as well." What a letdown. I know I am not a George Beverly Shea, but still want to believe those ladies liked the way I sang bass on those songs.

Most of my office staff in Washington called me "Boss." Cathie McCarley, and a few of the others would call me "Congressman," and one or two would call me by my first name, Earl. It did not matter to me what they called me. Back in our home district, I think all my staff called me by my first name. The point is that we had real genuine collegiality. I have already indicated the closeness of our staff.

Generally, when I hired a staff person, they had been interviewed already by my administrative assistant in Washington or my district administrator back in Northwest Florida. After that screening, I always wanted to personally interview those under consideration, because I felt very strongly that the people we had working with us must be compatible with me and the rest of the staff.

My management style was to make everyone feel comfortable in what they were doing and take pride in their work. I tried to show appreciation for their service, though I probably did not praise them enough individually. When we gathered in my office, or elsewhere, I always told them I was proud of what they were doing and, in my opinion, they were the best staff on Capitol Hill. I really believed that.

I conveyed to my staff that what we were doing was important work for our nation and the good people of Northwest Florida. I expressed to them that no problem or request for assistance was to be considered trivial, because in the minds of these constituents their problem might be the most important thing in their lives. I wanted my staff to put themselves in their shoes and not be bureaucratic, but show a personal interest in trying to assist them.

There were a lot of interesting and amusing things that involved my staff, and me sometimes. Let me allow Tom Culligan to tell a couple of these stories:

"Coffee is bad for you. This I learned while sitting at my desk in the Cannon Building, which has been known to be infested with Washington rats and other creatures, talking with Carol in our Pensacola office. I watched a roach run across my desk and up the side of my coffee mug. Upon reaching the top of the mug the creature started down the inside of my mug and enjoyed a drink of my coffee. I described this in detail to Carol as the events unfolded. Upon finishing the drink, the roach literally flipped over backwards and landed flat on my desk on its back and laid there not moving. After about five minutes, the roach flipped back over and ran for cover in my bookcase. I will probably never know if it was the office coffee or the saccharin I was using in the coffee.

"One of the strangest things I remember was that an office pen pal would write his letters so that we would have to hold them up to the mirror in Earl's office to read them. This gent claimed that he was coding his letters this way because the CIA was watching him through his television. He wanted Earl to stop the CIA from spying on him."

Besides studying and briefing me on upcoming and impending legislation, my staff was often burdened down by a constantly ringing telephone and an avalanche of mail, which we tried to answer in a timely manner. Culligan likes to tell about the time he facetiously stated if we had a fire in the office we could put out a press release advising that the mail was lost and we would be unable to answer it. A young intern working with us that summer, who seemed to be a little off the wall, overheard Tom and moments later came dashing through the office carrying a metal trash can with a roaring fire. He was laughing and saying, "Write the press release!" Then the container got hot, and he let out a big scream when his fingers got burned. Thankfully, the fire was extinguished without the alarm going off. Culligan said, "After that, we were very careful about our conversations around this kid."

Occasionally, there were some threats made to our offices in our home district that were quite frightful for the staff. We assisted one disabled veteran numerous times in getting the Veterans Administration to provide him with a proper prosthetic device. But the VA could never satisfy him. He was constantly hounding my office about not getting the proper device and we again interceded for him with the VA. On one or more occasions, this man came to our office, threw his artificial leg inside and departed. Several times he staged sit-ins and would not leave until police removed him.

Ben Collins, who headed my Pensacola office, was actually the victim of another irate constituent. This fellow came into the office, asked for Mr. Collins, and when Ben came to the waiting area to greet him, the man said nothing, but proceeded to beat him up. He knocked Ben over the receptionist desk and inflicted injuries, which fortunately healed in a few months. Apparently, the man, who was arrested, had been dissatisfied with a response several years earlier on a matter in which we were trying to assist him.

Earl Hadaway, who headed my Panama City office, got indoctrinated quickly to constituent complaints when he was confronted by some 30 irate fishermen waiting in the office for him as he arrived for his very first day of work. He listened to them complain about how the Vietnamese fishermen were running them out of business. The fishermen were still sounding off about three hours later when the local TV station news crew walked in. When a reporter asked Hadaway for an interview, he referred him to my AA in Washington, Randy Knepper. Randy told Hadaway afterwards, "That wasn't unusual. We break in all our staff members that way." Hadaway responded, "yeah, sure." ...and he still wonders to this day who set up that meeting.

Hadaway tells about another tense situation while working out of my Shalimar office: "A citizen who was sponsoring a Cuban refugee came into the office with the refugee, telling me that the guy was essentially a nut case, was irrational, and could explode into a rage at any moment. He did not speak English, so could not understand what we were saying, though he knew we were talking about him. The constituent wanted to know what the congressman could do to get this fellow out of his life since he had gotten physically out of control and hurt a couple of his family members. So, I called Tom Culligan in Washington and told him the background and that I had a potentially explosive situation on my hands. Tom said, 'Well, gee, I don't know of anything we can do...but let me know how it comes out.' Thanks a lot, Tom. But, it did turn out peacefully, as the two visitors left after a few more tense moments."

It was a joy to see our staff working together, committed to their work, caring about one another, having fun, and being happy in their jobs. My chest swelled with pride when I received many compliments on my staff. In fact, oftentimes I received high praise about my office and the way it functioned. It was a compliment to all of us that there were quite a few staffers working in other offices who envied the harmonious and loving reputation of our office.

In the real world, there is no way a member of congress can please all the people all the time. That is an understatement. I sometimes took positions on certain issues where the public might be split about 50-50. So, it is six of one and a half dozen of the other and whatever you do there are those who won't like it.

A continuing issue which divides the nation is that of abortion. My position,expressed in the Florida legislature and in congress, has always been the same. I am against abortion except in three cases--to save the life of the mother, rape, or incest. My voting record was pro-life. It did not mean I could not be friends with those on the other side of the issue.

Another hard stand I took was on the "notch" Social Security issue, which was only made an issue by those who exploited senior citizens for their own financial benefit. It would have been easy to co-sponsor one of their bills to curry favor with a lot of misled elderly people. Instead, I blasted those who were ripping off our seniors and advised senior citizens not to send money to these organizations.

Among other issues, I was the only one in the Florida congressional delegation who supported offshore oil drilling until, later, another member saw the light. To demonstrate how mean it is getting out there, some tried to say I was heavily supported in my elections by the oil industry. Completely false! I took my position because we are heavily dependent on the Oil Producing and Exporting Countries (OPEC) and need new energy sources. Also, we could not prohibit drilling by companies who paid millions of dollars for leases.

Let me point out that I was also alone, back in the early seventies, when I fought for a beach setback line, and I would certainly not do anything to harm the world's most beautiful beaches along the Gulf Coast of Florida. I was applauded by environmental groups at that time. The fact is that drilling is safe. Interior Secretary Bruce Babbit, in a meeting with the Florida delegation, told us that state-of-the art technology makes offshore drilling clean and safe. Oil spills come from tankers. From our gulf the oil, or natural gas, would be pumped to shore through pipelines without tanker involvement.

I maintained a reasonable position on the issue. I supported a 30-mile buffer zone and believe this might have been achievable, but the environmental groups wanted a 100-mile buffer and most of the Florida politicians climbed aboard. I had supported the presidential ban on drilling in fragile areas of the southwest coast of Florida. Also, at my request, I prevailed on the House Appropriations Committee to prohibit further lease sales in the gulf for several years running. I felt that since a vast number of lease tracts had been sold in previous years, there was no need for further sales. Somehow, I do not think diehard opponents of drilling gave me much credit for that.

While in Congress, I was often asked questions like, "How do you decide how you are going to vote on bills? What organizations or individuals influence you the most? Does writing or calling you have any effect on how you vote?"

There are many hundreds of bills that are voted on by congress each session. There is no way a member can be fully informed on every measure. In my case, and I think this is typical, I tried to stay abreast of the news regarding the issues. I tried to read as much as I could about the bills coming up, but usually this was summaries of bills. I had my staff study and brief me on bills and amendments that would be voted on in my committees and on the floor. I also kept my eyes and ears on the debate being shown on the TV set in my office

It is impossible for a Member of Congress to be in the

chamber for all the debate and do his work of answering phone calls, reading and dictating letters, meeting with constituents, and attending committee meetings. When it comes time to vote, there are a series of bells in the offices and around the capitol area that alert members to get to the House floor to cast votes in the electronic machines, staggered throughout the chamber on the backs of the seats. The computerized voting card can be used in any of the machines.

As to what organizations or individuals I listened to, my answer is " all of them." And yes, we certainly paid attention to phone calls and letters that came to our office concerning the issues before congress. All of these things I have mentioned were in the mix as to my decision process in voting. Occasionally, when I still had questions about something being voted on, I would head for the floor a little early and ask questions of the bill sponsor or someone who was a member of the committee that had that legislation when it came through the committee process.

Lobbyists certainly play a part in the process. Contrary to some opinions, most lobbyists are not evil people. Nor, do they congregate in a member's office and strong arm him on how to vote. These lobbyists are well versed on how legislation will affect their business or industry. They provide valuable information. I think the key to it is not to get locked in with any person or group. I could not have served in Congress if I were not my own person. There were several lobbyists with whom I was friends. I always felt, even when in the Florida legislature, that I could be friends with most anyone, but I was careful about being too buddy-buddy with someone having interest in legislation contrary to my point of view. In short, I listened to lobbyists as I would anyone else, then make my own decision.

There were a couple of other elements in my decision process on voting. I sometimes called a friend back home to get his or her read on which way I should go, or I would call someone that might be affected by the pending legislation. Another, and the most important element, was prayer. Often, I prayed specifically for guidance on how I should vote. More often, I adhered to the Biblical admonition of praying without ceasing, which I interpret as maintaining an attitude of prayer.

My staff and others could not understand how I could be so calm in the midst of some of those critical times on controversial issues. We were often besieged with angry calls and letters and accompanying media coverage of key votes coming up.

I believe the reason I was calm and cool at those times is the same reason that I am this way daily in whatever I do. My thinking was that this, too, would pass. I took each so-called crisis seriously, but had faith that I would be led to do the right thing. Sometimes in the midst of turmoil, I would get up from my desk and stroke a few putts on a golf ball on my carpet. Another thing I sometimes did, to avoid getting too emotional or upset, would be to call a member of the family, or a friend, and talk and laugh about something entirely unrelated to the matter at hand.

One of my former legislative assistants, Mark Kronenberg, remembers the pressure on members concerning President Reagan's tax cut proposal. Mark wrote to me, "What I remember is not the vote, but the tremendous pressure from both sides. Dan Rostenkowski, Chairman of Ways and Means, paid a visit to your office in an attempt to persuade you to vote for the Democratic alternative. Even his chief counsel stopped by later that day to respond to additional questions you may have had. It was hard for me to imagine the enormous pressure you were under from Democrats and Republicans. Yet it did not seem to faze you in the least. Your ability to keep perspective, despite the enormous pressure of casting such an important vote, was a lesson of true grace under pressure."

Another question I was often asked by my constituents back home was about the spiritual atmosphere in Washington and my reply was, "It is about the same as it is here." The mentality in the nation's capitol pretty accurately reflects the many diverse areas of our nation.

The House of Representatives holds a Thursday morning prayer breakfast when Congress is in session. I confess that I was pretty spasmodic in attendance in my early years. My excuse was that I lived 17 miles away from the capitol and with Nancy and me having to get two small children off to school, it was too difficult for me to get into the capitol so early.

Along about 1990, the prayer breakfast group elected me to be its secretary. I joked that it was a conspiracy to get me to attend regularly. The prayer breakfast on Thursdays is for members only. There are no Democrat or Republican signs outside the door. It is good to meet in a bipartisan way to enjoy fellowship, sing a hymn, hear reports of prayer needs, pray, and hear a member, who is not necessarily a regular attender, speak about his or her spiritual life.

The officers of the group are rotated from year to year between Democrats and Republicans and the secretary advances to vice president and then to president. I followed that procedure through each position. The House group and the Senate prayer group, which meets on their side each Wednesday, jointly sponsor the National Prayer Breakfast held at the Washington Hilton Hotel in early February each year, a tradition that started when President Eisenhower was in office.

The president and first lady and the vice president and his wife are always in attendance. The event, which packs in 3,000 people in the main ballroom, with overflows watching closed circuit TV in other rooms, should really be known as the International Prayer Breakfast because people come from all over the world. In recent years, Russia and other former Soviet republics have been represented. The program features music and songs from outstanding choirs, reports from House and Senate prayer groups, and a well-known speaker.

Emceeing of the National Prayer Breakfast is rotated between the House and Senate. In 1994, when I was president of the House prayer group, it was the Senate's turn and Senator Howell Heflin (D-Alabama) was the emcee. Senator and Mrs. Heflin were seated to the right of the podium next to President and Mrs. Clinton and Nancy and I were seated to the left with Vice President and Mrs. Al Gore, with whom we had served in the House. My part on the program was to bring greetings from the House prayer group. Our speaker that year was Mother Teresa, who is so tiny that she was practically hidden behind the microphone, even though she stood on a step that had been pulled out for her. That was the first time the breakfast had been televised nationwide by C-SPAN and Mother Teresa gave a good message which was well received and in which she appeared to be preaching to the president and vice president about abortion.

In the early 1800s, a noted French author and statesman, Alexis de Tocqueville, made an observation about our beloved country. He said, "America is great because America is good. If she ceases to be good she will cease to be great." Will that prophecy hold up? To say the least, most Americans, including myself, are concerned about the things that are happening in our nation. We have always stood tall as a nation of values. We need to get back to those standards that have been a part of us since our founding. In our hometown of Pensacola it was good to see Mayor John Fogg appoint a task force on core values, headed by retired Vice Admiral Jack Fetterman, in which special emphasis has been placed on community awareness of values, a step in the right direction.

As an optimist, I cannot be totally negative about our posture at the present time. Some changes have been for the better and my belief is that there is still a lot of good in people. There is definitely more tolerance with regard to races and skin color. As I grew up in the south, segregation of blacks and whites was an accepted thing. But, contrary to a belief among a lot of folks outside the area, there was not a lot of hatred. Some people seem to think that we had, and still have, Ku Klux Klansmen active in every community. The fact is that I never saw one Klansmen in Alabama. I know, from news reports, that the Klan does hold rallies in certain localities, but it is a misconception that this is a way of life in our part of the country. Someone has said, with apparent good reason, that there is more discrimination outside the south.

Make no mistake about it, though, there is a lot of hate throughout the world and unfortunately there seems to be more and more hate and divisiveness in our beloved United States of America. This is reflected in every community and every level of government, including our federal government. Even when I was in the Florida legislature, I did not like the partisanship that sometimes surfaced, but it was not nearly as bad then as it is now, according to reports. There was more comity and the two parties worked together on many issues. When I got to Congress, the partisanship was greater, but still the members were more respectful of each other and the leadership of both Democrats and Republicans frequently joined forces to pass important legislation.

The level of partisanship, bickering, and gridlock has increased greatly the last several years. Both parties seem to work only for political advantage. They get in very rigid, unyielding positions. If one party is for something, the other is automatically against it. That mentality has filtered down to the grass roots level and seems to be polarizing the nation.

I do not believe the average American cares whether the idea or solution is Democratic or Republican. They want members of congress to work together for the good of our country. I never did like the rank partisanship that was often manifested in congress. I also believe that the Democratic Party should be big enough to accept the conservative wing of the party, which it did until recent years. As a conservative Democrat, I never ran on the platform of the National Democratic Party and, like many of my conservative cohorts in the party, didn't accept funding from DNC. I did accept help a couple of times in my 16 years from the Democratic Congressional Campaign Committee (DCCC), which understood the diversity of the party.

Although I pride myself on keeping my powder dry and being calm and cool under any circumstance, that does not mean that the bickering atmosphere I was in in congress was to my liking. The demeanor we see now is mean. It is getting to the point that a lot of good people, who would make excellent candidates, will not run and subject themselves and their families to the nasty campaigns. Even letters to the editors of newspapers are more often negative diatribes without benefit of truth. I had some of those negative letters against me during my time in the political arena and remember how it affected my family. I am, however, appreciative of many positive letters that were written on my behalf.

My service in Congress was enjoyable and a wonderful experience for which I would not take anything. But, I was getting tired of being in the midst of the intensity that now is the order of the day in Washington. It is even worse now than when I retired at the end of the 103rd Congress. The arrogance of many of the people in our lawmaking bodies is unbelievable. One can understand that now I do not spend a lot of my time watching C-SPAN's floor coverage.

The issues should be debated--no question about that. But the disparity of position should not get personal and contentious, as we see so often. I am pleased to have been friends with practically all the members of the House, on both sides of the aisle. I worked with conservatives and with liberals, including women members, from time to time on issues that we agreed on. For example, I remember working with Representative (now Senator) Barbara Boxer (D-California) on an issue relating to security guards at military installations and I worked with Representative (now Senator) Barbara Mikulski (D-Maryland) on Coast Guard matters while we both were on the Coast Guard and Navigation Subcommittee. For the last couple of years in congress, I sat next to Representative Pat Schroeder (D-Colorado)on Armed Services and we both chaired subcommittees. In the Florida legislature, I was friends with a number of lady legislators, including Elaine Gordon and Elaine Bloom, both of Miami, although we differed on the Equal Rights Amendment. The fact that I voted differently than these folks did not keep us from respecting each other.

It is probably quite obvious by now that I do not like conflict. I am wholeheartedly in favor of the resolution of problems in a civil manner with trust in one another. This does not mean, at all, that individuals should not have strong opinions and positions and be willing to fight for them. But, this can be done without rancor and personal animosity.

I am grateful that I had the respect of my colleagues. It was respect that helped me pass so many bills, without fanfare, in the Florida House of Representatives. It was respect that assisted me in winning my big battle in the U. S. Congress on Whiting Field and that was responsible for many other victories as well as in dealing with the executive branch of government, including the Pentagon.

I believe I was respected for always running positive campaigns. I would respond to false and misleading attacks on me by setting the record straight. But, I never attacked my opponents or even mentioned their names in my political ads. Sadly, nearly all campaigns are now negative. I think one of the reasons for this is the advent of political consultants, who package their candidates, investigate opponents, take things out of context, and smear the opposition. These tactics are, unfortunately, putting a lot of people in office who should not be there. Previously mentioned campaign reform should take place and maybe civility and decency will return.

There was mutual respect and admiration between my staff and me. This is reflected in this paraphrased paper written by Tom Tamura. I will blush while you read it. Tom says, "Earl made things so much easier for us to do our staff work because 'people liked him.' This tells volumes about why Earl was an effective Member of Congress -- because other Members liked him. He probably would have won the 'Congeniality Award' had there been one among Members of Congress. With this liking of Earl came the absolutely essential features of trust and confidence, without which the process of good, honest, and productive politics would not be possible. Other Members were comfortable with Earl because he was believable, consistent, honest, humble and a man of integrity. They knew he could be trusted and counted on when he gave his word. Earl won trust and confidence through consistent behavior, his friendly ways, and personal warmth.

"Earl would have won the 'Best Boss Award,' too, if there was a way to pick one fairly. Never once, in nearly seven years with Earl, have I heard any cross words from his lips about any of his employees -- and I mean even in the privacy of our car as we car pooled home. He was always, and I mean always, kind towards his staff members. Earl was as humble a Member of Congress as you can find -- a rare breed as far as I'm concerned -- and this came naturally for him."

Tom, you embarrass me. But, thanks, I really do appreciate your comments. If you were still working for me, I would be inclined to give you a raise. I could say the same for Tom Culligan, who wrote the following words in describing how our office team worked together in handling the helicopter fight and other issues in my early years in Congress: "We were lucky we had a Member like Earl who was always a gentleman and willing to listen and do the right thing. It allowed for prompt resolution of issues that arose and kept us on an easy-to-follow path. If it were ethical and right, it was done. If there was any question, it was not done. I have tried to emulate Earl in this way since that time. Leadership sets the tone for the office and the organization and provides the moral compass for all personal and professional decision-making. Throughout his tenure in Congress, Earl was known for these qualities and deeply respected for them."

I feel undeserving, but am humbly grateful for those kind words from the two Toms and it especially means a lot to me, coming from two outstanding gentlemen like them. These comments will be very nice for my future grandchildren to read.

Toward the end of my congressional career, I was also honored by kind words from my colleagues in the Senate and House. But, unfortunately, I do not know what those words were, because I was not there to hear them. It happened while we were in the conference committee to resolve differences in the defense bill for 1995. During our discussions, the bells rang for the House members to go to the chamber and vote. The conference was delayed until we voted and returned. I was a little late getting back, due to some phone calls I was returning, but when I did get back, I was told that Senator John Glenn, with whom I had worked closely in conference, had said very nice things about me and told how much he had enjoyed working with me. I understand that Senator Sam Nunn had spoken likewise. There were others who chimed in, including our own Senator Bob Graham. This was a much appreciated tribute, although I missed most of what was said.

Through the years, I have received many trophies, plaques, and awards. I will certainly not bore you, nor would it be possible, for me to mention all of them. I am grateful for these honors, but they created a problem of where to put them after my retirement. We had a rather large office built upstairs in our dream home where I hoped to put these mementoes, but it was not nearly large enough. So, Nancy and I have filled our garage walls with plaques and pictures.

Allow me to mention, however, five national awards made to me in 1994, the last year of my congressional service. In September, at a luncheon in Washington, Minority Leader Bob Michel (R-Illinois) and I, both retiring from congress, were presented great big trophies, the Lifetime Achievement Award from the American Security Council Foundation. Making the presentations were two good friends of mine, Rep. Duncan Hunter (R-California) and Rep. Buddy Darden (D-Georgia), co-chairmen of the foundation.

On Saturday, September 2, with troops gathered for lunch at an armory in Pensacola on a drill weekend, I received a much-cherished honor from the National Guard Association of the United States. Nancy and Homer were present as General Ron Harrison, Adjutant General for the state of Florida, presented me with the Charles Dick Medal for my support of the National Guard.

October 8, 1994, was a special date for me as the Air Commando Association of the United States, at its annual convention, unveiled a new award in honor of me that will be presented annually to the person contributing most to the Air Force Special Operations Command. This outstanding group, with a large crowd in attendance at the banquet at Hurlburt Field, presented me, as its namesake, and with Nancy at my side, the first annual Earl Hutto Award. The award has a large gold commando hat on a plaque with attractive engraving.

Later in the month, Nancy and I flew to San Antonio, Texas, to the National Convention of the American Logistics Association, where I received the organization's Distinguished Service Award for 1994, a distinct honor for my logistical support to our armed forces around the world.

Then, in mid-December, I flew to Washington for the

American Defense Preparedness Association's convention at the Washington Hilton Hotel. I was very pleased and honored to be present at the banquet with many distinguished Americans and to receive the Lynn Rylander Award for my contributions to special forces. I was humbly grateful for all these awards which are prominently displayed in our home.

In our first year of retirement, we experienced several interruptions to our happiness by some unforeseen times of sorrow. In June, our close friend, Homer, succumbed to a sudden case of acute leukemia, and in July, as previously mentioned, my only brother, Rex, passed away. We sorely miss these two people, who were near and dear to us. The finest tribute to Rex came from Carl Pylant, Stan Powers, and Mitchell Grantham, who grew up with him and had known him all their lives. They said they had never heard Rex utter a negative or unkind word against anybody.

On August 3, 1995, Erin became the first hurricane in 69 years to give Pensacola a direct hit. On October 4, Opal was even more devastating to the beaches area and for a hundred miles eastward along the Gulf Coast, but did much less damage to Pensacola proper. There was a great deal of damage and a lot of inconvenience, such as our five days without electricity, but thankfully we were spared with minimum personal losses.

In reflecting back on my years of public service, there are many wonderful memories. The opportunity to serve my country in this way was special. Less than four years ago when I led my subcommittee on a trip to observe special operations forces of other nations, I shall never forget sitting next to King Hussein of Jordan in Amman and a day later across the table from the late beloved Israeli Prime Minister Yitzhak Rabin in Jerusalem. For this cotton pickin' lad from Ewell, Alabama to have served in such a position as U. S. Congressman, to have walked among kings, presidents, prime ministers, and world leaders, says something about our great nation.

The greatest satisfaction, though, is to continue to hear a simple "thank you" from hundreds of people, including the downtrodden and the many who have had problems which my staff and I have been able to assist along the way.

It did not take Nancy and me very long to get into the routine of being ordinary citizens again. We miss our friends in Washington, but we do not miss the busy life of a congressional family. Life in

Northwest Florida is wonderful! We stay busy and active, but it is not in the same way as when I was employed. It is good to set my own agenda for the first time since I was a teenager selling newspapers at Fort Rucker, Alabama.

What do we do? We are active in our church. I am active in the Pensacola Rotary Club, and on the Boards of Baptist Hospital, Boy Scouts, the Trustees of the National Naval Aviation Museum, have worked in fundraising with several local charities, play tennis in the Over 50 But Under the Hill Tennis League, and hit the golf ball when the notion strikes me. We are helping a few deserving students to get a college education with scholarships from Earl Hutto Foundation through a trust from my left-over campaign funds. What else? Well, Nancy and I also take walks around our beautiful neighborhood, swim in our pool, travel some, and enjoy our family and friends.

Being a public official for 22 years is most gratifying to me. Although we are all chagrined at some of the things going on in our great nation, I come away with a still strong feeling that there is none to compare with us. I am still very proud to be a citizen of the United States of America, the greatest nation on earth!

Captain Supreme did all right, didn't he?

INDEX